WILDWOODS WISDOM

WILDWOODS

WISDOM

ENCOUNTERS WITH THE
NATURAL WORLD

Written & Illustrated by

Doug Elliott

Paragon House
New York

First edition, 1992

Published in the United States by
Paragon House
90 Fifth Avenue
New York, N.Y. 10011

Library of Congress Cataloging-in-Publication data

Elliott, Douglas B.
       Wildwoods wisdom: encounters with the natural world/written & illustrated by Doug Elliott.—1st ed.
              p.   cm.
       Includes index.
       ISBN 1-55778-529-5
       1. Natural history. 2. Natural history—United States. 3. Outdoor life—United States. 4. Folklore—United States. I. Title.
QH81.E65 1992
508—dc20
                                                                                                                91-35712
                                                                                                                CIP

CONTENTS

Acknowledgments

A lot of folks have blessed me with a generous sharing of their friendship, hospitality, knowledge, and wisdom as well as their stories. I want to acknowledge their help and thank them for being who they are. Without them, the world would be less rich of a place, and much of this book would not have been possible.

I particularly want to thank Theron and Doris Edwards, Ron Evans, Bessie Jones, J. E. McTeer, Carlson Tuttle, John Connors, Roy and Edith Hill, Hawk Littlejohn, Lee Edwards, Lyge Hylemon, Clyde Hollifield, Greg Rogers, Michael Madden, Mary Bloom, Paul Geouge, Elizabeth Rose Campbell, Gary Shapiro, Sam and Katherine Gray, Ginny Tyson, and George Barnes.

Thanks, too, to Greg Guirard and Joel Arrington for use of their photos as references for my illustrations, and, of course, thanks to Barrie Van Dyck and Andy DeSalvo for their faith and persistence. In addition I wish to gratefully acknowledge *Wildlife in North Carolina* magazine and *Katuah Journal* in which a few portions of this book appeared.

I also want to mention my parents for their love, support, and willingness to help me develop into who I am.

Lastly, I dedicate this book to my beloved Yanna, for her bright mind, keen editorial perspective, and her loving heart.

DOUG ELLIOTT, *Painter Gap, 1991*

Introduction

Of Hitchhiking, California Dreaming, Negative Space, and the Spruce Grouse's Message

This book is about nature—about the denizens of the woods including groundhogs, skunks, turtles, snakes, bats, bees, flowers, weeds, roots, and trees. It is also about traveling—exploring, wandering, and journeying in the larger sense. And it is about being home, about dwelling on the earth as part of an ecosystem teeming with life and death and change. It is about kinship with the creatures who share the world with us—our codependents—or as the native Americans say, "all our relations." It is about recognizing our place as individual beings—as actors, observers, storytellers, and mythmakers—as well as recognizing our place as a species participating in the tangled network of relationships we call life on earth. It is about finding that sacred dwelling place within ourselves, from where we interact with the environment and the world at large.

Wood Sorrel Leaves

Once I was wandering in that particular part of the North Carolina mountains that I call home with a Chippewa-Cree Indian friend from northern Canada. This was the first time he had visited my home. We were hiking along the wooded trail behind my cabin, and I was asking him about the various plants we encountered; most of them, however, were southern species that were unfamiliar to him. Then we came upon a small wood sorrel (*Oxalis sp.*). The leaves of wood sorrel are distinctive. Each of the three heart-shaped leaflets are joined at their points so that, all together, they form a heart circle with smoothly scalloped edges. Seeing this little plant brought back fond memories for me. It was probably the first wild green plant I ever tasted. My dad pointed it out to me when I was a youngster: he called it sour grass. There was a patch of them in the yard that I visited regularly to nibble from. I loved the green cylindrical seed pods. I used to call them pickles. The intense tartness teased my young palate with a hint of the stimulating piquancy and richness of the natural world.

Wood Sorrel with Flowers and Seed Pod "Pickles."

"How 'bout this one?" I asked my friend from Canada. He smiled. Yes, he knew that plant. One like it grows up north, he told me. He used to gather it by the basketful when he was a child. His people often eat it mixed with other greens in salads. The sour flavor works like a dressing.

"What do you call it?" I asked. He answered with a softly rolling collection of syllables that sounded like "cah-see-yo-ta-sko-si-ya."

When I asked him how that name might translate, he thought for a moment and said, "It means, 'It's all there.'" And then, as if he had never really thought about it before, he said, "I wonder why we call it that?" And we continued on our way. A little while later he stopped and said, "Ah, I know why it has that name. We consider the number six to be a representation of completeness, in the same way the six directions—North, South, East, West, Sky, and Earth—represent completeness to my people.

"When you look at this plant, you can see that each stem has only three leaves [leaflets], so it seems incomplete. But when you look a little closer, you will see that each of the three leaves is divided into two lobes. The complete number six is there. So when we see this plant we say, 'It's all there.' This plant teaches us that if we look closely enough within our own selves, we will see that we, too, are complete beings."

It took my breath away to realize the deep truths that a common weed can provide when viewed from a mythic perspective. The wood sorrel's message is a broader one than just that of personal completeness. It is about the wholeness and completeness of nature as our source. It is all there—not only food, clothing, and shelter, but personal answers, mythic lessons, and deep spiritual truths are there, too; though sometimes it takes a peculiar squint of the eye for us to see and realize all this.

A lot of this book is about squinting—about adjusting our way of looking at the world, and trying to rearrange and broaden our perspective in order to see nature with new and different eyes, which just might soften our rigid concepts about the way things are and shed new light on many of the beings that share our world.

We will explore the world using the eyes of traditional people who embody ancient wisdom as well as those of people from our modern industrial society who have created deep and special connections to the natural world. Whether it be a native American, an Appalachian mountaineer, a coon hunter, a hoodoo root doctor, a Pentecostal snake handler, a biologist, a farmer, a 'possum breeder, a stock broker, or a New Ager on a vision quest, we will try out their points of view for a while, and in the process, learn ways to expand our own vision, and deepen our relationship with the natural world. And after looking through all these eyes, that "peculiar squint" just may become wide-eyed wonder.

I am often asked when and how my passion for the natural world developed. All I know is that it has been there ever since I can remember. I was always a nature kid. My dad used to say, "That boy knows what's under every rock between here and town." I was raised on the Severn River, an estuary of the Chesapeake Bay. I spent all my spare time on the river or roaming the woods, and the swamps. Sometimes, I brought home strings of fish or baskets of crabs for supper, or wildflowers and ferns for the garden, or frogs, turtles, insects, and snakes to study and keep as pets.

When I went to college, I wanted to continue to pursue my interests so, of course, I wanted to study biology. That is when the realities of the academic world smashed in on me. In order to study biology one had to get through math and chemistry courses. These hard sciences were more than my soft, right-brain dominated, liberal-arts mind could master—I barely made it through the first semester. So, in a series of rapid-fire changes in majors, I switched from biology to journalism to sociology to anthropology, and finally, to art. Studying art really worked for me. I had always enjoyed drawing and painting pictures. Studying it in a disciplined way not only honed my skills, but it taught me new ways of seeing. I learned to squint my eyes and watch crisp details dissolve into the light and dark forms that are the basis of everything we see. I learned about seeing and defining negative space—that the space around an object is as important as the object itself. The right side of my brain was finally getting some training.

This art training, combined with the tumultuous protest years of the 1960s nurtured in me a spirit of uncompromising idealism. When I finally graduated in 1970, I was radical, unruly, artistic, idealistic, excited about life... and unemployable. All I wanted was to live in the woods, commune with nature, and create art. I had the opportunity to stay in an old family house in the White Mountains of New Hampshire for a low rent, so there I went. How I would make a living, I did not know. All I knew was that I had a few hundred dollars in the bank and the longer I could make that last, the longer I could do what I wanted to do. I owned no car, so I walked, rode an old clunker of a bicycle, or hitchhiked wherever I needed to go.

That first year I spent lots of time alone, roaming the woods and mountains—snowshoeing in the winter, hiking, swimming, and camping in the summer—painting pictures, sketching, and taking photographs wherever I went.

I planted a garden, but soon it was overrun with weeds. Dandelions, lamb's-quarters, amaranth, purslane, and wild mustard greens were coming up everywhere. Then I realized—these weeds were good to eat. They were at least as good as the garden vegetables I had planted, and unlike the vegetables, they were no trouble to grow. Wild plants were speaking to me. This began to change the way I was seeing the world. Coming to terms with the weeds surrounding my garden vegetables was like seeing the negative space around an object I was trying to draw.

My time was rich and full there in the North Country. But I had an urge to travel that was getting stronger all the time. In those days, everybody was "California dreaming"

Lamb's-quarters

Amaranth

Purslane

and "looking for America." I wanted to look for America, too. I wanted to see California—explore the wonderland. I wanted to hit the open road, stick my thumb out, and see where it would take me.

Sure enough, on April Fools Day 1972, I extended my educated thumb, and was on the road. And what a trip it was! I met folks from all walks of life. They opened unseen worlds to me and carried me on unheard-of adventures. I visited the Maine coast and the canyons of New York City. I worked in a factory in Memphis and heard mountain music in the Ozarks. I felt the Oklahoma wind come whipping across the plains. I rode a freight train over the Great Divide and across the Mojave Desert. I hitched down into Baja, Mexico, and sailed back to Los Angeles on an aged thirty-foot yawl. I learned to play the blues on my harmonica. I spent a week in the Big Sur backcountry sleeping in a giant, fallen, hollow redwood log, living on dandelion greens and granola. I spent time on a Christmas tree farm in the Santa Cruz mountains, and hung out at a Taoist retreat center listening in puzzled awe to sunrise readings of the *Tao Te Ching*.

Wherever I went, I looked at the plants. Hardly any of them were familiar. I had no field guides, so I couldn't identify them. All I could do was crush little pieces of the leaves between my fingers and sniff. And such smells there were. A few, like bay leaves and eucalyptus, I could recognize and sometimes I knew the family, but the species were all new, and each was a new sensory experience. There were many kinds of pungent sagebrush, aromatic mints, flowery-smelling composites, sweet-scented umbellifers, and more. Each plant had a unique fragance that filled my head and tingled the recesses of my brain. It is said that the sense of smell provides a direct link to our unconscious, and I think that having those sensory experiences with totally unfamiliar plants accessed a deep connection. The plant world was speaking to me. I knew that I wanted to become more involved with plants in some way.

Later, while exploring the streets of Berkeley, I wandered into my first herb store and was astounded to see an entire wall covered with jars containing all kinds of chopped and powdered roots, barks, leaves, and flowers. I stood quietly reading one label after another; I knew some of these plants. People were coming into the store and actually buying them! I shyly approached a young woman who was scooping out quantities of various herbs.

"You use this stuff?" I asked.

"Sure," she said.

"Like, what are you buying there?"

"Well, this is peppermint," she said. "It makes a good tea, and it's settling to the stomach. This is yarrow. I mix it with eucalyptus for colds. This is golden seal. I use it as a douche for vaginal infections."

"Oh," I said, blushing and speechless. As speechless as I was, it made such sense to me. Natural herbs used to heal natural ailments. Of course.

I left town the next day, heading north. With my pack on my back, I walked across the Golden Gate Bridge and soon caught a ride through northern California, then on through Oregon and Washington, and in a few days I crossed the border into Canada. I wanted to visit a friend of a friend who was homesteading in British Columbia. This was a lifestyle I wanted to witness. I traveled on northward into the backcountry, and before long, I was hitching down one dirt road after another. There was hardly any traffic, and I walked for hours. Whenever vehicles did come along, however, the drivers would usually pick me up because they were so surprised to see someone there on the road. I finally made it to this fellow's rutted driveway, and I followed it back to his cabin. It was a beautiful place. The cabin was set in among the trees with snowcapped peaks all around. But

no one was home. I waited around, and eventually I spent the night there. I left a note on his table and headed out early the next morning. The first ride I got was with a young couple about my age. They knew the fellow I was trying to visit. They said he was working for the summer in Nelson, the nearest sizable town about one hundred miles away.

I told them where I had come from and that I was trying to get a taste of the British Columbia backcountry. They said that they were waiting to move into a cabin in a few weeks and until then, they were going to camp beside a river near there. They had plenty of food. Did I want to come and camp with them?

Having come this far, I gratefully accepted their offer. We camped beside a beautiful rushing stream in a narrow valley ringed with the majestic, snowcapped Rocky Mountains. We hiked around and explored the valley. We harvested wild greens and cooked over a camp fire. It was a restful time for me. One reason it was so restful was because my companions, as friendly and hospitable as they were, were not very verbal. I, on the other hand, had lots to say. Each evening, I'd ask them questions about their life, about the area, and the animals and plants. I tried to make conversation about the grandeur of the mountains and our adventures of the day. They gave short answers or would simply nod in agreement and stare off into the crackling camp fire. We listened to the river a lot.

I found out they were going to have a baby, and I said, "There must be a lot of things going through your mind about being pregnant and having a baby out here, living in a cabin."

She said, "Yeah."

And we listened to the river. And that river had a lot to say, too. At first, when we had pulled into camp there, the river provided a rich and textured background sound for our activities, but after a few days our own conversational murmur became the background noise to the river while it gurgled, chanted, and sang. It rushed, it pooled, and it poured out its soul. We drank deeply, and it began to quiet me down.

After about a week I thought, "Here I am in the middle of the Rocky Mountains. I ought to at least try to climb one of them." So one day I loaded a day pack with a lunch and my sketch pad. I waded the river and started up the mountain. There wasn't any trail. I just bushwhacked upward through thick growths of spruce and fir. After several hours of working my way up that mountain, I came out onto a rocky ridge that had a breathtaking view. As I looked up I realized that there was no way that I would reach those snowcapped peaks in one day. So I sat there for a while, taking in the vastness and the quiet. Then I made some drawings, working with the interplay of the dark rocks against the brilliant white of the mountain snowfields. In some places, the whiteness of the snowfields merged with the bright sky and you could not see where one started and the other stopped. Which was the negative space here? The mountains and the sky knew no boundaries. The spruces jutted up all around, bringing the earth and sky together, their rich green branches eating light, exhaling oxygen, and embracing the sky, while their roots grasped the dirt, entwined the rocks, drank from the soil, and became the very fiber of the earth. There was quite a bit of material to work with, and I stayed busy sketching for quite a while.

While I worked, I could see the shadow of the mountain stretching out across the valley below. I knew I had better head down soon as I was not prepared to spend the night.

As I started back into the spruce forest, an explosive flut-

"The whiteness of the mountain snowfields merged with the bright sky…"

ter of wings startled me. A large bird had burst out of a thicket at my feet and landed on a branch about fifteen feet away. It was a big bird, like a grouse, but it did not look like any grouse I'd ever seen before, nor did it act like one. It just sat there on that branch and looked at me, while uttering a peculiar cooing whistle.

I was amazed. I thought, "If it's just gonna sit there, I'll get out my sketch book." I had never had a grouse pose for me before.

So I slowly eased the pad out of my pack. I opened it carefully and started sketching. The grouse perched there and watched while I drew. Then it turned around on the branch, giving me a new pose. I kept drawing.

I found out later that the bird was a spruce grouse. White settlers called them "fool hens" because they are so tame, they can often be killed with a stick. Because of their inherent tameness, spruce grouse cannot survive near civilization, so they are only found in remote northern regions.

I made a few more sketches, then the bird flew off. It had hardly disappeared into the trees when a realization came over me. It just hit me. "I'm a wildlife artist! Here I am, deep in the Canadian wilderness surrounded by snow-capped mountains with my sketch book on my knee, drawing pictures of rugged wilderness landscapes and wild fowl I have never seen before. I'm a wildlife artist!"

If someone had told me when I was about to flunk out of college that in a few years I would be a wildlife artist in the Canadian Rockies, it would have seemed like the fulfillment of the most wonderful life dream I'd ever had!

"The Grouse perched there and watched while I drew…"

I thought, "How did I get here? Did *National Geographic* hire me? Well, no. Let's see, did I get an NEA grant? No. Uh, let's see, how did I get here?" I had hitchhiked up here and had just climbed up into these Rocky Mountains and started drawing pictures of wildlife. That's what a wildlife artist does. That's what I was doing. I realized right then and there that if I really wanted to do something, all I needed was to do it! Don't wait to be hired. Don't wait for authorization or validation—just *do it* with clarity, humility, determination, and passion. At some level, that brief revelation in that mountainside spruce thicket gave important direction to my life.

I returned to New Hampshire and dove into my art work. I began to devour wildflower and herb books, learning all I could about how to identify, gather, and use every wild plant I could find. In a couple of years, I knew most of the local plants and was gathering great quantities of herbs for teas and remedies. I was starting to outgrow my backpack; I needed a vehicle. But cars and engines, like math, chemistry, and science were hard for me to relate to, and I did not want to be dependent on a machine I couldn't understand. Then a local mechanic befriended me, and I hung out at his garage and learned basic mechanics. I bought an old Volkswagen van for three hundred dollars, and soon I was on the road again. For most of the next decade, I made my living as an itinerant herbalist. I fitted the van with drying racks and traveled around the country gathering plants. I would set up herb booths at folk festivals and country fairs to sell my wares. Between fairs, I would

"The spruce grouse often brings a message…"

go on extended field trips and gathering expeditions, studying plants and exploring various natural environments from the Canadian forests to the southern swamps and deserts right on down to the Central American rain forests. Since those days, I have written and illustrated books and magazine articles, performed as a storyteller in concerts, lectured at museums and universities, and worked as a wilderness guide.

The spruce grouse, the bird that started me on my path, flew out of my memory until a few years ago, when I was talking with an Indian who asked me if I had ever seen a spruce grouse. I said, "Yeah, as a matter of fact, I did see one once. Why do you ask?"

He told me that in the North many Indian people know the spruce grouse as a messenger bird. "They say when a spruce grouse comes into your life, you should pay attention because it often brings a message."

I stood speechless, thinking back to that spruce grouse cooing and peering down at me, repeating over and over its message; a message that shaped my life.

Now, when I'm in nature, I still try to pay attention. I try to listen with my heart and keep my eyes wide open to the wonder of it all.

And when I'm in the modern world, acting out my particular part in this bundle of contradictions we call life in the twentieth century, I try to do whatever task I'm doing with clarity, humility, determination, and passion. All the time, I try to remember that it's all there.

In this book I will introduce you to quite a cast of characters, each with wisdom to share and tales to tell. Like precious herbs, I have tried to gather, nurture, and preserve their stories and words of wisdom. Whether these are ancient legends, traditional lore, personal anecdotes, or outrageous adventures, I have been nourished and healed in many ways by their truth and beauty, which I hope will sprout, take root, and continue to grow in you.

1

Confessions of a Snake Boy

WITH A FEW WORDS ABOUT HORSE GIRLS AND OTHER CHILDHOOD PASSIONS

Youngsters are often struck at an early age by a particular primal passion. It may manifest itself as a deep interest, a craving, or a special aptitude for a particular aspect of the world. I was a snake boy. For a number of years in my youth, there was nothing more interesting, amazing, or desirable to me than a snake.

Some kids love sports while others become enthused about music, dance, art, mechanics, computers, or building things. What it is that attracts and focuses certain youngsters so strongly in a particular direction is part of the great mystery that gives texture and richness to the human family. These childhood affinities might develop into a hobby or they might turn into a career, a profession, a calling, or the basis of a lifelong quest. Certain common interests are often aligned with particular age groups, and as such, these affinities can provide a young person with a means of coming to terms with, or getting through, a particular stage of life.

That teenagers identify with certain types of music is an obvious example. But there are other examples not so tied in with popular culture and the mass media. Take young school children and dinosaurs, for example. An attraction to dinosaurs seems to strike a lot of youngsters between the ages of five and nine years. Some think the dinosaur "craze" is a recent phenomenon, but when I was a second grader several decades ago, I definitely knew a stegosaurus from a triceratops! I think this broad-based fascination with dinosaurs comes from a primal need in youngsters to contemplate and hear stories about great mythic monsters—the sort of tales that have been told around hearths and camp fires since ancient times. In the mythic void of our modern scientific society, dinosaurs are the only monsters that are acknowledged. Thus, wide-eyed youngsters with expanding imaginations devour anything they can find that has to do with those giant beasts that lived on the earth once upon a time, long, long ago, before there were people.

As children grow older, their interests and affinities begin to divide along gender lines. Boys like certain things while girls are drawn to others. Whether or not this is the effect of societal sex-role conditioning can be debated ad infinitum. Rather than debate anything, I would like to explore two recognizable interest groups that seem to develop along gender lines in boys and girls from grade school age through puberty. There are the "horse girls"—those girls who have a thing about horses, and their counterparts, the "snake boys"—certain boys who have a thing about snakes.

I remember horse girls from my school days. They read horse books; they drew pictures of horses; they galloped around on the playground. Some of them actually got to ride horses. It is difficult to know what it is that strikes certain girls and gives them this passion for horses. I often ask grown-up horse girls about it. Some tell me that it was the specialness of having a relationship with such a strong, sensitive animal. "Horses are on such a grand scale," one woman told me, "especially to a small girl; they seem larger than life." Another woman said that while riding up on her horse she gained a sense of power, strength, and invulnerability. She could ride far off into the countryside or through parts of town where she would never feel safe to walk. Another former horse girl confided that she enjoyed the intimate and rhythmic qualities of riding a horse. For her there was a strong sensual thrill in straddling, as she put it, "safe, hot meat." Perhaps riding horses is a way of coming to terms with budding womanhood.

A girl can learn much about life from riding a horse—about strength, control, vulnerability, and mastering fear. As well, she can learn about relationships—the pleasurable intimacy of mounting, riding, guiding, and being carried by one of these powerful creatures.

There is really little more I can say about horse girls. It is not for me to glibly speculate from a distance about someone else's passions; probing my own are enough of a challenge.

As I said, I was a snake boy. I loved snakes. You have probably encountered snake boys. These boys dream about snakes, read about snakes, hunt for snakes, and keep snakes as pets.

It is difficult to say what it is about snakes that seems to hold such an attraction for certain boys. The male experience certainly does have a lot to do with coming to terms with a certain mysterious, powerful, phallic entity that seems to have a will of its own. Handling snakes might be seen as a metaphor for growing up male.

There is something about the silent, graceful, glistening beauty of a serpent that has always attracted and stirred me deeply. As I talk to other grown-up snake boys, I get the impression that there is something empowering about capturing and possessing a snake, a creature that evokes terror in so many people. To catch a snake, a youngster must learn thoroughness—to literally leave no stone unturned. He must cultivate stalking and observation skills, as well as the ability to identify the species and enough courage to actually grab the beast. To do this, he must gain enough strength and conviction to overcome whatever personal and societal fears that may be ingrained in him. Catching a snake might be seen as a rite of passage in some cases. It provides a way for some youngsters to confront and master their own fears, as well as the fears and misconceptions of the world at large, and to come into their own as independent beings.

Some young boys learn that they can take a snake home and that it can make a good pet. As such, it provides important lessons about life and relationships. Although a snake can be held captive, it cannot truly be tamed. A snake has a will of its own. It can be restrained and controlled, but if it is not handled with understanding, it will writhe and struggle and sometimes bite. A snake fancier soon learns that to hold a snake properly one must gently support its body while giving it freedom of movement, allowing it to slide freely through the hands. These are important lessons, especially for young boys; perhaps similar to the lessons girls learn by riding horses.

As a youngster, reptile field guides were like "wish books" for me; I would leaf through them by the hour. I read about the natural history of snakes, and devoured the writings of Raymond L. Ditmars (*Snakes of the World*), Karl Kauffield (*Snakes and Snake Hunting*), and Roger Conant (*Field Guide to the Reptiles*). Much of my boyhood was spent ranging the countryside, hiking through the woods and fields, wading through swamps, and turning over rocks, boards, sheet metal, and other debris in search of snakes. Sure, frogs, turtles, insects, and other creatures were of interest, but snakes were the real prize. For me, snake dreams were always good dreams; though sometimes adventurous, they were never nightmares.

I still run into former snake boys. Some have become naturalists and biologists but, often as not, they have unrelated careers—teachers, doctors, lawyers, musicians, carpenters, etc. We have read many of the same books and can describe in vivid detail all the particulars of certain prize snakes we knew many years ago.

My own snake memories are very clear. My first snakes were worm snakes. Hardly bigger than earthworms, these gentle subterranean creatures had tiny black eyes, pink bellies, and gray backs. I could almost always find them under certain large flat rocks in my front yard.

I remember, as a preschooler, visiting relatives in east

"My first snakes were worm snakes…"

Texas. I was exploring the edge of a bayou that bordered their property when I heard a rustling in the leaves. I looked over toward the noise and saw a huge snake crawling into the water. It was larger than any python I had ever seen in a zoo. Wide-eyed with terror and panic, I ran back to the house and breathlessly told my grandfather what I had seen.

"Let's go have a look," he said fearlessly. He took me by the hand and we went down to investigate. There in the bayou was the snake. It was a water snake barely two feet long. It floated in the quiet murky water while we looked down from the bank.

"There in the bayou was the snake."

"I guess that's your great big snake," my grandfather said. I think I learned at that early age the amazing capacity for the human mind to exaggerate encounters with serpents. In my mind's eye I can still see a thick-bodied python slithering down the bank of that bayou. How fortunate I was to have a calm-natured elder to help me gain perspective.

As I grew older, a regular procession of snakes came into my life. There was an assortment of garter snakes and there was a Dekay's snake that was so tame it would eat earthworms from my hand. The chicken snake that someone brought me from South Carolina was over six feet long. Its body was yellow with dark longitudinal stripes and could swallow whole Grade A hen's eggs. It became a neighborhood event to watch the progress of an egg as it moved down the snake's grotesquely distended gullet. To me, the black rat snakes were the local treasures. These agile tree climbers are glossy black on the back and the belly is white near the head with patches of gray, black, and an occasional fleck of orange and pink toward the tail. They were never common, but it seemed that every summer I could catch at least one. Most of them were calm and gentle. Sometimes, when I first caught them, they would strike defensively and

"Black rat snakes were the local treasures…"

struggle, but most of them responded to my gentleness and quickly became used to and even seemed to enjoy being handled. But there was one I had that was never tamed. It would always coil and vibrate its tail against the wires of the cage with the ominous sound of a rattlesnake. (Many snakes vibrate the tips of their tails when they feel threatened. In dry leaves this can sound much like a rattlesnake. The rattlesnake's rattle accentuates and amplifies this vibration. Rattlers are bulky, slow-moving snakes and it is believed that their rattle evolved to protect them from being stepped on and injured by large, grazing animals.) This particular black rat snake steadfastly resisted my efforts to calm it. My gentleness and slow approaches were met with tail rattling and repeated frantic striking.

I learned from this snake (and from a few others) how to receive a bite from a nonpoisonous snake. To aid the swallowing of prey, a snake's teeth are recurved back toward its throat. So if you react with the normal amount of human horror to being snake-bit and snatch your hand away, you will actually yank some teeth right out of the snake's jaws. This can damage the poor snake's gums as well as leave a few teeth embedded like splinters in your own sweet flesh. (The bites of nonpoisonous snakes are usually less serious than minor scratches.) Handling agitated nonpoisonous snakes taught me a lot about gaining control of my own reflexes. I learned to let the snake bite and to allow it to release itself, without pulling away. In the process of learning to accept a snake's bite, I also learned to cultivate a calming presence around snakes which, I'm sure, keeps me from getting bitten more often. Now I often find that I can handle snappy "ill-tempered" defensive species of snakes, like water snakes and garter snakes, without inciting them to bite.

During most of my high school years I had a pet boa constrictor. I had gotten it from the zoo in exchange for a somewhat rare local mole snake, a species I had found.

This boa was a beautiful tawny color with black and yellow saddlelike markings on its thick body. It was less than three feet long when I got it. I kept it in a glass-fronted cage in a back utility room with the washer and dryer. I made a pact with my mother that it would never, that is, NEVER escape (and miraculously it never did). My dad was a heating and cooling engineer, so we rigged up a thermostat on a light bulb to keep the cage at a tropical 78 degrees.

I fed the snake a live mouse once a week and the snake began to grow. By the time I was in my senior year, that snake had grown to six feet long with a body nearly four inches thick. It was eating a large rat every week and feeding time was quite an event. When I placed a live rat in the cage, the snake would immediately come to rapt attention. Its tongue would flicker as the unsuspecting rodent curiously explored its new environment. Sooner or later, the rat wandered within striking distance. Suddenly, there was a fierce, lightning-fast lunge punctuated by a squeal from the rat; in less than a second the rat was snatched off its feet and completely enveloped in the glistening coils of the reptile. Depending on the angle, sometimes you could see the rat's nose and bulging pink eyes extending out one end of the coils and its twitching tail out the other. Within a minute or so the tail would stop twitching and go limp, and the life would go out of its eyes. The snake would relax its grip and slowly swallow the rat whole. It was a powerful event—high drama in the utility room.

Along with my interest in snakes and other wildlife, as a rapidly maturing adolescent I was also interested in girls. I didn't know nearly as much about girls as I did about reptiles, but there was one thing I was sure of and that was that girls didn't like snakes. I knew that if I ever wanted to get anywhere with girls, I had better keep this snake thing under wraps. So I became a closet snake boy. Only my family and a few of my closest friends knew about my snake. At school I tried to appear as normal as I could. I got involved with a few student activities and managed to carve out a little bit of a social life and even managed to have a few not very exciting dates. But of course, I never mentioned my snake.

For a special zoology course in my senior year, we had to do a year-long project where we studied something in depth. I decided I would research boa constrictors for my project. I would keep records on my snake, collecting data as to when it ate, when it shed its skin, and how much it grew. I would record my observations on its behavior and anything else I could think of.

At the end of the year we had to write a paper and do a report or a demonstration for the class. I realized that I was at the end of my high school career, so showing my snake was not going to ruin my social life. It was time to come out of the closet.

The showman in me started to conjure up a plan. Wouldn't it be an amazing thing, I thought, if I could stand in front of the class with a hungry boa constrictor draped on one arm, present it with a live rat, which the snake would attack, kill, and swallow right in front of my classmates' eyes. If I was going to come out of the closet, I might as well come out with a flourish.

I had never handled the snake at the same time as I fed

it, so at a feeding session a couple of weeks before my report was due I decided to do a practice run at home to see if this would be possible.

One day after school I brought home a rat. I was home alone. I took the snake out of its cage and allowed it to coil around my arm in a comfortable position. Then I reached in the box, lifted the rat out with my other hand, and presented it to the snake. In a flash, the snake had that rat entwined in its coils. I held out my hands and arms to support the snake's body as best I could while the snake squeezed the life out of the rat. Then, when the rat was dead, the snake tried to position itself to swallow its meal. The snake was unaccustomed to such a nonrigid perch, and it was having trouble getting itself into a position where it could ingest its meal. The snake held the rat in its jaws and kept dragging it back and forth while trying to get into a comfortable position. I kept trying to adjust my hands and arms to support the snake's body.

Eventually, I had my wrists crossed in front of me with the snake cradled in my arms. The snake still seemed a trifle confused. Then, before I knew it, the snake had a couple of coils looped around my wrists, and I suddenly felt a powerful contraction. My boa was constricting *me!* My hands were tied! First, I quickly tried to snatch them apart but the snake only clamped down harder. Then I tried, ever so gently, to slip one hand out of its grip, but even the slightest twitch was met with an ever-increasing pressure. If I moved even so much as a little finger, the snake could feel it in my wrist and it responded by squeezing tighter...and tighter.

I must have really confused this snake. It was in the middle of this process of killing and eating an animal when it felt this warm live thing in its coils. To the snake it must have seemed like its supper was still alive. It apparently decided that it hadn't finished its job. Yes, this was definitely one strange rat it was tangling with today!

This was amazing! I was really experiencing the snake from a new perspective. So this is what it felt like to be crushed by a boa constrictor. I could feel the power and strength of its thick glossy coils like few people ever have.

However, my herpetological reverie was tempered by the fact that my hands were turning pink. A tingly, numbing sensation was setting in and the feeling in them was decreasing with each successive contraction. I knew that I had better think of something soon. I wondered if I could simply use all my strength and wrench my arms apart. I'm sure if I had wanted to get violent I could have gotten the snake to release me, but this snake was precious and I wasn't feeling that desperate—yet. I went to the phone and removed the receiver. Then, I contorted myself in such a way so that I could call up my friend Bruce who lived a couple of houses away. It's not easy to dial or talk on the phone with your wrists bound, but I managed.

"Hey Bruce? This is Doug. Glad you're home, ol' buddy. Can you come over for a minute...? Yeah, I've got a little problem here maybe you can help me with....Okay great....Yeah the sooner the better."

I sat on the back steps with my hands bound in front of me, and humbly awaited rescue. Bruce came jogging around the side of the house and screeched to a halt. Bruce was not a snake boy. He certainly had been exposed to enough snakes, being the same age and living in the same neighborhood, but it had been a while since he had seen my boa and how large it had grown. It took him aback.

"Glad you made it ol' buddy," I said as casually as I could. "Seems like I'm sorta tangled up with this here boa constrictor and I was thinking you might help me get untangled."

Bruce's eyes widened and never left the snake. He fidgeted and seemed a little pale, especially compared to my pinkish-blue hands. "What do you want me to do?" he asked weakly.

"Oh, I was thinking you might just unwind him. Yeah just take him by the head…there…"

Bruce, ever so gingerly, with thumb and forefinger, gently lifted the snake's head to unwind it, and the snake immediately released its grip on my wrists and dropped the rat. It then started crawling around in my arms like nothing had happened.

I put the snake back in its cage and put the dead rat back in with it. I thanked Bruce and tried to explain what had happened. He went home shaking his head.

That particular performance never got beyond the dress rehearsal. I did take the snake to school and show it to the class. They all seemed quite interested in my report and most of them enjoyed the opportunity to handle the snake—the girls as well as the boys.

This experience taught me some important lessons about my snake and about myself—lessons about letting nature take its course, and the potential repercussions of trying to manipulate a natural process for ego's sake. It also became clear that if you keep something about yourself in the closet too long, it can be immobilizing. Indeed, you might just find your hands tied.

❧

I never saw a poisonous snake in the wild till I was in my teens. A couple of snake-hunting buddies and I came upon a pair of copulating copperheads and we quickly pinned their heads down with our snake hooks. (These were made from broom handles that had a stout metal hook embedded in one end. Snake hooks are used for turning over debris, extracting snakes, and pinning their heads.) Our rude pinning of their heads quickly put a stop to their nuptial reverie. They disengaged, and we watched in amazement as the male's paired, visceral-looking, wart-covered copulatory organs were everted and reabsorbed into his cloaca.

Although we had their heads secured, we never picked them up. We knew we could have. We had studied about how to hold them down and grab them behind the head. We had read about it in books, seen it demonstrated, and practiced it hundreds of times on nonpoisonous snakes. But we had also read many accounts of the pain and misery caused by a venomous snake bite, and knew that even the experts get bitten sometimes. So, we had made a pact among ourselves that, because of the risk, we would not pick up poisonous snakes. We knew we couldn't take them home with us anyway. Each of our personal reptile collections already had our folks' tolerance stretched to the breaking point (sort of a teenage homeostasis) without adding venomous serpents to our menageries. While keeping their heads firmly pinned, we stroked their tails longingly, and we examined the row of undivided subcaudal scales on the underside of the tail (a characteristic of pit vipers). We hefted the weight of this posterior section of the snakes. It was as if just touching these powerful beings gave us a charge. We finally stood back, lifted the sticks that were pinning their heads, and watched the snakes disappear into the brush.

The first time I actually did pick up a venomous snake was one warm summer night on a deserted country road in a swampy area in north Florida. I was in my twenties and touring through the South, when the headlights of my Volkswagen van illuminated the thick body of a large water moccasin that was crossing the road from the other lane. I stopped and backed up, so the pavement around the snake was well illuminated. Then I dashed to the back of the van, fetched my aluminum-handled dip net, and ran out to confront the serpent. I had no particular plan. I just wanted to "mess with it"—to learn more of its nature and its being. To my surprise, the snake was very calm and moved with a slow, dignified grace. I later learned that this calmness is characteristic of many venomous snakes. Armed as they are, they can afford to be slow and dignified.

In southern swamps and waterways, there are many species of nonpoisonous water snakes that share the same habitat as the poisonous water moccasin. Like water moccasins, these harmless water snakes have thick dark bodies with faintly marked rough scales. Many southerners know that the nonpoisonous water snakes can be differentiated from the poisonous water moccasin by their behavior. The nonpoisonous ones retreat the instant they are disturbed. They drop off their trees and logs and disappear into the water almost before you know they are there.

Poisonous water moccasins, on the other hand, either calmly hold their ground or slowly retreat, swimming high on the surface of the water.

I quickly pinned that large water moccasin's head beneath the rim of my net. Then I grasped it firmly behind

"The water moccasin's jaw gaped and its fangs came forward..."

the head and picked it up. Supporting its writhing body with my other hand, I held it up to the headlights. My body quivered with intensity and excitement as I looked into those dark shining eyes.

I examined the heat sensitive pit between the eye and the nostril. These pits, one on each side of the face, detect changes in nearby infrared activity, and enable the snake to accurately locate and strike warm-blooded prey—even in complete darkness. Rattlesnakes, copperheads, and water moccasins all possess this feature and so are called "pit vipers."

The snake writhed and twisted as it tried to free its head

Head of Timber Rattlesnake Showing Heat Sensitive Pits.

and neck. I restrained the middle of its body and allowed the tail to flail about. My willful handling transformed every bit of its dignified calm into a flailing, defensive fury. It would have bitten me if it could have, but my technique, rehearsed hundreds of times in my mind and with harmless snakes, was flawless. Its jaw gaped and its fangs came forward unsheathed and drops of venom, clear and glistening, dripped from their needle-sharp tips. I definitely had control of this snake. But what kind of control did I have? I had captured this snake with the skill of a professional, something I had dreamed about since childhood, but there was something less than satisfying about it. Is this the way I wanted to relate to nature and to the world in general? I carried the snake across the road in the direction it had originally been heading and gently tossed it off the shoulder of the road so that it might return safely to its watery realm.

I spent some time in eastern Kentucky, where I attended several churches of a denomination known as the Pentecostal Holiness Church of God. These are the "people who take up serpents." These devout churchgoers who take the gospel seriously and literally, find a passage at the end of Mark of particular interest. In this passage, Jesus, after his death, appears to eleven of the disciples and tells them to "go into the world and preach the gospel to every creature...." He said that those who believed and were baptized "shall be saved" and nonbelievers would "be damned." Those who believed would be associated with certain signs: They would "cast out devils...in my name; ...speak with new tongues...they shall lay hands on the sick, and they shall recover." Most notably, he said, "They shall take up serpents; and if they drink any deadly thing, it shall not hurt them." Mark goes on to conclude, "they went forth and preached everywhere, the Lord working with them, and confirming the word with signs following." (Mark 16:14–20)

To this day, this passage of the Bible has given meaning and direction to many Christians' lives. They are still out there, preaching the word, speaking in tongues, laying on hands, and looking for signs. A few isolated congregations still take up serpents and some even drink strychnine as a sign that they are saved. These folks wholeheartedly believe, and regularly demonstrate, that if you are anointed with the power of the Holy Spirit you can take up deadly serpents and they cannot harm you.

I'll never forget the first of these churches I attended. The congregation was gathered together in a converted corncrib covered with tar paper on the outside. Two bare light bulbs dangled from the ceiling. It was a church only in the true sense of the word, "a place where two or more are gathered together in my name." This congregation of poor white mountain people was seated on benches, boxes, and folding chairs. The preacher talked, shouted, exclaimed, and exhorted about salvation and the glory of God. The congregation shouted back encouragement and affirmation: "That's right! Thank you Jesus! Praise God!" People stood up and testified about the joy that came into their lives once they were saved. Occasionally, they broke into song—a rousing gospel hymn accompanied by a red electric guitar and crashing cymbals. Sometimes, the preacher just opened the Bible at random and started reading the Word, elaborating and exclaiming about the truth of what he read. Then everyone fell to their knees and prayed loud personal prayers and the church house reverberated with an eerie, cacophonous moaning and murmuring—the mournful yet joyous voices of redeemed sinners. As the service went on, the energy seemed to build. Several people started speaking in tongues—loud unintelligible syllables spewed from their mouths. One woman swooned and fell to the floor, convulsing and crying, and was lovingly cradled in the arms of her brethren.

Then, amid shouts, whimpers, the crashing of cymbals, and the vibrato twang of electric guitar strings, out came the snake boxes, and before I knew it, copperheads and rattlers were being taken up and passed around by a small group in front. People crowded around and I rushed forward for a closer look. The snakes were quite alive and appeared to be in good health, and they seemed rather calm in spite of the noise and religious frenzy they were a part of. As they were passed around I became amazed that none of them were reacting defensively. (Copperheads, especially, are known for their ill temper.) They weren't always handled gently. One man held a copperhead up in front of him. Occasionally, his body would jolt with cosmic energy as the spirit took hold of him. Then he would jump and ecstatically shout, "Oh Jesus!" and the snake's head would bounce around in his hands—hardly what you would call conscious, careful reptile handling.

One of the strongest images I came away with was of an older man holding two large rattlers. He was lost in a spiritual rapture and was saying, "Oh Jesus, when I see 'em in the woods I'm scared of 'em, but now I'm anointed with your power, I know they won't harm me....Whoa Jesus!...Thank you, Jesus!" On his face was the most peaceful, beatific smile I have ever seen. All the while, those rough-scaled, thick-bodied snakes gracefully twined around his arms, their tongues flickering in and out.

the Lord for bringing me here.") Testifying gave the preacher a feeling for the group's consciousness and gave the congregation an opportunity to express what was in their hearts and minds. Only when the conditions are just right and the participants feel a special unity of spirit are the serpents handled.

After attending a few of these services I was left with questions: How are the snakes viewed? Are they seen as an incarnation of evil or a creation of God? How do they view the occasions when someone does get bitten during a service?

I finally visited one of the handlers at home, and he was delighted to talk to me about his faith. He said that snakes were part of God's creation and if you are "anointed with the power of God, nothing God made can harm you." I asked how it is that people who take up serpents in church sometimes get bitten, and he responded with the story of Peter walking on the water, one of the great biblical lessons about faith. According to Matthew (14:24–33):

In the course of visiting several of these churches, I was struck by their free-form, spirit-dominated approach. The services were electrifyingly raw, intense, and sincere. Nothing was done for show. They seemed to be interested only in getting in touch with the Holy Spirit. Little value was placed on style, protocol, or the setting. This was quite different from the suburban High Episcopal church my family attended. On one occasion, I saw people come into the church before the service carrying the snakes in their hands, and at other times, I was at services where the snakes never came out of the boxes. At all the services I attended, every person was asked to testify. (I usually told about how far I had come and how I considered it a privilege to pray with them, and concluded by saying, "Praise

The disciples were on a boat trying to cross a large body of water. They were battling a strong head wind and heavy seas. They had been sailing most of the night when, in the wee hours of the morning, Christ appeared to them. He was out in the storm, walking on the water. The disciples didn't know what they were seeing. They thought it was a ghost and cried out in fear. Jesus spoke to them and said, "Be of good cheer; it is I; be not afraid." Peter asked if he could walk out there, too. Christ said, "Come on." Whereupon Peter stepped right down off the storm-tossed deck and started walking across the water, heading for Jesus. He was doing quite well until he felt the strength of the storm and realized where he was. That is when he lost his nerve. "He was afraid," and for a split second his faith failed him. And when his faith failed him, so did his footing, and he started sinking. "Lord save me!" he hollered. "And immediately Jesus stretched forth his hand and caught him" before he went under. Jesus hauled Peter back to the boat muttering, "O ye of little faith...." As soon as Jesus and Peter climbed back on board, the wind stopped. Needless to say, the disciples were quite impressed. They bowed down before him and said that truly "thou art the son of God."

I am impressed, too, when I think of the strength and purity of the faith of these modern-day devotees, and of how these humble people (from a snake-fearing culture) regularly demonstrate their faith in their salvation by walking a thin high wire over a storm-tossed sea of fear and faithlessness. They fully believe that the consequences for a glitch in the impeccability of their faith is as sure and as deadly as the strike of a rattlesnake.

If your faith falters for second, you've got the hypodermic, needlelike pearly whites of a fat and sassy pit viper sunk into your sweet hide, pumping the fatal fluid into your veins. Now that's keeping the faith!

There is a unique snake consciousness among many of the natives of the Pine Barrens in New Jersey. The Pine Barrens are famous for their relatively high population of king snakes and pine snakes, and snake hunting is somewhat of an institution there. For the last few decades, reptile dealers have been buying snakes turning snake hunting into a part-time occupation, even a way of life for some.

King Snake

Now, as anyone who has hunted snakes knows, you can't depend on being able to find a snake. But as it turns out, the traditional people from the pines (often called Pineys) have another type of work that ties in nicely with snake hunting. During the summer, they gather the wild, high-bush blueberries and huckleberries that grow prolifically in the understory of the extensive pine forests. They carry washtubs into the woods and, with sections of hose mounted on pieces of broomstick, they beat the bushes, knocking the berries into the washtubs and buckets. A hard day's work beating the bushes can usually earn a meager day's wages when the berries are sold to a local pie company. Someone who spends that much time in the woods is likely to see a snake, and if an opportunistic berry-bush beater can catch a couple of snakes to sell for ten or twenty dollars each along with his berries, he has done quite well that day.

Once when I was working with a folk-life project in the

Pine Barrens, we went to visit a man whom I will call Freeman Baylor. It was in the late fall of that year and he and a couple of neighbors were butchering some hogs they had raised. As the home butchering of hogs is considered a disappearing folk art in New Jersey, our job was to photograph and document what he was doing. I was particularly interested in visiting him, not so much because of the hogs, but because I had heard he was a snake man. There were rumors that he kept rattlesnakes in his basement.

When the butchering was done, they put the carcasses to be delivered in the back of his pickup truck. As we were walking back to the house to get cleaned up, I asked him about his snakes.

"You keep snakes?" he asked with interest.

"Well, no, not now," I told him, "but I used to." I said that I had heard he had rattlesnakes, and I wondered if he'd show them to me.

"Yeah, I got a couple in my basement," he said. "I'll show 'em to you."

We walked into the house and he told us to wait right there in his kitchen. He disappeared down the basement stairs. I thought he would take us down with him and show us a couple of cages with snakes in them. You can imagine my surprise when he came back up out of the basement carrying a live and healthy thick-bodied south Jersey timber rattler in his hand. He was holding it casually with one hand around its middle; its head was not restrained in any way.

I could not believe my eyes. "Freeman," I said, "aren't you supposed to hold them behind the head?"

"Nah, they don't like 'at," he said. "It hurts their neck."

"But aren't you worried that it might bite you?"

"Nah, they don't bite," he said and then he flopped the snake down at our feet in the middle of the kitchen floor.

As we casually pressed ourselves up against the kitchen walls he disappeared into another room, saying he was going to change his clothes. With flickering forked tongue, the snake calmly regarded the group surrounding it, and it proceeded to slowly crawl toward the kitchen cabinets. It crawled along the edge of the kickboard space under the counter and started crawling into an opening it found above the kickboard. By the time Freeman came back, the front two thirds of the snake had disappeared in behind the cabinets and only the posterior third of the snake, complete with two inches of rattle, hung out into the kitchen.

"Why didn't you tell me that snake was crawling back there?" Freeman asked as he reached down, grabbed the snake with both hands, and started pulling. He tugged for a moment and said, "I can't do that. It'll hurt the snake. It'll cut his skin on the corner of that wood if I try to pull him out of there. I didn't know there was a hole up under there for him to get into. Oh well, I've got to deliver those hogs," he said, as the last bit of that snake's rattle disappeared under the counter. "I'll have to get him out later," he said as he ushered us out and locked the door.

I was speechless. I had never seen a venomous reptile handled so casually. A few days later, after my mind settled down long enough to formulate a few questions, I went back to talk to him.

Yes, he did finally get the snake out from behind the counter. "Yeah, I had to rip out the bottom of that cupboard."

Knowing that many snakes are defensive when first caught and then settle down later, I asked him if when he first catches rattlers he pins them and holds them behind the head. "No," he said, "I just pick 'em up. They never try to bite me."

I asked if anyone ever taught him to handle snakes like that. "No, Daddy always told me to be scared of rattlesnakes, but I just never was."

Did he think he could teach someone else how to handle snakes like he does? He didn't think so. He remembered the time a snake man from Florida brought a box with some Florida rattlesnakes in it and wanted Freeman to show him how to 'free-handle' them. Freeman said, "I could just reach in that box and pick 'em up but as soon as that Florida fellow started to put his hand in the box, they coiled up, started rattling, and reared back ready to strike. I told him he'd better not try."

So here is an example of a completely secular snake handler who could safely "take up deadly serpents" not because he was empowered with a biblical belief, but simply because he "never was scared of 'em." His ability is beyond faith. He simply knows they won't bite him.

In the summer of 1984 I was working as a guide, taking a group of people backpacking into a remote part of the southern Appalachians. We were exploring an old ghost town when I spied a scattered pile of sheet metal roofing, which was the remains of a cabin that had long ago burned and fallen down. The snake boy in me drooled with anticipation. Sheet metal in an overgrown field is one of the best places to find snakes; it creates an ideal habitat. Not only is it warm, dry, and comfortable for the snakes, but also the mice, voles, shrews, and other small animals that snakes like to eat seek shelter there.

"Come on gang, let's look under that sheet metal," I suggested. "There's always something interesting under sheet metal."

And we started lifting it piece by piece, with me jabbering away in my enthusiastic naturalist mode. "Oh, look at those ants. See them rushing around. See they're carrying their babies—larvae and pupae, back down under the ground.

"Hey, look under this one. See this ball of soft grasses and shredded plant fibers here. This is a mouse's or maybe a vole's nest. See the runways leading to it." After we lifted each piece of metal, we replaced it exactly where we had found it so as not to disturb the life underneath any more than we already had.

When I had carefully lifted the third piece, up reared a handsome, eastern timber rattlesnake. Its creamy yellow body was elegantly marked with a pattern of regular dark patches. The snake must have recently shed its skin and the coloration of its scales was so rich they looked like velvet.

"Oh, now, looky here!" I enthused. "Will you look at this magnificent beast!" Most of the group scattered like quail. "Come back, you all, and look at this critter." As my fellow adventurers cautiously regrouped around the snake, it started to crawl off under some rocks and other debris. I quickly borrowed someone's hiking stick and slipped it under the snake. I gently lifted the snake and moved it a few feet onto more open ground. Its head was raised and curled over the forward part of its body. The snake looked around at this group of shamelessly gawking two-leggeds with a timeless, emotionless self-assurance, infusing us with its hypnotic intensity. It did not rattle nor did it coil up defensively. Just its tongue flickered out, probing the highly charged atmosphere for a molecule of meaning. Could it sense that we meant no harm?

The posterior part of the snake was stretched out, its tail pointing in my direction. I slowly reached out and touched the tail. The snake did not show any sign of irritation. Gazing into its eyes, I slipped my hand underneath the tail and lifted gently. The snake's tongue flickered curiously. When I glanced down at my own hand, there in my palm was the snake's tail, complete with a magnificent rattle over two inches long.

A snake's rattle is made of interlocking segments of a dry horny material. These segments are loosely connected and move back and forth against each other, which produces a distinctive buzz when the tail is vibrated. A new segment is added each time the snake sheds its skin. Sometimes, during the normal course of a snake's life, part of its rattle breaks off. This does not hurt the snake any more than clipping your fingernails hurts you.

As I looked at that rattle in my hand, I carefully grasped it between my fingers and gently twisted the last four segments off the rattle. I let the tail go and looked at the section of rattle I now had in my possession. I could hardly believe what I had done. It was certainly nothing I had planned to do. *Planning* to take the rattle off an unrestrained live rattler would be even more foolish than actually doing it. The snake was not restrained in any way. It was free and able to pull away or strike, yet it lay there and watched while I took its tail in my hand and removed that piece of its rattle.

I felt like I had received a sacred gift. I made a quiet offering of thanksgiving to this elegant being. Its head was still lifted and it was looking back at me. The pupils of its eyes, "the windows of the soul," were unfathomable vertical slits. Its tongue flickered in and out. I carefully lowered the sheet metal.

I felt that this experience was in some ways the culmination of a lifetime fascination with snakes, as well as a metaphor for my own personal maturation. It seems like I had grown a bit since that day on the bank of the bayou when, as a young child, my perception and fear created a snake that was larger than life. Here I had just faced a potentially deadly rattlesnake with calmness, respect, and compassion. Those four segments of its rattle remain with me as a token of how each stage of my ever-developing affinity with these "mysterious phallic beings" reflects my relationship with the world at large.

Later, one of the guys in my group said, "So how long have you been handling rattlesnakes like that?" He was quite surprised when I told him this was the first, and probably the last, time.

2

Oh Groundhog!

OF WHISTLEPIGS AND WORLD POLITICS

Shoulder up your gun and whistle up your dog,
We're gonna hunt for the ol' groundhog...
Oh Groundhog!

So goes the first verse of an old traditional song—a jocular folk litany of praise and thanksgiving for this pert member of the squirrel family. In the next few pages we'll go on a groundhog hunt of sorts. We'll hunt down some groundhog legends and lore, dig up some groundhog natural history, sing a few more verses of that groundhog song, and I'll tell more than a few groundhog tales—like the one about the special gift I received from an old groundhog hunter....

One afternoon I looked out the window to see my white-haired, mountain neighbor, Lyge, treading up the path to my cabin. He was wearing his well-worn bib overalls and he seemed to be leaning to one side, as though he were carrying something heavy in one hand. As I greeted him at the door he flopped his load on the doormat. It was a freshly killed, fat groundhog!

"Doug, didn't you say you was a' wantin' one of these critters?" he asked.

In a way, I had. I had often heard Lyge and his family reminisce about catching groundhogs in the old days. They had raved about how delicious roast groundhog tastes. Figuring I might get invited to a groundhog supper, I hinted that I'd like to try groundhog sometime. It seemed like that "sometime" was now. My groundhog supper had just come to me!

Meat on the table, butter in the churn,
If that ain't groundhog I'll be durn...
Oh Groundhog!

Lyge instructed me on skinning and cleaning the beast. He told me the meat would taste better if I removed the

I allowed as how I was glad to know that, but I didn't have any banjos under construction.

"Well, then make you some shoelaces," he said. "Groundhog hide makes the best shoelaces there ever was!"

He explained that all I had to do was put the well-scraped hide in a dishpan and cover it with wood ashes and water.

In a couple of days, the hair would slip off and I could tan the hide by working it over the back of a chair until it was soft, dry, and flexible. The hide could then be cut into a long spiral strip to make the laces.

"In the old days we made all the laces for our shoes and boots out of groundhog hide," said Lyge. "You can't hardly break 'em."

> We'll eat the meat and save the hide,
> Makes the best shoe strings you ever have tied…
> Oh Groundhog!

I was intrigued, and I determined right then and there not only to clean and cook that groundhog, but to try working the hide into shoelaces. If I wanted to learn about groundhogs, this was an opportunity—to start from the ground up.

As Lyge was walking out the door he said, "Now don't forget to render out the grease."

"The grease?" I asked. "What would I do with that?"

"Oh, thar's a thousand and one things you can do with groundhog grease. H'it makes good medicine," he said. "We always use it when the young'uns take the croup. I've took many a spoonful of it when I was coming up. Now thar's things I've had that tasted better, buddy, but it'll he'p ya'. H'it'll cure what ails you."

My head was reeling. This grizzly little buck-toothed

Tanning Groundhog Hide

scent kernels from under the forelegs. (And I thought *I* had gamey pits.)

"Save that hide," said Lyge. "Thar's a thousand and one things you can do with a groundhog hide."

"Like what?" I asked.

"A young, thin groundhog hide makes a good banjo head."

varmint lying at my feet was not only a source of food, but also of banjos, shoelaces, cordage, and even medicine.

Lyge left me to my task. I skinned the animal, then trimmed masses of fat from the meat. I parboiled the meat with spicewood twigs, juniper berries, and bay leaves until it was tender. Then I put it on the grill over some hot hickory coals. I slathered barbecue sauce on each piece and let them sizzle until well done. The meat was succulent with a rich wild flavor—talk about delicious!

After supper, I carefully rendered the fat in a skillet over low heat. That groundhog had spent the summer feeding heavily on tender wild greens, fruit, acorns, and Lyge's garden produce. By late September when it was killed, it had accumulated a thick layer of fat that could carry it through a winter of hibernating deep in its burrow. It yielded almost a quart of grease that was as clear as store-bought cooking oil. I put it in to small jars, as gifts for my neighbors. I was amazed at the many uses they related for it when they received those jars.

One old-timer told me about how he uses it as a liniment for his rheumatism. "Yessir, buddy, h'it'll work right in them joints and loosen 'em right up. H'it's a penetratin' oil."

Another neighbor uses it as a skin conditioner to prevent chapping in cold weather. He told me, "Now I don't take a lot of baths in the winter, but if I'm gonna be out in the cold, the night before, I take me a bath and then stand there right next to the wood stove till I'm pink as a newborn baby. Then I lay the groundhog grease to me, buddy. I rub it in good. I'll tell you, the next morning my clothes slide on smooth as silk and I can stay out in freezing weather, hunting or dragging in firewood all day long and not get cold."

I know one family that mixes the groundhog grease with Vick's Vap-O-Rub for coughs and chest afflictions. (They swear the Vick's doesn't work without the groundhog grease.) Still another person uses it to soften leather.

> Here comes Sally with a snicker and a grin,
> Groundhog grease all over her chin…
> Oh Groundhog!

A groundhog's burrow is a masterwork of excavation. The main entrance is usually under a rock, a stump, or a building. This prevents dogs, foxes, or irate gardeners from digging into the nest.

> Here comes Sally with a ten-foot pole,
> Gonna twist that whistlepig out of its hole…
> Oh Groundhog!

The burrow's main entrance is easily recognized by the large heap of excavated dirt piled in front of the hole. The tunnel may reach as deep as six feet beneath the surface in soft ground, but in rocky soil it may be less than three feet deep. Its total length may be from ten to forty feet, with as many as five alternate emergency openings. These side doors have no telltale dirt piles because they are dug from within and are usually well concealed with brush or tall grass. Inside the tunnel, various chambers serve as toilets and bedrooms. To protect it from flooding, the main sleeping chamber is usually in the highest part of the tunnel. Sometimes its roof is within two feet of the surface of the ground.

We'll dig down, but we won't dig deep,
We'll find that whistlepig where he sleeps...
Oh Groundhog!

The groundhog is a true hibernator; a fat individual may begin its winter slumber before the first frost. Curling up into a ball, it drops into a deep sleep, breathing once every six minutes. Its heart rate drops to four beats per minute. The animal's temperature may drop as low as 38 degrees Fahrenheit and remain this low the entire winter. It would take several hours to wake up even if it were dug up and taken to a warm place. The thick layer of fat sustains the groundhog until spring, and when it finally awakens, it will have lost as much as one half of its body weight.

In considering groundhogs, we must not forget February 2, Groundhog Day. I've searched my calendars and can assure you there's no 'possum, coon, squirrel, or fox day—only Groundhog Day. It has always seemed mighty peculiar to me that this animal, which for all intents and purposes should be sound asleep in its burrow during this, the coldest time of the winter, should have a day in February that commemorates its being.

But it turns out that Groundhog Day concerns more than just groundhogs. February 2 marks the halfway point between the winter solstice and the vernal (spring) equinox. It is a remnant of an ancient pagan celebration called the "Return of the Light," a festival of rebirth and renewal.

Pagans have been getting some bad press lately, and before we pursue this concept of Groundhog Day much further we had better define our terms. I looked up *pagan* in various dictionaries and found an assortment of definitions. One of these is "an irreligious person, a heathen"; another is "one who is neither a Christian, a Muslim, nor a Jew." It is intriguing to think that if you are not a member of one of the three monotheistic desert religions, you are classified as a pagan. So I probed the word further. It is derived from the Latin *paganus* which means a peasant, a rustic, a civilian, a villager, or a person of the countryside. (*Heathen* is an Anglo-Saxon word that means essentially the same thing: "a person of the heath.")

The word came into being during the Roman Empire, when the western world was experiencing a radical restructuring of civilization. Cities were growing and society was becoming more organized, urbanized, and militarized. The Emperor, with his powerful army, ruled every aspect of people's lives through law and decrees. The spiritual life of the people reflected the society in which they lived, so even religion became hierarchical. Urban people began to worship one supreme god who reigned from above through a complex set of laws.

Meanwhile, out in the *pagus* or countryside, in the rural districts and villages, things hadn't changed much. Pagan folk planted their crops, tended their herds, gathered wild foods, and hunted game in the forests. They were deeply aware of the sun and the moon traveling on their mystical journeys and of the earth's seasons marking time. The spirituality of the country folk reflected their life and their environment. Pagan religions tended to be nonhierarchical and pantheistic and demonstrated a deep spiritual connection with the earth and its cycles.

Pagan peoples living in the northern hemisphere realized that the period around the beginning of February, even though it is in the heart of the cold weather, marks a return of the light. The days are getting longer. With the new light will come the warmth and the world will be born anew. The seeds are not yet germinating, but the spark of new life is being kindled.

Celtic peoples celebrated this time of the year with invocations to Brigit or Briid, the goddess of fire and fertility. It is an old custom among farmers and herders of Celtic stock to make a bed for Briid on their hearths and perform a ritual inviting her to spend the night. If, in the morning evidence indicates that she had been there, this would ensure health and fertility to the crops and livestock (and if things went well, perhaps even an October baby). Among rural people in Scotland, this custom persisted until recent times. But the old heathen goddess has undergone a few changes: She now wears a Christian cloak and is known as St. Bridget or St. Bride.

Groundhog Day is exactly forty days after Christmas. The Law of Moses prescribed that a Jewish mother's firstborn son belongs to God and he must be presented at the temple after his birth to be redeemed with an offering. This holy day, also forty days after Christmas, is known to many Christians as the "Presentation of the Lord in the Temple."

Some Christian sects refer to February 2 as Candlemas. On this day they melt down all their used candle stubs and make new candles as a way of celebrating the coming of the light.

In rural folklore, it has often been said that if you still have more than half your firewood, stored food, and other supplies on Groundhog Day, you'll have enough to last until spring. An old folk verse puts it like this:

> February 2nd, Candlemas Day
> Half the grain and half the hay
> Half the winter is passed away
> We eat our supper by the light of day.

Of course, the most famous legend about the groundhog is about how it emerges from its den on Groundhog Day to predict the arrival of spring (based on whether or not it sees its shadow). We've all heard it said that if Groundhog Day is beautiful and sunny, Mr. Groundhog will see his shadow and return to his den, and we'll get six more weeks of winter. If it's a blustery, overcast winter day the groundhog stays out and spring is on its way.

This puzzling tale is actually an ancient myth that comes down to us from early European bear and badger cults. In the life cycle of the hibernating animal these folks saw a metaphor for the human spiritual journey; autumn and winter are the time of death and darkness, while spring and summer are the time of rebirth, new life, and growth. Through all the days of our lives, human and animal alike, we are accompanied by our shadow—our dark side. This shadow lengthens as autumn arrives, and soon the creature must return to the earth. When it enters its burrow and the darkness of the underworld, it loses its shadow. This symbol of the soul is set free, and the creature remains inert and formless, deep in the earth, until it is time to be reborn. When the animal finally emerges, if a portion of its old shadow still adheres, it has not fully slept the sleep of death. The rebirthing process is not complete and it must go back into the underworld until not a trace of the old shadow remains. Thus, if the animal sees its shadow on February 2, we say that we can expect six more weeks of winter; if it sees no shadow, we say that spring will soon be here. Settlers arriving in the New World adapted the groundhog to this ancient legend, and it is still with us today.

Ancient legends and verses aside, what would any self-respecting groundhog be doing out in February anyway? It's the heart of the cold weather, the ground is frozen, and there is little greenery to eat.

One bright blustery day after a February snowfall, I headed to the woods near my North Carolina mountain home.

I love following animal tracks in fresh snow. In the summer, when I am fortunate enough to glimpse a wild animal, it is usually for just a fleeting moment, but in the winter when I'm following a clear set of tracks, I feel like I can "be" with that animal for hours and witness every detail of its activities.

I was hiking along the mountainside when I found paw prints with distinctive fingers. "Raccoon," I thought, until I looked more closely. The front feet had only four toes; a raccoon has five. I was on the trail of a groundhog! What was a groundhog doing out in the snow? I followed these tracks around the mountainside, where they led to a burrow. The snow was trodden down at the entrance, and I could see where the animal had entered and then exited, staining the snow for a yard or two with its freshly muddied feet.

I followed on, as the tracks led on around the mountain and arrived at the mouth of another den. Again I could see

Raccoon Tracks

Groundhog Tracks

where it had walked into and departed from the hole. The snow was packed and disturbed at the mouth, but those same muddy footprints had entered and left, continuing around the mountainside. Eventually, those tracks led me to the mouths of seven different dens. I never once saw any sign of feeding. I later learned that food was the last thing on that groundhog's mind. I had been on the trail of a lusty young boar groundhog on a mating quest: he was looking for love in all the right places. Of course, what happened in each of those dens is more than tracks can tell.

A Cherokee Indian friend told me that when the male groundhog arrives at a female's den, he rapidly pounds his feet at the entrance and whistles. If his intended is receptive, she will come out and greet him. This same friend told me that, when he was a youngster, he would go into the woods during those hungry months of February and March and creep up to a groundhog's den. Then he would drum his fingers on the earth in front of the den and whistle. If he could lure the female out, he greeted her with a swift blow from a stout stick and brought her home for supper. He was highly praised by his family for being cunning enough to bring home meat during those months of scarcity.

My Cherokee friend and Indians of other tribes have told me that the groundhog is an important medicine animal because of its intimate knowledge of herbs and healing plants.

I had an interesting confirmation of this once when I was in upstate New York visiting a historical park with a mansion and extensive lawns. Out in the middle of one grassy area I spied a fat groundhog grazing contentedly. Normally, groundhogs are very wild and shy but a season or two living in these genteel surroundings, with acres of delicious shaded lawns and no hunters or irate farmers, had taken some of the wild edge off this critter. It had become used to people and was somewhat approachable.

When I realized this, I promptly forgot about the man-sion and decided to spend some time hanging out with the groundhog. So I quietly walked over and sat down nearby. Its nose was to the ground and its mouth was working constantly. Like a quiet, miniature lawnmower, it was busily eating its way through a patch of clover. Clover can be eaten by people, too. It is rich in protein, and can be cooked like a green vegetable or dried and ground into a kind of flour. A tea of the leaves and flowers is a favorite healing tonic of herbalists.

I slowly crawled closer. The groundhog kept an eye on me, but it never stopped eating. Then it moved to an area thick with dandelion leaves and started eating them.

Dandelions are one of my favorite wild greens, especially in spring. Dandelion is one of the richest natural sources

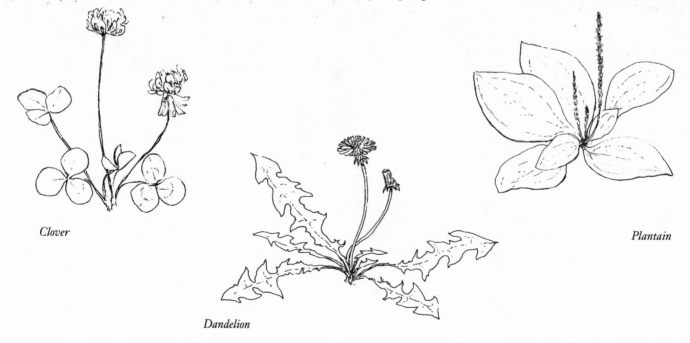

Clover

Dandelion

Plantain

of vitamin A, potassium, and a multitude of other nutrients and healing agents.

For the next course, the groundhog concentrated on plantain leaves. I eat plantain leaves, too. Occasionally I'll mix some in a salad, and I really like them sautéed with other vegetables. A plantain poultice is a great remedy for insect stings and skin irritations.

Then, as if it wanted a little tangy dressing for this lawn salad, the groundhog devoured a few wood sorrel leaves (the *Oxalis* or "It's all there" plant I discussed in the Introduction).

Next, the groundhog waddled on over to the edge of a brushy area and began to browse on large, succulent violet leaves. I had been crawling alongside the critter all this time. Little by little, I was managing to get closer and closer. I could have reached out and touched it. Suddenly, the groundhog looked over at me and stopped chewing, as if it had suddenly realized that the huge lout who had been slowly creeping closer might be a threat. How could I show that I meant no harm?

I quickly bent my head down, bit off a mouthful of violet leaves and started chewing as obviously as I could, while trying out my own brand of interspecies communication. "Who me?" I thought, as telepathically as possible. "Don't worry about me. I'm a vegetarian (this week anyway). See, I eat the same things as you. Mmm, good leaves. Yessir, I love them leaves." As their mild, green, slightly sweet flavor

"Suddenly, the groundhog looked over at me and stopped chewing…"

filled my mouth I remembered how much I really do like violet leaves. I bent down and ate a few more. This apparently satisfied the groundhog, and the two of us continued munching away there side by side for quite a while. As I munched I felt like I was beginning to understand why the groundhog is known as a medicine animal. The plants that the groundhog had just shown me are five of the most useful and abundant wild healing plants on the North American continent.

Some Indians see the groundhog as an intermediary between Grandmother Earth and Grandfather Sky because it spends half the year deep within the bowels of the earth, yet when it emerges from the depths, it looks skyward and bursts forth with the whistle of the eagle — the high-flying, far-seeing, master of the heavens.

This shrill, explosive whistle gives the groundhog its nickname "whistlepig," a colloquialism common throughout the southern mountains. The Algonquian name for groundhog is *wujak*. This name was corrupted by English speakers to "woodchuck," and that is what groundhogs are called in most of the northern states and Canada.

Woodchuck, whistlepig, call him what you will,
We'll sell that hide for a two-dollar bill…
Oh Groundhog!

My Chippewa-Cree friend told me that his people see

the groundhog as an image for a warrior. Since this timid, chubby vegetarian did not fit my stereotype of a warrior, I asked him to explain. He said that the groundhog is very alert and vigilant and heads for the safety of its den at the first sign of danger. It avoids trouble whenever possible. "This is sound strategy for any warrior," he said. "But if a groundhog is trapped or cornered away from its den, it will fight like a wildcat."

That statement took me back a number of years to a time when I lived in New Hampshire and knew a woman who had a feisty border collie. This dog was an inveterate groundhog chaser who lived and breathed his ongoing vendetta with groundhogs. He wasn't large enough or skillful enough to kill them, but that only fueled his fury.

He would often chase groundhogs from dawn to dusk. This was generally not a problem, except when the dog was chasing them on the property of a particular neighbor, who didn't care to hear the dog raising a ruckus in his back pasture.

One morning, we heard the dog's barking coming from the direction of this neighbor's land. The barks were fierce, frantic, and unrelenting. We could tell there was high drama going on over there. My friend ran down the road to retrieve her dog. I saw her leap up and climb over a low stone wall that bordered the small pasture where the action was taking place. She no sooner got over that wall when she let out a whoop and scrambled back up on the wall again, calling for help. When I arrived, the dog and the groundhog were about three feet apart in a critical face-off. The dog was barking furiously, and the groundhog's teeth were whirring like a buzz saw. We called the dog, and for a second he turned and started to come to us. As soon as the dog's attention was diverted, the groundhog charged. The

dog had to whirl around to defend himself. He couldn't afford to turn his back on that groundhog. The only way I could figure to break up the fight was simply to wade into the fracas and drag that dog out of there. As I leaned over to grab the dog, the combined threat of this looming human plus the furious dog became too much for that groundhog to bear, so it turned to make a run for it. The minute the groundhog turned its back, the dog leapt forward, and for a split second it had that groundhog by the hindquarters. But the groundhog twisted loose and landed on its feet looking right at the dog, and they resumed their furious face-off. These two animals were locked in a fight or flight confrontation, and neither one could afford to advance or retreat.

I finally got down on my hands and knees, crawled up behind the dog, grabbed him by the hind legs and pulled him backwards away from the groundhog. As soon as they were more than their critical distance apart, the groundhog scurried off and disappeared into the bushes. And that was that.

I have some other friends who also have a groundhog-chasing dog. They tell me their dog often gets into the same kinds of face-offs, except they live in open farm country and one of these confrontations might take place out in a hay field a half-mile away. In their neighborhood, absolutely no one cares if their dog messes with groundhogs. So, when their dog and a groundhog get into one of these conflicts, they often leave them out in the field locked in their characteristic raucous, nose-to-nose, teeth-rattling altercation. This might go on for an hour or two with both animals becoming more and more exhausted. Yet neither party dares to advance or retreat. The noise subsides a bit, but they are still in their face-off.

"Guess what they do next," my friends say. "They start grooming!" Each animal grooms itself, licking and scratching its fur in meticulous detail, getting every hair in place.

These animals are caught in a desperate, life-threatening deadlock, and they respond to it by grooming?! It made no sense to me or my friends what this grooming behavior could have to do with their conflict.

Then I talked to an ethologist—someone who studies animal behavior—who told me that this phenomenon is known as displacement. This is usually observed when an animal is caught in a frustrating or indecisive situation. When it faces an opponent and is undecided whether to attack or flee, or when a male approaches a potential mate, and has strong tendencies to both intimidate and court, it may choose a third, seemingly irrelevant act, like grooming. Under these circumstances, grooming is considered to be displacement behavior.

A classic example of this can be observed in the breeding colonies of sea gulls. Gulls nest close to each other. Each pair's nesting territory covers several square yards, and it is maintained and guarded by the male. Occasionally, one of the males will get into a confrontation with a neighboring male and they will face-off, each bird in his own territory with the boundary between them. Neither bird is about to cross into the other's territory, but nevertheless they stand their ground and display a series of aggressive territorial behaviors, including head movements, wing lifting, and certain vocalizations. Each of these threatening behaviors evokes the same in the other bird, and often this goes on for quite a while. Neither bird advances or retreats and, like the groundhog and the dog, they grow frustrated and weary and begin displacement activity. They start grooming and preening and then begin a displacement behavior

unique to gulls known as grass pulling, where they start tugging on and pulling up grass and other plant material. (Gulls eat fish and garbage, not grass.) This grass pulling is classic displacement behavior.

Displacement behavior is also found in the human animal, according to Robert Ardrey, the author of *The Territorial Imperative* and other pop-anthropology books. Ardrey's works were popular in the 1960s but evoked little more than scorn and aggressive territorial behavior from academic ethologists, who claim he draws too many unfounded conclusions (in their territory). Nevertheless, he has some interesting observations. He points out that, when faced with a frustrating, seemingly unsolvable problem, we humans often respond by grooming—scratching our head, biting our nails, or engaging in some other form of displacement activity.

If you want to see a group of human animals displaying a wide variety of displacement behaviors, confine a somewhat random aggregation of them away from the security of their kinship group and home territory. Provide them with a frustrating variety of stimuli where they are not sure whether they should be feeding, courting, displaying aggression, or retreating. Watch them at a cocktail party. You will see many forms of grooming, subtle territorial posturing, and highly ritualized courtship displays. Smiling, laughing, grimacing, and the other "bared-teeth" and "open-mouthed" displays that are common in other higher primates can usually be observed, as well as smoking, drinking, unconscious eating, and other symbolic oral gestures. You'll see a lot more than grass pulling.

When these behavioral motifs are viewed on an international level, they still look familiar. During the Cold War years, we could see two world superpowers locked in a fight or flight confrontation. Neither one dared to fight or flee; each was unable to attack and unable to retreat. They were trapped in a frustrating, deadly face-off. The tension was great and they both were getting weary and depleted. What did they do? They engaged in displacement activities. Unfortunately, they didn't just start pulling grass. Instead, they invaded and wreaked havoc in small countries nearby.

It seems that the Cold War is over now. (I think Japan won.) Much of civilization's destructive urges have moved to the harsh environment of the Middle East, where the three monotheistic desert religions began. As we have felt the frustration and anguish of the hostage crises and witnessed the horror of Operation Desert Storm and its aftermath, there has been little that most of us could do, except perhaps participate in a display of institutionalized displacement behavior and hang out a yellow ribbon.

The ceremonial smoking of the "peace pipe" between two bands of Indians has been classified by one ethologist as a displacement activity that diffuses tension between strangers. It might behoove us to look at how a so-called primitive society has transformed this seemingly inherent interspecific behavioral motif, displacement, into a metaphysical gesture.

A pipe ceremony is a prayerful delving into the Great Mystery—a conversation with, or an invocation of the Powers: the Four Directions, and Father Sky and Mother Earth; the Winged, the Four-Leggeds and the Many-Leggeds, and the Little Ones who creep and crawl the earth; the Swimmers and the Green and Flowering and Fruiting Ones, who penetrate the earth and reach upwards to the sky and the waters that flow through us all. Smoking the peace pipe—I guess that's more than grass pulling, too.

Wherever you may be, displacement behavior seems to be there, manifesting itself at many levels, in a variety of forms. Whether in front of a groundhog burrow, in a bird colony, at a cocktail party, with a band of aboriginals smoking the medicine pipe, in the nuclear no-man's land between two world superpowers, or sitting at home watching a war on the tube, displacement is there, rearing its ubiquitous, multifaceted head above the clamor and confusion.

So, whatever you want to understand, whether it's international politics, biology, psychology, sociology, ethology, traditional medicine, or mythology and metaphysics—you'll understand it better if you just hang out with them groundhogs!

> Little bit of corn bread lying on the shelf,
> If you want any more you better sing it yourself...
> Oh Groundhog!

Beaver Psychology

One day I was exploring a beaver colony with a friend who is a psychotherapist. The dam was an intense tangle of brush, sticks, and rocks. Every place where water had been running over the top was freshly daubed with mud and other debris. Wood chips littered the ground. Fallen trees lay everywhere. A number of the trees, after being cut, had lodged in the branches of neighboring trees and had died without ever falling to the ground and so were of no use to the beavers. The trunks of other trees

Beaver Lodge

"Those beavers chewed through this log in five places…"

had been gnawed into and apparently forgotten. The water around the lodge was thick with freshly cut branches.

"Beavers are compulsive and scatterbrained," I was proclaiming. "Look at how they gob up every little leak. Look at all these half-cut trees. And look at how they chewed partway through this tree and then got distracted and forgot to get back to it. Look at these logs here. After they cut them down and they were already on the ground, they chewed through them just to be gnawing, and then they left them just lying here. Now there was no reason for that. Look at all these unfinished projects lying around here. I tell you, these critters are scattered and compulsive."

"It seems like you identify with beavers, Doug," my friend replied in his therapist's voice.

I chuckled at this observation, then realized that maybe I needed to think about beavers, spend some time with them, and look at them a little closer. Not only might I come to know beavers better, but I might even learn something about myself.

On a few occasions in my life my eagerness and enthusiasm earned me the nickname "Beaver." But this was based on our society's popular conception of beavers. What are they really like?

I asked my Chippewa-Cree friend about beavers: "What do they teach us?"

"Beavers are a lot like people," he said. "They live in dome-shaped lodges, like we do. They cut trees, dam streams, and change the landscape. They are community builders."

Unlike modern humans, however, beavers do not create "exclusive" communities based on age, race, or social status. A multigenerational extended family of beavers will often occupy a single lodge. Beavers usually mate for life. Young beavers stay with their parents well into their second year, sometimes longer, and they help in caring for the newborns. Beavers do mark their home territories with scent mounds, but sometimes several different family groups will occupy neighboring lodges on lakes or adjoining ponds.

Beavers also coexist peaceably with countless other species. In fact, a beaver colony in a section of forest will greatly increase the diversity of plants and animals that can live in that area.

As soon as a stream is dammed and the water backs up and floods an area, a multitude of different aquatic habitats are created. The slower warmer water nurtures different species of fish. Marshes are created. Frogs, toads, and other amphibians come to live and breed in these swampy areas. Turtles also thrive in the ponds, and they bask in the sun on the many fallen logs. Snakes, herons, mink, otters, and raccoons are attracted by the turtles, frogs, and fish. Ducks soon discover the pond weeds and other aquatic food plants as well as nesting areas in the surrounding marsh.

When beavers topple trees, more sunlight can reach the earth. This encourages the growth of many other species of plants, including various kinds of berry bushes and seed-producing grasses and sedges, which attract sparrows, finches, and other songbirds.

The beavers feed on the bark of the trees they cut. They use the smaller branches for constructing their dams and lodges. These fallen dead trees, as well as those killed by the high water or girdled by the beavers and left standing, attract many kinds of wood-boring insects, which in turn become food for woodpeckers. The woodpeckers chip nesting cavities in the standing dead trees to raise their young. After the woodpeckers finish using them, these holes provide nesting places for other birds—like tree swallows, crested flycatchers, owls, wood ducks, and bluebirds—that require cavities to nest in but cannot make their own.

As the standing trees rot and become hollow, bats seek daytime shelter in their interiors and forage at night in the insect-rich air over the pond. Bears occasionally lumber along the shore, feasting on berries and breaking apart the well-rotted logs and stumps in search of ants, termites, and other creatures. Foxes, coyotes, and wildcats stalk rabbits, mice, and other small mammals in the grassy areas. Deer, elk, and moose find plenty of browse in these clearings as well as shelter in the shrubby edges. Even after beavers have moved out of an area and their dams have washed away, the ponds they once inhabited become grassy open areas known as beaver meadows, which continue to support life that could not exist in the depths of the forest.

After spending many hours watching beavers at their ponds, I have come to realize that even though their working areas might look as disorderly and chaotic as my office or workshop, beavers are really not frenetic or compulsive. They are slow, methodical, and dignified. They might occasionally forget to get back to a tree they started gnawing, but nevertheless, for me, they have been teachers because of how they live their lives with grace and dignity.

They move slowly, but they still accomplish a great deal—a good example, especially for an "eager beaver"–type who has assimilated a strong dose of the Protestant work ethic.

A beaver's first task upon leaving its lodge for an evening's activities is a slow patrol around the pond to inspect the shoreline for intruders. These could be potential predators such as bears, wolves, or other carnivores large enough to risk a beaver's sharp incisors, or it could be a bumbling human like myself, arriving late for the first feature of the evening beaver show. On a number of such occasions I have been the object of a beaver's scrutiny.

I'll never forget the first time that happened. The sun had just set behind a distant mountain and I was sneaking through the bushes, intending to slip behind the roots of a fallen tree right at the edge of the pond. I had my binoculars ready and I was hoping to get settled before the beavers emerged. As I crossed a clearing about fifteen feet from the water's edge a slowly swimming beaver material-

"Then like a toy ferry boat the beaver turned to face me...."

ized from behind the stump of a downed tree. It was close, and it was swimming closer. I froze in mid-stride, trying my best to resemble a gnarled tree stump (with binoculars).

With just its head and some of its back above the surface, the beaver was moving along, parallel to the shore. When it came even with me, it paused. Then, like a toy ferry boat, it turned to face me. It swam closer and paused again, staring right at me. It lifted its nose and tried to scent the air. I stared back intensely. That beaver was CLOSE. I held my breath and did not move. My leg muscles started to cramp. I gritted my teeth and held my position, determined to not even blink.

As I stood there like a strained statue, looking deeply into those beady little beaver eyes, I realized that my psychic presence, that is, my stressed-out ego—that part of me that sees myself as separate from, rather than as part of, the environment—was probably much more disruptive to the peacefulness at the beaver pond than my mere physical presence. I knew I could fit in so much better if I could somehow soften the discordant chords of this cacophonous ego of mine. But how?

I released my breath. I relaxed my eyes and softened my gaze. This felt better. I tried to release my thoughts and quiet the excited internal narrative rattling on in my busy little brain. And I relaxed my leg muscles and allowed my body to float, ever so slowly, into a more comfortable position.

The beaver just kept staring. It seemed like it was playing "What's wrong with this picture?" Something here just didn't quite look right. Then, KAPOW!! Its tail came crashing down on the surface of the water, sounding like a combination rifle shot and belly flop. I just about jumped out of my skin. Water splashed everywhere, and the beaver disappeared in the splash.

I was so startled that I completely lost my balance and fell over into some brambles. The beaver surfaced a few seconds later. It was a little farther out in the pond, and it calmly surveyed the shore to see if the scene had changed. Earlier I wrote about some of the ways beavers alter the environment. Here was another way: This beaver had actually altered my psychic environment and my consciousness as well.

Not only had it induced in me the beginnings of a meditative experience, but with the help of this furry, buck-toothed psycho-drama coach, I had just acted out a personal existential metaphor—that of a startled being, falling out of control into the unknown.

This little flat-tailed guru had transformed me from a poor imitation of a gnarled tree trunk into an embodiment of my true self, falling into a brier patch. With the help of this beaver, for a few short seconds I had experienced eternity. I had lived purely in the moment. This living in the moment (or "being here now") is, for practitioners of yoga, meditation, and other spiritual disciplines, the goal of years of devotion. That beaver had brought me to that place with a mere tail slap. Not bad for a second's work.

I first learned about beaver tail slapping at a Disney nature movie when I was a small boy. The film said that this tail slap is a warning and that when one beaver slaps its tail, they all disappear.

Hanging out with beavers taught me that this behavior is not quite that simple. Besides being a warning for other beavers, it appears that this tail slapping is also meant to evoke a startled reaction and cause the intruder in question to reveal itself and its true nature. I sure had revealed mine. A cougar or a wolf would have acted differently, I'm sure.

That beaver came over and slapped its tail again and again as if to emphasize its point, and then it continued slowly on its way around the pond, smoothly crawling over a few submerged logs and diving under some floating ones as it made its rounds.

During a beaver's rounds, the lodge and dam are inspected as well as the shoreline. If repairs are needed, the beaver usually dives to the bottom and comes up carrying a double armful of mud, rocks, and/or waterlogged sticks between its front legs and chest. It nudges this load into place at the edge of the dam, or if the lodge needs work, it waddles up out of the water on its hind legs, looking like a pear-shaped senior citizen with a load of groceries. Steadying itself with its broad, stiff tail, the beaver trundles up the sloping side of the lodge and deposits its load of debris.

In summer, beavers spend a great deal of time in the pond eating lily pads and other succulent water plants, as well as grasses, raspberry canes, and other tender herbs on the water's edge. Beavers go ashore primarily to cut wood. All during the warmer months they cut shrubs and small trees and haul them back to the water. Once back in the water, the beaver cuts the trunks and branches into convenient lengths (from a few inches to a few feet long). Then, squatting in shallow water or floating on the surface, the beaver holds the stick in its front feet and leisurely munches off the bark, eating it like you or I might eat corn on the cob. These newly cleaned branches often become part of the lodge or dam.

Wood-cutting activity peaks in autumn as the green plants die back and winter approaches. Not only do the beavers rely more on bark for food at this time of year, but they also store food for winter by stockpiling branches underwater near the entrance of the lodge. This enables the beavers to swim out of their lodge, cut one of the submerged branches, and carry it back to the lodge to eat, even when the pond is completely frozen over.

When cutting a tree, a beaver works hard and fast. It can cut a five-inch willow in three minutes. Beavers have been known to fell trees with trunks several feet in diameter. Usually a beaver works alone, but for large projects several individuals might work together.

The trunks of trees and those limbs larger than five inches in diameter are usually left lying where they fall, though some of the bark might be eaten on the spot. Smaller branches are cut into portable lengths, seized in the mouth, and dragged to the water's edge. Once the limb is afloat, hauling it is much easier. Beavers often dig canals into areas where they are working. These canals save labor in dragging logs and branches but they are probably built

This cross-section of a beaver pond in winter shows the beaver family coming and going from their lodge and swimming under the pond's frozen surface. A food storage area of submerged branches is in front of the lodge; the dam is to the far left.

more as a function of the beavers' discomfort at being far away from water. Beavers are water creatures. They would much rather swim than walk.

In its watery realm, the beaver feels secure. It has large webbed hind feet, a thick coat of impermeable fur, and the ability to swim a hundred yards under water and stay submerged for as long as fifteen minutes. When the water is deep enough, a beaver is safe from all predators (except perhaps, alligators in the South). The function of the dam is to maintain sufficiently deep water to cover the entrances of the lodge and for the beavers to be able to submerge and move about under water—and under the ice in winter. By building substantial dams, beavers are able to ensure their watery security. Could these engineering projects, as extensive as they may be and as effective as they are in maintaining the water level of the pond, really be monuments to the beavers' insecurity, discomfort, and fear of being on land?

A large, well-maintained beaver dam is indeed a wonder to behold. One on the Jefferson River in Montana was 2,140 feet long. Leonard Lee Rew III reports that one near Berlin, New Hampshire, was 4,000 feet long and created a lake on which forty beaver lodges were built.[1] Some dams are more than 12 feet in height, though most are not more than 4 or 5 feet high. Often a colony of beavers will build an elaborate series of ponds and canals with dams at separate locations, maintaining different water levels in each pond.

Observers of beaver works often portray the Northern Hemisphere's largest rodents not only as hardworking animals but also as engineers of great vision. Although the function of the dam is clear, the actual concept of a dam across a stream and the advanced planning necessary to build one seems rather abstract for the minds of most rodents. There is much speculation and controversy about whether beavers' abilities to "engineer" such elaborate projects are derived wholly from instinctive behavior, as is the case with most rodents, or if they actually plan their work and acquire skills through learning.

Hope Ryden, a naturalist who spent four years watching a beaver colony and wrote a book about her experiences,[2] observed a three-month-old beaver kit as it joined in to help its mother tow branches across the pond to their lodge. On the first trip, it held the leafy branch by the middle and had quite a struggle pushing the branch against the resistance of the water. It finally delivered the branch to the lodge, but only with great difficulty. Later, while fol-

lowing its mother, it learned to drag branches by the butt end, so the leafy end would easily trail behind. This is the way it carried all subsequent branches.[3]

She also observed a senior male member of the colony acting as a kind of foreman. While he didn't actually direct the other beavers, he would often move some of their piles of sticks and mud to what were apparently more strategic locations on the dam.

Her observations indicate that older beavers might actually take more responsibility in the planning and execution of a project than younger ones, and that many of the skills beavers use are learned. Learning, planning, and thinking may be part of the beaver's world.

Yet other researchers have observed beavers acting as if they have an instinctive aversion to running water; they try to stop it by piling sticks and mud on it. Could this seem-

ingly simple, instinctive response to running water be the basis from which these rodents build great dams that can alter entire watersheds, change the landscape, enrich the soil, and augment wildlife populations?

As a way of trying to learn more about the instinctive basis of beaver behavior, Swedish ethologist Lars Wilsson played recordings of the sound of running water to captive beavers that had been raised away from other beavers. The beavers responded by piling mud and sticks onto the loudspeakers.[4] This does imply that some of the beavers' mud-and-stick-piling behavior is instinctive. But there is a lot more to building a dam than simply heaping up mud and sticks.

Ryden points out that young wildcats are born with a "pounce response," which is triggered by the sight of scurrying objects, but it takes many months of following their mothers before they learn when, where, and how to use this simple motor response to kill prey and feed themselves. The fact that young beavers typically spend about two years with their parents leads her to suppose that beavers also must acquire know-how from adults and their older siblings on when, where, and how to use their stick-and-mud-piling instinct.[5]

Although Wilsson's work with captive beavers produced interesting results, his experiments may simply illustrate the vestiges of natural behavior in experientially deprived laboratory animals.

The problems of using the laboratory as a place for investigating the nature of reality was well illustrated by the late biologist and philosopher Gregory Bateson in his classic "Dog in the Lab" story. In an interview with Stewart Brand, Bateson discussed the phenomenon observed in laboratory animals known as experimental neurosis or

"Pavlovian nervous breakdown." He explained that when the animal is brought into a laboratory the dramatic environmental change alters the animal's emotional state—"the smell of the lab and the feel of [its] harness…are context markers which say that [it is] supposed to be right or wrong, for example."

First, you train the dog to "discriminate between an ellipse and a circle, say…. Then you make the discrimination a little more difficult and he learns again, and you have underlined that message. Then you make the discrimination impossible.

"At this point discrimination is not the appropriate form of behavior. Guesswork is. But the animal cannot stop feeling he ought to discriminate, and then you get the symptomology [of experimental neurosis] coming on."

Bateson notes that it is impossible to induce this response in animals in the wild. "In the field none of this happens. For one thing the stimuli don't count. Those electric shocks they use [in the lab] are about as powerful as what the animal would get if he pricked his leg on a bramble….

"Suppose you've got an animal whose job in life is to turn over stones and eat beetles under them. All right, one stone in ten is going to to have a beetle under it. He cannot go into a nervous breakdown because the other nine stones don't have beetles under them. But the lab can make him do that, you see."

"Do you think we are all in a lab of our own making, in which we drive each other crazy?" asked Brand.

"You said it, not I, brother," said Bateson with a chuckle.[6]

Back at the beaver colony, the debate goes on. What is the true nature of these industrious beings? Is a beaver pond and lodge a richly productive home environment for the beaver clan as well as a habitat for multitudes of other species, or is it more like a monument to fear and insecurity? Are beavers hardworking engineers of great vision, or are they insecure, slow-moving, yet compulsive neurotics who can't stand the sound of running water?

And back in the midst of human society, when I ponder human endeavors, such as great cities, nuclear arsenals, works of art, and concepts such as xenophobia, charity, and racial bias, I find myself asking the same questions about myself and my species that I ask about beavers. I wonder, are we beings with great vision or are we instinctively insecure, compulsive neurotics? Is our primary endeavor as a species to build monuments to our own fear and insecurity; or are we conducting ourselves as the manifestations of a great vision?

Both. We are both. Like my Indian friend said, beavers are like people and people are like beavers. We are a reflection of our world. We can place ourselves in a lab of our own creation where we can drive ourselves crazy or we can learn to resonate with the natural harmony and vision of which we are a part. We are multifaceted beings, each retaining within ourselves everything from the ridiculous to the sublime; from the neurotic to the visionary. Like the wood sorrel, which teaches "We are all there," the beaver teaches that we are not only "all there" but that, whether neurotic or visionary, we can accomplish a great deal and nurture others, too—if we learn to live with grace and dignity.

Whatever we do, we can certainly do worse than live like the beaver. We can learn to observe our surroundings carefully in order to understand and bring out the true nature of the beings we encounter in our daily lives. Like the beaver, we can endeavor to live in such a way that we create a community of nurturance and respect, not only for our own kind but also for other species as well. Might we also be better off if we learned, like the beaver, to cover our TVs, radios, and other loudspeakers with mud and sticks?

1 Leonard Lee Rew III, *World of the Beaver* (New York: J. B. Lippincott, 1964).

2 Hope Ryden, *Lily Pond, Four Years with a Family of Beavers* (New York: William Morrow & Co., 1989), p. 181.

3 ——. "The Beaver Is One Smart Rat," *Audubon* V.90. #5 (Sept. 1988).

4 Lars Wilsson, *My Beaver Colony* (New York: Doubleday & Co., 1968), p. 140–49.

5 Ryden, *Lily Pond, Four Years with a Family of Beavers*, p. 132–34.

6 Stewart Brand, *Two Cybernetic Frontiers* (New York: Random House, 1974), p. 25–26.

4

Beaver Legends and Coyote Tales
OF MYTHIC RODENTS, THE FOOLISH CREATOR, AND ONE SORRY SUCKER

When I first heard native American "Coyote" stories I was puzzled. In these stories Coyote, the Creator, is portrayed not only as a trickster but also as a greedy, pompous fool. To someone who was raised in the Judeo-Christian tradition, where one of the greatest sins is to take God's name in vain, it seemed strange to think of native Americans calling the creator foolish, continually making fun of him and even telling bawdy stories about his seemingly scandalous antics and trickery. When I asked an Indian friend about this he said, "Look at this crazy world we live in today. How could it have been made by anything but a foolish creator?"

And there's more to it than that. In many of these tales, a Coyote's actions, thoughts, and deeds are displayed on a

Wooden Coyote Mask from Key Marco, Florida.

mythic scale and recounted in hilarious detail. He becomes involved in one comedy of errors after another. When he has made a complete fool of himself and become the laughing stock of creation, he will indignantly proclaim, "You can't laugh at me; I created the world."

These stories are so entertaining because we recognize all of Coyote's qualities and behaviors as our own. Coyote is the quintessential human; he has all the same attributes, as well as the same flaws, petty vanities, and greed as we do. His mythic foolery is held up for us as a mirror to look into deeply, laugh bawdily at what we see, and perhaps, learn from the reflection. Coyote, the Foolish Creator, is a reflection of ourselves; we each are our own creator. Through our perceptions and our actions, we each create our own world—

"Crooked Mouth," a Foolish Creator Image of the Algonquin.

and we often act downright foolishly.*

As the plots unfold in these stories, the different characters teach archetypical lessons about life by embodying different values and different ways of being and relating to the world.

Incorporated in many of these tales are "origin myths," which tell how certain things came to be the way they are today. These stories often point out interrelationships between species, as well as subtle intricacies that occur in the natural world, and "explain" them through the tale. This encourages a special awareness of one's surroundings and allows every aspect of the environment to become part of a rich mythology that contains a plethora of personal lessons.

These origin myths often describe events that may seem like casualties or mishaps, but they end up changing the world. This reminds us that in our own lives, we build upon the events of yesterday. We can learn from our mistakes

For Natives of the Pacific Northwest, the Creator is a Raven.

(especially if we can laugh at them) and this changes us and makes us into what we are today.

"Long time ago" in many native American legends (like the "Once upon a time" of European fairy tales) refers to mythic time, the time before this world. Sometimes, Indians call it "Real Time," the time of the "Real Beings," the shape changers, the ones who changed the world into what it is today.

There is a legend that the Algonquian peoples from north-central Canada tell. Long time ago, a man was traveling through the countryside along a stream when he came to a dome-shaped lodge. He was invited into the lodge to share the pipe and smoke tobacco. He was shown certain tobacco ceremonies, and given tobacco seed to take back to his village. His people planted the seed, and from then on, they had tobacco. When he went back to the lodge and went inside, he realized that beavers were living there. This gift of tobacco, a principal medicine plant, established the spiritual connection between people and beavers. The beaver-people of this legend had a lodge large enough for this human to walk into. They were as large as bears, it is said.

What amazes me is how much this ancient Indian legend of the "Real Beaver" resembles the modern, scientific origin myths of paleontologists, who tell us of the giant beavers, *Castoroides ohioensis*, that

---

*Although most native American cultures have a trickster-creator in their mythology, Coyote is not the only embodiment that this figure takes. For Northwestern peoples, the creator is Raven. Southeastern tribes have Rabbit. In the Northeast it can be Raccoon or Gray Jay. Many Algonquin tribes see the wild-haired character known as "Twisted-Face" or "Crooked Mouth" as the foolish creator.

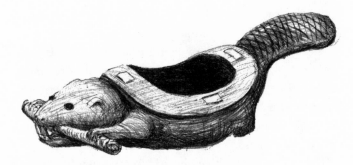

Beaver Effigy Bowl

roamed the continent during the Pleistocene Epoch several hundred thousand years ago. This was the time of the ice ages, when Paleolithic humans made their appearance. It is intriguing to think that this story of Real Beaver, which is still told today, might have been passed down from the Pleistocene. Of course, many native Americans would say that the stories were there even before the people (a common theme in other mythologies, including the Christian Bible).

Paleontologists tell us that fossil evidence confirms that these giant beavers were as large as the black bear of today and that they became extinct during one of the glacial ice ages.

According to the native American tale, when it came time to leave this world and recede into the mythic realm, Real Beaver resisted. He had given the people tobacco, but he wanted to leave more. Finally, the Thunderers, those great birds, were called

Beaver Totem Figure

in to take Beaver back into the mythic Real World. They hooked their claws into his back and flew off, carrying him from the eastern edge of the continent to the West. They stopped once in what is now Minnesota, and Beaver's blood soaked into the ground. Today, in that place where they stopped, there is a deposit of blood-red soapstone. Geologists call this peculiar soapstone catlinite. For many tribes this is the preferred material from which to carve ceremonial medicine pipes, and Pipestone National Monument is located here today.

I once heard another apparently contradictory Indian legend that says that this deposit is the congealed blood of the Earth Mother. When I asked a native American about these two completely different explanations for the same phenomenon, he told me that his people always say,

"Anything that is real has more than one explanation."

A favorite Chippewa-Cree tale starts out "Long time ago...."

Everyone—all the creatures—were sitting around looking up. They were looking up through that big hole in the sky, wondering what kind of world was up there above the clouds. They wanted to go up there and look around, and they were trying to figure out some way to do it.

They talked to Porcupine. He was a good archer and always carried lots of little arrows. They wanted him to shoot an arrow into the sky to see if he could get it high enough so that it would stick in there. He tried, but he couldn't shoot high enough. So then he climbed up on Eagle's back and Eagle flew up and up, as high into the sky as he could, and when he reached the apex of his heavenward flight, Porcupine shot an arrow and it stuck solidly into the sky.

Then he shot another arrow into that arrow and another into that one and another and another, until they had a ladder, a scaffolding of sorts, made entirely of porcupine quills, going all the way up into the heavens—sort of a native American "Tower of Babel." Unlike the Judeo-Christian tower, however, there was no problem getting this ladder tall enough to reach heaven; it started there.

They were all getting ready to start climbing up when that trickster Coyote, the foolish creator, came along.

"Just where do you all think you're going?" he asked.

"We're gonna climb up through that hole in the sky and look around," they told him.

"Well, you can just wait for me," he ordered. "I'm the creator around here. I made the world, so I get to go first."

"Well, go ahead then!" they all chimed in at once.

"No, I'm hungry; I'm gonna get something to eat first."

"You're always hungry," they said. "We don't want to wait around for you to find something to eat. Who knows when you'll be back. We want to climb up now."

"No, you have to wait for me," Coyote insisted. "I made the world...."

So they waited and waited, and waited some more. Coyote never returned. After a very long time, they finally decided to start climbing without Coyote. Up the ladder they climbed, all the way to the top, and soon they all made it through that hole in the sky. And when they looked around up there, they found another world, and they liked it. It was a lot like the earth below, where they had just come from. There were trees and lakes and grassy prairies. All the grazing animals really liked the grass that grew there. They spread out grazing, while the others roamed all over exploring this new world.

Meanwhile, back on earth, Coyote finally returned, and when he realized that everyone had climbed up there without

him, he got mad and tore down the ladder. When it fell, it left such a huge pile of debris that it became some of the jagged, rocky mountains that are still down here on earth today. Some people say that even in summer those mountains have patches of snow on them, but others say that those white patches up high come from the white coloring that was on Porcupine's crumbled quills.

When they saw that their ladder had collapsed, everybody wondered how they would get back down. Some of the grazing animals said that they liked it up there—that the grass really was greener up there on that side of the sky. So they decided to stay. Sometimes, you can still see herds of them up there moving across the night sky with little points of light glinting off their hooves.

But most of the other animals still wanted to go back down, and they were trying to figure out how when Beaver said, "I know, I'll make a big boat and sail down in it." And he immediately began cutting trees, dragging them around, and chopping and working the wood.

In the meantime, the other animals started talking to one another. They realized that there were about the same number of winged ones as there were of the four-leggeds and others who didn't fly. So they decided that if they could pair up, each winged one could carry one of the flightless ones and sail down, with their wings spread wide to assure a gentle landing. So that is what they did. While they were gliding down with each bird carrying another creature in its feet, many of the birds had trouble holding on and they started to lose their grip, and they had to keep grabbing tighter to keep their hold. This loosened the fur on some of the four-leggeds, and to this day, at certain times of the year, many of the four-leggeds shed their hair.

So almost all the animals made it back down to earth except Snake, who had been somewhere else; Suckerfish, who hadn't been paying attention; and of course, Beaver, who had been busy working on his boat.

"No problem," said Beaver as he dragged his newly finished craft over to the hole in the sky. "We'll just sail back down to earth in my new boat."

To his surprise, however, the boat was too big to fit through the hole. He had gotten so involved in the project that he had forgotten to measure the hole. Besides, if he hadn't been so involved working on his boat, he could have easily gotten a ride down with one of the birds. So there the three of them sat, looking down through the hole.

"I guess we'll have to jump down," said Snake, ever so slyly. "Why don't you go first, Suckerfish?"

Suckerfish agreed, and as he slipped over the edge and began to hurtle down towards earth, Snake shouted, "See you later, Suckerrrr!"

Sucker landed with a splat on a rock and every bone in his body was broken into little pieces. He couldn't move. When Snake saw what had happened to Sucker, he decided that he would just stay up in the sky. And he is still up there to this day. You can see the zigzag pattern of stars up there. Some people call that constellation Cassiopeia, but many others know that it is really Snake.

Everyone wanted to help Sucker when they saw him with his bones all crumbled, so they all got together and each one gave him a bone from his or her own body. Soon Sucker had enough bones, but many were still lined up, ready to give him more of their bones.

When somebody is offering you a bone from their own body, this is a great gift. It didn't seem right to just say, "No, thank you." So Sucker graciously accepted all the bones they offered and even to this day, Sucker has too many bones. If you've ever tried to eat a suckerfish, you know this is true. The meat is sometimes mushy in texture, too.

Now Beaver decided that he might as well jump down too, and when he did, he landed right on his thick round tail. Sure enough, the tail squashed flat and that is the way it is today. Beaver's still a worker and gets involved in his projects, but instead of personal projects, he is a community builder. And that's the way beaver colonies are today.

This story, as ancient and traditional as it may be, speaks to me about my own personal development. I think about how Beaver became so compulsively involved in his poorly planned project that he missed a ride down with the birds. This type of story might save me from allowing my own industrious nature to cause me to fall through a similar hole in the sky. I also think about the healing and the growth that this story implies, as Beaver with his newly flattened tail learns to use his same industrious spirit to create community. Whenever I visit a beaver pond and see the plethora of life-forms it supports, I can see these lessons of community clearly, intricately, and beautifully demonstrated.

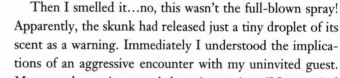

5

The Night of the Living Skunk

I was sound asleep up in the loft of a little log cabin at the foot of the Black Mountains in western North Carolina. It was in the late 1970s. In exchange for living there rent-free, I had been working on the place. I had finished the chinking, sealed the windows, and hung the doors. I was pleased with my progress; winter was coming and I knew the cabin was tight. As I lay on the mattress in the loft, I had one hand extended out of the covers and I was dreaming that a small animal was licking my fingers. When I woke slightly and rolled over, I heard a rustling in the back of the loft and realized that I was not alone. I quietly groped for my flashlight, pointed it at the noise, and flicked it on. There in the beam was an impeccably marked, sprightly little spotted skunk!

"How did YOU get in here?" I asked, thinking not only of the

skunk, but also of my bedding, my expensive down sleeping bag, and all my good clothes hung up there in the loft.

Then I smelled it…no, this wasn't the full-blown spray! Apparently, the skunk had released just a tiny droplet of its scent as a warning. Immediately I understood the implications of an aggressive encounter with my uninvited guest. My second question wasn't long in coming. "Never mind how you got in here. How are you gonna get out?" I asked.

The skunk, who was at least as uneasy as I was about our surprise meeting, slinked along the wall behind some boxes, then gracefully scampered the width of the cabin along an open log rafter, and went out a small hole under the eaves. I stuffed a rag in the hole and breathed a long sigh of relief.

The next morning, I recounted the night's adventures to my landlord and he said, "Oh yeah, we call

Spotted Skunk

This skunk was hardly bigger than a large squirrel, which is the normal size for this, the smallest member of the skunk clan. The spotted skunk is known for its agility and its ability to climb. It is often called civet cat by mountain folks. Of course, it's no more a cat than is its larger cousin the striped skunk, which is known as the polecat. (These are actually names of musk-bearing Old World animals. When the first European settlers encountered skunks, they applied these familiar names to them, and they are still used to this day.)

Skunks are actually in the family Mustelidae, the musk carriers. Included in this family are weasels, mink, marten, otters, badgers, and wolverines, all of which have musk glands. This very vigorous and diverse family has dispersed its members to every conceivable niche on the continent and each has its specialty. The river otter and the mink have adapted to fresh water, where they live on fish and frogs. The sea otter lives in the kelp beds off the Pacific coast and dives for mollusks; the marten lives in northern treetops, where it leaps from tree to tree in hot pursuit of red squirrels. Weasels are agile predators, easily able to slip into narrow rodent burrows. Badgers are powerful diggers. The wolverine is the most fierce and powerful of all and lives in subarctic regions. Skunks, however, thrive in almost all parts of the continent except the extreme north. Their only specialty is their highly evolved (and extremely accurate) musk glands. With one gland located on each side of its anus, a skunk rarely misses. While looking straight at its target, the skunk can swing its rear end around and fire away! As powerful as this spray is, the quantity is limited to about five or six shots. Perhaps because of this, or simply because of its mellow temperament, a skunk shows restraint. It would much rather avoid a confrontation.

him 'the inspector.' He comes around to check on your work to see if you've done a good job closing in the cabin. If you've left any holes anywhere, he'll find 'em." You can believe I went over that cabin with a fine-tooth comb and closed up every possible skunk-sized opening. And it's lucky I did, because sure enough, the inspector was back the next night; he came snooping around quite regularly after that. I started to enjoy his visits (outside the cabin, that is) and would leave offerings of food for him. He would eat most table scraps but seemed to especially enjoy meat and peanut butter. It wasn't long before I could sit quietly at the back door and the skunk would come right up to me, prop his front feet on my knee and eat peanut butter off a stick I was holding. (At first I let him take food from my fingers until I learned he had trouble discriminating where the food stopped and the fingers started.)

When it first senses danger, a skunk will try to retreat, waddling away with its characteristic ambling gait. If it is still being molested, it then gives warning. The striped skunk may stamp its front feet on the ground, growl, hiss, or click its teeth. The acrobatic spotted skunk may even do a "handstand" when agitated and walk about on its front legs. Then up goes the tail—straight up like a magnificent bushy plume. This is the moment for you to head for the hills! In a flash, the skunk whips into its U-shaped battle position, its head and rear on target, facing the enemy. It can shoot up, down, left, right, or straight ahead. It holds its gorgeous tail daintily aloft, as it would not want to soil its own fur or block the carefully aimed stream of spray.

The two vents of the glands protrude like twin nozzles as the powerful hip muscles contract and squeeze two fine streams of oily yellowish liquid toward the target. These streams merge about a foot away from the animal into one spray of very fine droplets. This spray is aimed at the face of the attacker, and it is amazingly accurate up to about twelve feet. If the wind is right, the spray can actually carry six or eight feet farther.

If the spray gets into the eyes, it will burn like fire, but it does no permanent damage. Flushing the eyes with fresh water will hasten recovery, but even without this, the stream of tears will wash out the spray within ten or fifteen minutes. (That's usually enough time for the skunk to be

Striped Skunk or "Polecat"

long gone.) I have talked to a number of folks who have caught an eye-full of skunk spray. Though they all agreed that it hurt at the time, many of the victims believe it has actually improved their eyesight!

Of course, the most noteworthy quality of the spray is its overwhelming musky stench. Sometimes it can be smelled from a half-mile or more away. Most people find it disagreeable and some find it nauseating. Numerous ways are recommended to remove the smell from one's clothes and person, including washing with tomato juice, vinegar, gasoline, ammonia, or chloride of lime. There is even a commercial preparation sold in pet stores for this purpose. Old trappers were known to bury their clothes in the ground for a week or so and then smoke them over a fire of juniper and cedar. Equal parts of citronella and bergamot oil have been used to neutralize the scent on one's body. In dissipating skunk odor, time is your best ally. I have a couple of skunk hides hanging on my wall. They were road kills, and when I first prepared them, they were rather strong. Now, however, if they remain dry, the aroma is not noticeable. If the air is humid, or if you sprinkle water on them, it is a different story.

One cool, drizzly evening, I happened to be in New York City. I was walking down Fifth Avenue behind two elegantly dressed women. One was wearing a beautiful, silky, black fur coat. I couldn't help but notice that mixed in with their scent trail of expensive French perfumes the distinctive odor of skunk was emanating from that costly fur wrap. She might not have known that what was sold to her under the furrier's trade name of "Alaskan Sable" or "Black Marten" was really skunk. The odor surrounding her was the skunks' posthumous revenge and it seemed like poetic justice. And to tell you the truth, to my simple tastes that mild, musky whiff of skunk was preferable to those fancy perfumes!

To some extent striped skunks are still trapped for their fur throughout most of their range. Those hides with the least amount of white bring the best price.

Unless they are starving, very few predators will risk a spraying for a meal of skunk meat. The great horned owl, however, is an exception. These huge nocturnal birds often capture and feed on skunks. Apparently, they are immune to the smell and often carry the odoriferous residue of their prey on their feathers for months at a time. If you aren't squeamish, you might even find out for yourself that skunk meat, cleaned VERY carefully, is tender and delicious. You might even want to render out some of the grease. Like groundhog grease, when rubbed on the chest it is a traditional home remedy for respiratory ailments, and it is used as a liniment for arthritis.

February and March is the mating season for skunks. When the females come into heat, the males will travel long distances looking for them. This is a time of frenzied activity, and sometimes of large unruly gatherings of fighting and squealing male skunks. Sometimes, they even spray each other!

The spotted skunk tends to be bolder than its larger striped cousin and during this "mating madness" it can act even more outrageously. One such skunk was reported to have run right up to a reclining bull and sprayed it in the face! Another invaded a wolf's den and shook the young wolves by their ears.

In skunks and other mustelids, copulation is repeated and very prolonged—up to one or two hours. Apparently the female skunks will not ovulate unless she is thoroughly aroused by long and vigorous copulation. The penis is stiffened by a bone, the baculum, which facilitates the process.

The young striped skunks are born after about a two-month gestation period. Because the implantation of the fertilized egg on the wall of the uterus is delayed, the spotted skunk's gestation can be twice that long. The litters are usually from three to eight in number. Once the young have reached approximately seven weeks of age, they can be seen on hunting expeditions following the mother in single-file caravans. By summer's end they are on their own.

Once I was sitting in the woods when I heard a rustling in the leaves coming my way. As I watched and waited, a large striped skunk moseyed by. I sat very still and, as I was downwind, the skunk did not know I was there. After it passed, I carefully got up and followed. The skunk was poking along with its nose to the ground, hunting for food. Occasionally it stopped, scraped away the leaves, or dug into the soil, and quickly munched down a beetle, worm, or some other insect. I was about twenty feet behind, trying to be as silent as possible. But the leaves were dry and before long, I crunched down on a dry twig and made a loud rustling noise. When I did, that tail flew straight up and the skunk whirled around ready for action. I froze in place and did not move a muscle! The skunk squinted in my direction, lifted its moist black nose, and sniffed the air. (A skunk's eyes are rather weak and unable to discriminate color or fine details if an object is not moving.) I held my pose like a statue. Soon the skunk was satisfied that nothing was there. It turned around and continued its foraging, with me tiptoeing along behind like a big clumsy shadow. Several more times I created a disturbance and the skunk whirled around ready for action. But I immediately did my statue routine, freezing until the skunk continued on its way. Then the skunk started digging a hole and soon its head was down in the earth; it continued digging deeper. Before long, it was up to its forequarters in the excavation. With its head down in the hole, it couldn't hear well and I was able to creep up very close. I was curious to know the object of this furious digging. I peered cautiously around a tree, right behind the skunk, and watched. Soon the skunk had half its body down in the hole and then it rolled out a gray object, the size and shape of a large potato. I could see its jaws smacking as it pulled this thing apart and ate the contents. Small insects were buzzing around its head. After the skunk departed, I examined the excavation and realized that it had just devoured an entire nest of yellow jackets. Its long, thick fur coat must have given it some protection from their stings, but still, any critter that can take on a nest full of these powerful stingers has got my respect! Indeed, insects of all kinds make up the major part of a skunk's diet. In fact, skunks' efficiency at destroying the hop grub in New York State earned them legislative protection in hop-growing areas. (Next time you sip a delicious cold beer, you can thank a skunk!) A foraging skunk is nimble and quick. They catch and eat mice, rats, voles, and other small mammals as well as snakes and other reptiles. (Some evidence suggests that skunks are immune to the venom of the poisonous snakes they sometimes eat.) They appreciate all kinds of fruits and berries and occasionally eat the eggs and young of ground-nesting birds. (Now, before you bird lovers start a campaign against skunks, remember that they probably save the lives of many ducklings and other water birds by digging up and eating the eggs of snapping turtles.)

Sometimes a skunk will cause problems for farmers by slipping into a poorly fenced henhouse to eat eggs, and occasionally one will raise the ire of a beekeeper by visiting a hive at night and scratching at the entrance. When the bees come out to investigate, the skunk swats them and gobbles them up. The remedy for this is to tack a large piece of wire mesh to the front of the hive, so the skunk can't get at the entrance, or place a board full of protruding sharp nails on the landing board at the front of the hive. This will make bee swatting a painful experience and will soon discourage the skunk.

If you ever want to get rid of a troublesome skunk without incurring its spray, use an enclosed or covered live trap. A skunk will feel secure in the dark enclosure and it can be gently transported and released far away from trouble.

It is possible to pick up a skunk by the tail without getting sprayed; I have done it several times. Apparently, in order to spray, a skunk must hold its tail at a right angle to its body. When being held by its tail, the tail extends straight back and the skunk can't spray. Of course, it is difficult to approach a skunk close enough to grab it. I have only been able to do this when the skunk is partially concealed and thinks it is hiding. You must grab the skunk's tail firmly and swiftly lift it off the ground. (There are no second chances in this game!) Once you are proudly holding the skunk by the tail, the next question that will occur to you is, "How do I put him down?!!"

If you find yourself in this position, just give me a call

(I'm in the book), and if you don't get my answering machine, I'll be glad to tell you!

Seriously, all you need to do is toss the skunk with a gentle underhand swing so that it lands about ten or fifteen feet away. It usually lands on its feet, and in an unruffled, dignified manner, it will calmly walk away. (And if it doesn't—run like hell!)

The skunk's scientific name, *Mephitis*, is a Latin word, meaning a noxious vapor. Our word skunk is derived from the Algonquian Indian word *segonkw*, which translates as "a stimulating puff of wind."

In the following Chippewa-Cree tale Skunk plays an important role:

One day Coyote, the magical, foolish, trickster Creator, was very hungry. He was outside his lodge when he saw Skunk coming his way. Skunk would make a delicious meal if he could just trick him, so he ducked back into his lodge and transformed himself into a beautiful and seductive female skunk. He came out of the lodge and called out to Skunk, "Hey cousin, you handsome one, you. Why don't you come visit me? We could have a good time together. We could make love. Then we could have a nice meal together. The pot is on the fire. *Heh, heh.*"

Skunk looked over and he liked what he saw. She was so pretty, and she sounded so friendly. He accepted her invitation and was almost at her door when Chickadee, who saw what was happening, warned Skunk. He flew down and said, "It's a trick, Look out-out-out-out!" He did this four times. (And to this day, if you listen carefully to a chickadee, you will hear it still repeating this same call.)

When Skunk heard this warning, he

became suspicious and cautiously resisted going into the lodge with this beautiful imposter.

"How about a little hug out here before we go inside?" he suggested.

When they embraced, Skunk reached over, snatched the mask off Coyote's face, wriggled loose, gave Coyote a good spraying, and escaped to freedom. Coyote was enraged at this treatment and was even madder when he thought of the delicious meal that had just slipped out of his grasp. It was all because of that meddlesome Chickadee! He caught Chickadee and said, "How dare you unmask me! Just for that, I'll unmask YOU!"

With that, he pulled the skin off Chickadee's face and threw him down on the snow. Later, Skunk came by and found Chickadee lying there almost dead.

"Oh, little Brother Chickadee!" Skunk cried. "You saved my life. I've got to try to help you." So he took Chickadee back to his lodge and worked on Chickadee's face. He took a piece of his own skin to graft as a patch. He trimmed the hairs short, and as Skunk had always been partial to a black-and-white color pattern, that was the way he repaired Chickadee's face. To this day, Chickadee has a distinctive black-and-white face and Skunk still has a little bare place at the base of his tail, where he removed that patch of skin to graft on to Chickadee's face.

In considering the ancient myths of traditional peoples, I am reminded of the roles these stories play in the life of a culture. These traditional tales are full of information and multifaceted interpretations about the natural systems of which the people are a part. They also illustrate how the natural world is full of daily lessons and spiritual teachings for humans.

As an active participant in a high-tech,

twentieth-century culture and lifestyle, it has always been interesting to me to observe ways in which the natural world can still offer these lessons for us, even if we live lives that give the illusion of being separate or removed from nature. I have heard three such stories that illustrate this.

The first was from a young New York stockbroker. He had been doing quite well with his career, and he had a wife and two young daughters. They had just bought a large house in a nice area of Brooklyn. With more discretionary income coming in each week, they were discovering the joys of consumerism. They found more ways to spend money, and always, more things they could buy. He often worked late on weeknights, but on Saturdays, the whole family would pile into the Mercedes and they would go on weekend shopping sprees to some nearby area of interest. One Sunday afternoon they were returning from just such a trip to Williamsburg. They were cruising along a secondary road in rural Virginia, when they rounded a curve and saw a large bird picking at something on the road. They screeched to a halt just in the nick of time as the bird lifted itself into the air with huge frantic wing-beats. It was a turkey vulture that had been feeding on a freshly killed skunk. As they slowly passed the skunk, its overwhelming stench filled the car. The oldest daughter, who was about eight years old, said, "Pee-YEW! What was THAT?!" They explained to her that it was a skunk. Whereupon she proclaimed, "YUCK! I'd never buy one of them!"

When the chuckles subsided, the husband and wife looked at each other and wondered aloud, "What are we teaching our children?" They realized then that their kids had the whole world neatly divided into two categories: what they do, and what they don't, want to buy. This one incident marked a significant reevaluation, of and change in, their lifestyle and values. Shopping is no longer their major family recreation, and they are finding more value in what cannot be bought. They now have a little summer place near the Delaware River and he takes the summer off so that the family can be together when the kids are out of school. The last time I saw them, they were fishing on the bank of a pond as the sun set over the Delaware Water Gap.

The second story comes from another New Yorker, whom I'll call Mary, who works in Manhattan helping homeless people. She also works with the Humane Society and the A.S.P.C.A., caring for abandoned, orphaned, and mistreated animals.

On the morning before Thanksgiving she received a worried call from a young man about a skunk that was living on the grounds around his apartment complex. The caller didn't mind the skunk; in fact, he had become rather fond of it and had been discreetly feeding it. He was concerned about the skunk's welfare, however, because he was sure if other people found out it was there, somebody would kill it. He had been calling various animal organizations all around the city and had finally been given her name. She was his last hope. Is there any way she would come and remove the skunk and take it somewhere where it would be safe? She regularly got calls about squirrels, raccoons, opossums, and occasionally, even owls, but she had never had a call about a skunk in Manhattan.

She met him in front of his apartment on Thirty-eighth and Broadway. He was somewhat secretive because he was worried that someone else would find out about the skunk. He showed her where he fed the skunk. When she asked where the skunk stayed during the day, he took her around back and pointed to a storage building. The door to the building was a locked gate made of steel bars (that a skunk could easily pass through) and there was a homeless man sleeping in the doorway. He said he thought that the skunk stayed in that building, but he was afraid to look because that "derelict" was always there.

Mary went right over to the man lying in the doorway and politely asked, "Excuse me sir, have you seen a skunk around here?"

The man sat up and blinked. He was not used to being spoken to so directly and when he was spoken to, it was rarely with courtesy and respect.

"Yeah, he's in there," the man said, gesturing through the bars into the storage room. "That's where he stays during the day. He comes out every night and walks right over me. When he comes back in the morning, he climbs right back over me. He don't bother nobody."

She went back and asked the uniformed doorman if he had seen the skunk. He said, "Oh yeah, I see him crawling around in them bushes there almost every night. Sometimes I leave him a piece of my sandwich. He sure likes ham and cheese!"

"Don't you think it's unusual to see a skunk here?" she asked.

The doorman gave her a sidelong glance and said, "This is New York, lady."

Then he added, somewhat sadly, "The super just found out about it and he's been on the phone all morning to every exterminator in the city. They'll come spray your roaches and poison your rats but there ain't a one of them that'll touch a skunk! They don't know nothin' about skunks! All he knows is he wants that skunk outa here and

soon. We figure it came in here on a delivery truck from Jersey about a month ago. They left an old tire here with all that stuff they delivered. That skunk musta been in that tire. Now the poor guy's stuck here in the city like the rest of us."

Mary located the superintendent and told him that she would remove the skunk. He gave her a key to the storage building. She got a "Have-a-Heart" trap that the Humane Society uses for cats, and baited it with peanut butter and pieces of ham and cheese. She told the homeless man what she was doing, excused herself, unlocked the gate, went in to the storage building, and set the trap.

The next morning she checked the trap and sure enough, there was the skunk. She had come prepared with an old blanket, and slowly approached the trap, talking soothingly to the skunk. Then she draped the blanket over the trap and gently carried it out of there. She secured it in the back seat of the car she had borrowed ("THAT was a very big risk," she confided), then drove upstate to have Thanksgiving dinner with friends. On the way, she released the skunk on a large wooded estate where she knew the caretaker and so was assured that it wouldn't be disturbed.

When the skunk mission was completed that afternoon, she phoned the man who had been feeding the skunk, the man who had originally called her. She told him that the skunk was now on its own in the country and out of danger. He was very relieved and grateful.

"How can I ever thank you?" he asked.

"Perhaps you could take a plate of food down to that homeless man now and then," she said. "And happy Thanksgiving."

Mary spends a great deal of her time and energy on this sort of mission. She finds good homes for unwanted pets, relocates wild animals, and each year raises dozens of orphaned ones till they can be released in the wild. She once told me that when an animal leaves her care and goes off to its new life, a little piece of herself always goes with that animal, but in return, a little piece of that animal's new freedom comes back to her.

The third of these stories is a tale of a more conscious and directed spiritual quest. For the last few years I have been part of the faculty at a "wholistic studies" center. This institute offers a veritable smorgasbord of "new age" classes and workshops from yoga, massage, acupuncture, and the healing arts to dance, music, meditation, and personal transformation. It also offers classes that explore various spiritual disciplines, including Taoism, Sufism, Buddhism, and native American, Jewish, and Christian mysticism. One year, when I was there teaching a course on edible and medicinal wild plants, a workshop on shamanism was creating a great deal of excitement around campus. The instructor had spent many years in the South American jungles and other remote parts of the world, studying the spiritual practices and psychic healing techniques of tribal cultures, and he was trying to teach these skills to modern Americans.

One of the initial steps in shamanic practice is acquiring an animal ally as a spirit guide. This animal becomes a source of power and strength that can be called upon in times of need, in everyday life as well as when one has embarked on a shamanic journey into other realms of reality.

During the first part of the week, the class members were involved in attempting to contact their individual spirit animals through meditation and guided imagery. Once the animal presented itself, each rookie shaman was to try to merge with the animal and become one with its spirit. This meant not only trying to learn the lessons that the creature had come to teach, but also becoming one with the physical body of their ally and learning its movements. Yes, the mellow meditative atmosphere of the campus was transformed that week as people got more and more in touch with their animal allies. There were soaring eagles, lumbering bears, prowling cats, howling wolves, dancing cranes, breaching whales, trumpeting elephants, and even a few seals flopping about on the ground. Some days the students would show up at the dining hall with painted faces and feathers in their hair. Other times, they could be seen stalking the woods singly or in packs. At night ceremonial bonfires blazed with eerie chanting and feverish dancing, accompanied by the ever-present pulsing of the spirit drums.

Toward the end of the week one of the class members (whom I'll call Michael) took me aside. He seemed very preoccupied, and he had a wild look in his eyes. He said, "Doug, I know you have a strong feeling about animals and maybe you could give me some advice. I think I've gotten in touch with my spirit animal. I think it's a skunk. It came to me last night: I mean, I really saw one! Tell me what you think I should do. They talked in class about native American shamans on a spiritual quest actually hunting down and taking the life of an animal to capture its spirit power. Do you think I should kill that skunk? Maybe I should make a medicine bag from its hide."

I agreed that a fresh skunk hide would certainly be powerful and probably would make some mighty strong medicine (phew!), but I suggested that perhaps he could be more creative than simply killing it. I told him it would seem much more in keeping with his quest to spend time with the animal, study its nature, and come to know its habits and ways. A live animal could probably teach him much more than a dead one. This advice seemed to resonate with him. He thanked me. That faraway, wild look returned to his eyes and he took off back into the woods.

I did not see Michael again for a couple of years. When our paths did cross, he seemed slightly less wild-eyed. He had the same excitement about life, but he seemed more centered and settled. When I referred to our last conversation about his skunk encounter, he said, "I never did tell you the whole story of what happened that night, did I?" And this is what he told me:

> I was learning a lot in that shamanism class, but I was learning it in my head and not in my spirit. Whenever we'd do those meditations and try to call for our spirit animal, everybody else would get one, but nothing would come for me. I knew I had one out there somewhere, but I just couldn't make contact. I was starting to lose sleep over it and I couldn't figure out what to do. Well, one night (I guess it was the night before I talked to you), I was tossing and turning, so I got up for a walk. It was warm and cloudy, but the moon was nearly full so I could see pretty well. There was a mystical quality to the soft night air— like it was bearing secrets. I realized that this was the ideal time for me to ask again for my animal spirit ally to reveal itself. So I went to a secluded area down by the lake. I wanted to bare myself, body and soul, so I took off all my clothes and sat down with a straight spine and my legs crossed in a lotus position. I tried to quiet my mind and let my heart and spirit speak. "Hey God!…Michael here….Yep, back again. Still tryin' to get in touch with my animal spirit guide. I think I'm ready, God. My heart's open, and I'll just be hanging out right here."
>
> So there I sat, that moist night air caressing my skin, trying to keep my heart open and my mind quiet. Then I heard a noise in the bushes, a rustling in the leaves. It was some animal in there, and it was coming my way! My heart started pounding! "Uh, oh! Is this it, God? My spirit ally?" And sure enough a little animal pokes its nose out of the bushes and looks

around. It was a skunk. "Aw come on, God. What is this, a joke? My spirit ally isn't really a skunk!…IS IT?" Seemingly in answer to my question that skunk headed right toward me! I wanted to get out of there quick, but I had chosen a warrior's path and that was no way for a warrior to greet a potential spirit ally, even if it was a skunk. I took a deep breath and waited. That skunk walked right in front of me and paused. It dug in the grass, looked right at me, and then started waddling off. If that wasn't a sign, I don't know what was. I knew I had to follow, so I started off on my hands and knees, crawling behind that skunk, doing the best skunk walk I could. The skunk and I were making our way across the lawn, around some clumps of bushes and into some tall grass, when I heard a weird guttural moan. What was that? My heart was pounding! I could barely make it out, but there in the dusky moonlight up ahead of us was a large, light-colored, amorphous mass between two clumps of bushes. That thing was hissing ominously and undulating! The skunk was leading me right to it! I was disoriented and I was terrified, but I had chosen a warrior's path! I had to follow that skunk and face my destiny!

> Closer and closer to that ghastly thing we crawled and it took my breath away when I got close enough to see it clearly. It was a man and a woman intertwined! They were on their own journey of spiritual union. Was I embarrassed! But that skunk was headed right for them! I had to warn them! So in a loud whisper I said, "Hey you two! There's a skunk coming! … Hey! There's a skunk! It's heading right for you!"

Michael shook his head, "They didn't even hear me," he said. "They didn't miss a beat. That skunk walked right around 'em and off into the thicket. I carefully backed off and tiptoed away. That was enough destiny for one night!

Michael said that when he got home, he called one of his close friends and told him about the workshop. He said he had made contact with an animal spirit ally but it was still pretty confusing. When his friend asked him what animal it was Michael said, "Now don't laugh. It's a skunk."

His friend paused for a moment and said, "You know, Mike, that's a perfect animal for you, because you really are like a skunk. You are generally an easy-going, friendly guy, but you will let people get only so close. If anyone gets too close, you piss on 'em!"

Michael thought about the events of his life, about his recent divorce, and about his other relationships. He realized that he really did have much to work out regarding issues of intimacy. When he had accepted that skunk as an ally, it took him on a journey to confront (quite literally) that which he feared most—the deep intimacy between a man and a woman.

Michael did a lot of personal work after that. He went for counseling and on vision quests. He worked hard with his ex-wife on healing some of the wounds left by their divorce. They might not be completely reconciled now, but they do have a good understanding of each other and completely share the parenting of their child. He volunteers at his child's school and is probably more a part of his child's life than many married fathers.

Michael says he is learning to give of himself more deeply and is more willing to accept intimacy and closeness in his relationships. "But people who are close to me know," says Michael, "that sometimes my tail still goes up. And when it does, they'd better look out!"

6

The Buzzard Lope

One sunny spring day I was exploring an abandoned old barn set at the edge of a woods. I was climbing up into the attic when I heard a ghastly sound—a wheezy, guttural growl. It came from a dark corner, where the roof met the attic floor. It had a threatening quality to it, and part of me wanted to bolt out of there. But I just couldn't leave. I had to know what it was that could emit such a dreadful sound. Warily, I crouched down and waited for my eyes to adjust to the light. There, huddled in the corner, was a baby bird, all covered with a soft fuzz as white as swan's down. This was no ordinary baby bird, however. This was a giant, gawky-looking creature with a hooked bill. It was almost as large as a chicken!

I had blundered in on a vulture's nest, and this young

Young Buzzard

vulture was doing its best to encourage me to blunder right on back to where I came from. That's just what I did. And after I learned of a certain unique defense mechanism of vultures, I'm glad I retreated. As helpless as they are, young vultures do have one very effective deterrent in their arsenal. If I had approached much closer, that soft, downy, baby bird would have puked all over me! A vulture can expel a load of vomit two or three feet—with considerable force and accuracy.

Buzzard puke as a weapon—what a concept! When I first heard of this, all I could think of was how the divine creator must have an outrageous sense of humor, but as I investigated further, I found that vomiting vultures is all part of an elegant plan. Vultures, as adept as they are at

"I'd like to see an ol' buzzard just a burpin' up them eggs!"

gliding and soaring, are awkward and ungainly on the ground. They have weak flapping muscles and take off from the ground with great difficulty. By emptying the contents of its crop into the face of a potential predator, a vulture can reduce its weight significantly, enabling it to take off more quickly. Any assailant unfortunate enough to catch such a load is not only left reeling from the indignity of the gesture but is burning wherever any of the vulture's powerful digestive juices have touched bare skin. One vulture's victim summed it up like this: "When you been puked on by a buzzard you KNOW you been puked on!"

This behavioral characteristic has spawned a strange bit of folklore. Because of vultures' legendary proficiency at vomiting, some folks believe that they have no anal opening and cannot defecate like other birds.

I once heard two old-timers discussing vultures, and it was not long before they got to this particular aspect of vulturine anatomy. One of them was saying, "Them buzzards don't have a bung hole." He kept adamantly insisting this was true, until the other one said, "Well, if that's true, then tell me how they lay their eggs." That stopped the first man in his tracks. He hadn't even considered that. The second fellow kept chuckling and saying, "Now buddy, that's something I'd like to see—an ol' buzzard just a burpin' up them eggs!"

As it turns out, vultures do defecate and lay eggs like other birds. They breed in the spring and raise one brood a year. There are between one and three (usually two) eggs in a clutch. They nest not only in deserted buildings, but also in hollow stumps, in cavities on cliffs, in the old nests of hawks, as well as directly on the ground. Sometimes, several pairs will nest in a colony.

However, due to man's encroachment, the forests that provided hollow logs and other undisturbed nest sites have been disappearing and even most of the abandoned barns that vultures used several decades ago have fallen down. Because of this scarcity of nest sites, vulture populations are declining through much of their range, and both the turkey and the black vultures, while not actually classified as endangered species, have been declared species of special concern in many regions.

Although you might see the turkey vulture anywhere in the states, the black vulture is most common in the South. The black vulture can be differentiated from the turkey vulture, because it flaps more often, has white patches

Vultures in Flight Top: Turkey Vulture, Bottom: Black Vulture.

under its wings, a shorter tail, and a black head. The turkey vulture has a red head (when mature), and its wings form a slight dihedral (a shallow "V") when it is soaring.

Vultures are famous for their seemingly effortless style of flying. You can watch a vulture for hours and never see its wings flap. A vulture's physical structure is aerodynamically ideal for a soaring lifestyle. The large size of the bird gives it the stability and the momentum to carry it through erratic air currents. The width of its wings gives it maneuverability, which is particularly important as vultures must be able to circle in tight spirals within the often small and undependable pillars of warm air. Their broad high-lift wings have slotted, fingerlike primary feathers at the tips. Each separately extended primary feather acts as a narrow high-aspect wing and each feather can be set at a steep angle for maximum lift. This makes them ideally adapted to high-altitude, low-speed soaring.

Gliding was probably the original form of bird flight, and it is still the simplest. Soaring flight is only slightly more complicated. A soaring bird is one that maintains or increases its altitude without flapping its wings. Vultures soar by gliding in or riding on updrafts.

Vultures exploit two basic types of air currents: obstruction currents and thermals. Obstruction currents are updrafts that occur when a prevailing wind strikes and then rises over objects such as hills or buildings. A wind coming down the lee side of a mountain may strike the plain and rebound in a series of "standing waves," very much like water flowing over a large rock in the rapids of a whitewater river. Each of these waves has an updraft component. When you see vultures soaring along the edges of ridges and bluffs, they are most likely riding the updrafts from these obstruction currents.

Sometimes, you may see a number of vultures circling over a field. If some are on the ground, it is probably because they have found something to eat, but if they are merely circling about in the air, they are most likely riding a thermal. Thermals (sometimes called convection currents) are updrafts caused by the uneven heating of the air near the surface of the earth. The air over cities, bare fields, or rock faces heats more quickly than that over forests or bodies of water. Since warm air expands and is lighter, it rises above denser, cooler air. Thermals, usually local disturbances in the form of slender columns or huge bubbles of rising air, are the domain of vultures and other soaring birds. This is where they spend most of their waking hours, where they are the safest and most at home.

There have been a few adventurous scientists who have studied the flight of vultures from motorless sailplanes. Not only is this an ideal observation platform for watching the vultures but, in order to stay aloft, the observer also has to search out and use the same currents of rising air. With their immense wingspans, sailplanes can glide farther and faster than the vultures, but they have less maneuverability than the birds. Speed is not as useful to a vulture as maneuverability. A vulture's ability to fly slowly is what allows it to fly in the tight circles necessary to take advantage of narrow thermal columns.

In order to soar on a mass of rising air, it is essential that the sinking speed of a bird be no greater than the rate of rising air in the thermal. The sinking speed of a bird is the speed it would fall if dropped with its wings spread (but not flapping) into absolutely calm air. This all sounds rather theoretical, but the observers in those sailplanes were able to calculate that the sinking speed of a turkey vulture is 2.28 kilometers per hour and that of a black vulture is 2.83 kilometers per hour.

The differences in the sinking speeds of our two species of vultures show that the black vulture, even though it is about the same physical weight as the turkey vulture, is aerodynamically slightly heavier. This small difference has striking geographic consequences. The range of the more buoyant turkey vulture extends up into the cool north as far as southern Canada, while the black vulture is restricted to the southern half of the United States and southward into the tropics, where the strong sun generates many and more vigorous thermals.

By traveling from thermal to thermal, vultures can cover hundreds of miles in a day and expend very little energy. They can be seen spiraling upward in the midst of a column of air until they are high in the sky, then they might head off in their intended direction, gliding slowly downward until they find another thermal in which to gain altitude. How they can tell where to find the next thermal is a bit of mystery, but they are known to have sharp eyesight and they watch each other carefully. And when one vulture starts ascending on a thermal other vultures in the area sail over, and they all rise up together.

Vultures use their powerful vision to locate food as well. They are scavengers and their diet is almost entirely carrion—dead animals. They are as well-designed for scavenging as they are for soaring. The bald, featherless head, as ugly as it may seem to us humans, is an elegant adaptation to the bird's diet. When a vulture plunges its head into a succulent, putrid carcass, it has no head feathers to soil.

Few birds use their sense of smell to locate food, and for many years ornithologists speculated about whether this was true of vultures. Researchers have conducted a series of experiments where they watched concealed animal carcasses. They found that turkey vultures would definitely come to investigate the smell of carrion and the "riper" the hidden carcass was, the faster the vultures would appear. However, it was discovered that black vultures have little or no sense of smell. They would come to the bait only if they could see it or if they could see other vultures swooping down to feed.

Many people have little regard for vultures. Because of their diet, they are thought of as little more than filthy vermin, or sometimes as omens of death. Of course, it is just this diet that makes them an important link in the chain of life on earth. Vultures are part of nature's sanitation system. They quickly clean up any dead animals, which if allowed to lie and rot might pose a health hazard.

In traditional Cherokee mythology the Great Vulture played an important role in the shaping of the earth. When the earth was new, the Great Vulture flapped its mighty wings, and where its wingtips struck the ground, they formed the mountains and the valleys that are at the heart of Cherokee territory today.

Vultures are seen as medicine animals by the Cherokee and other native Americans. Because they can thrive on carrion and decay, vultures are believed to have immunity from sickness and disease and so are important spirit allies or totems for medicine people, who often wear vulture feathers. In certain traditional Cherokee healing ceremonies, a small quantity of the vulture's flesh is eaten, and medicine is blown on to wounds through the hollow part of a vulture's quill. Vulture's down is then placed over the wound to stop bleeding and promote healing. (The skin from the gizzard of a vulture, stretched over the narrow end of a two- or three-inch hollow section of cow [formerly

buffalo] horn, is used as a suction device for snakebite and other ailments, which is somewhat reminiscent of the old European practice of cupping.)

Once I found the bones of a large bird in the woods. Although the skull was not there, I did find a portion of the lower jaw. I could tell from the curvature that it was from some kind of bird of prey. I kept the bones with me for a while and puzzled about their identity. One day I ran into an Indian from the North who was a native speaker of various Algonquian languages. I asked him about the bones. He looked them over thoughtfully and said, "I wonder if they could be from a peace eagle."

"A peace eagle?" I asked. "What's a peace eagle?"

"Oh, it's a big eagle," he said, "almost as big as the white-headed eagle. It has fingers at the ends of its wings. It circles in the sky above peace encampments."

As he spoke, my birder's brain was rattling up and down my mental checklist of northern raptors, trying to figure which species he could possibly be talking about.

"Why do you call it a peace eagle?" I asked, groping for a clue.

"It brings an element of peace to a tribe of warriors."

"How so?"

"It doesn't kill," he said. "It only eats animals that are already dead."

"Does it have a naked head?" I asked, finally getting the hint.

"Yes, that's him," he replied.

"Peace eagle!" I said. "That's quite a name for a buzzard."

I don't think I will ever look at an ol' buzzard the same way again.

❧

I once saw a bald eagle feeding with a flock of vultures—they were eating a dead calf in a pasture in north Florida. It was quite an image. It seemed strange to think of our national bird hanging out with a bunch of buzzards.

The eagle is a powerful symbol for many people and many nations. We usually think of this regal bird as a pristine being, one who soars high in the heavens and has great strength and clear vision. Many spiritually oriented people identify with the eagle and take on this great bird as a personal symbol of strength and vision.

Yet here was this majestic, spiritual being, hanging out with a flock of vultures, shouldering up to a carcass, trying to get itself a bellyful of the fetid flesh. It is said that, occasionally, an eagle will gorge itself so full of carrion that it can hardly take off, and not having the automatic vomiting response of the vultures, it can sometimes be killed with a stick.

Although the bald eagle is known as a great hunter, it is also a great pirate. Sometimes, when it encounters an osprey carrying a freshly caught fish back to its nest, it dive-bombs and harasses its smaller cousin, causing the osprey to drop its prey. Then the eagle swoops down to grab its stolen plunder, sometimes intercepting and catching the falling fish before it hits the ground.

The lessons the eagle teaches us are more profound and complex than that of merely flying high. The true lessons we can derive from an animal, or any being of nature with which we identify, do not come from our own narrow-minded projections. They come from a true relationship, which is based on paying attention to the being, spending time with it, observing its way of living, and feeling its spirit.

An eagle does indeed soar high—as do some spiritual people. Yet as it soars, it keeps its eyes focused on the earth. The higher it flies, the broader is its perspective on what is below. For all its soaring, the eagle is always aware that it must come down and touch the earth for its sustenance.

According to an ancient Cherokee legend, the vulture learned some lessons about flying high. A long time ago, Vulture was a high-flying, proud, and arrogant warrior bird with a beautiful feathered crest. But he was so excessive in his vanity and arrogance that he was stripped of his crest and lost the ability to hunt and kill. The details of the story that accounts for the vulture's baldness were too vulgar to record, according to James Mooney, a Victorian ethnologist who worked among the Cherokee in the late 1800s and collected many of their stories.

Today's vulture is a humble, homely, bald-headed creature. Those who know the bird well and understand some of its many dimensions know that the vulture not only provides the valuable services of cleaning up carrion and bringing the gift of healing, it is also a soaring symbol of humanity's greatest ideal, peace. Remember that the mighty eagle who soars high in the heavens with the vultures is more than willing to sail down to earth to dine with them.

My friend Clyde told me that once when he was a young teenager in western North Carolina, he and his cousin Charlie were out exploring in the mountains. They came to an open rocky ridge and spotted some vultures sailing back and forth along the cliff face. The birds were riding obstruction currents created by the ridge or catching thermals rising up from the warm rocks.

Both curious and adventurous youths, Clyde and Charlie got the idea that it would be fun to lie out on the rocks and play dead, to see if they could fool the vultures.

So when there were no vultures nearby, they both slipped onto an exposed area of rock and stretched themselves out, flat on their backs. They lay there as still as two corpses and waited patiently, occasionally peeking surreptitiously skyward through their eyelashes. After a while, a vulture silently glided by. It wheeled around and passed by again. Soon another vulture sailed over to join the first one. And then another. And another. Eventually there was a small flock circling the boys. Each pass they made was closer than the last. Back and forth they sailed, closer and clos-

er. Soon they were passing over not even three feet above them. At this close range, the vultures' fleshy red heads looked like raw meat. The boys could see their dark bulging eyes leering down at them. The birds' six-foot wingspans seemed enormous and ominous as they silently swept back and forth. This whole experience was becoming unsettling. What if the birds landed? What would they do? Would they walk up and bite? These boys did not want to find out.

"Hey, Charlie, next time they get close let's jump up and holler," Clyde whispered. "We'll scare 'em good!"

"Okay."

"Here comes one. Ready…. NOW!"

They both jumped up, shouted, and waved their arms. The terrified vultures flapped frantically, desperately trying to gain altitude, simultaneously vomiting and defecating.

"That stuff splattered all around us on the rocks," Clyde said, "but none of it hit us. Thank goodness."

I recounted Clyde's story to my Chippewa-Cree friend. He nodded and said, "The peace eagle circles around a long time and looks his food over very, very carefully before he lands to eat it. I'll tell you why." Knowing a good story would ensue, I settled back and got comfortable. He continued:

A long time ago, Coyote persuaded Vulture to take him for a ride. He climbed up on Vulture's back and off they flew, way up in the sky. Coyote enjoyed this for a while, but before long, he started acting like a smart aleck and a show-off. He started making faces and obscene gestures, ridiculing Vulture. Vulture kept looking back over his shoulder to see what Coyote was doing. But whenever he looked, Coyote would stop and deny that he was doing anything. Finally, Vulture realized what was happening and said, "Okay, so you wanted to go for a ride and sail through the air. That's just what you're gonna do!" He started on a high-speed dive, but just before they reached the earth Vulture veered off and sent Coyote careening earthward into the end of a hollow tree stump—where he stuck. When he finally extricated himself he was enraged at Vulture. He was Coyote, the Creator. How dare Vulture treat him with so little respect. He planned his revenge.

He went out to an open rocky area and changed himself into a dead deer. Before long, Vulture came sailing in and landed. This dead deer looked delicious. "It looks pretty fresh," he said to himself. "I wonder where to start? That hide is probably too tough to bite through."

Coyote threw his voice so it seemed to come from out of nowhere, and said, "Why don't you try the rear end, the anus would be a good place."

"Who said that?" Vulture inquired, looking all around.

"This is your medicine helper," the voice said. "I give you good advice."

"Oh," said Vulture, "thanks."

"You ought to try the hind end first," the voice continued. "It's nice and soft and if you reach in deep enough you'll be able to get some of those tender and delicious intestines."

"Gee thanks, Medicine Helper. I love intestines. That is good advice."

So Vulture walked to the back end of the deer and plunged his head deep into the rectum.

Suddenly the deer came back to life. He clamped down with his anal sphincter and Vulture was his prisoner. Was he ever getting his revenge now! But when Coyote looked around at his back end, and saw Vulture frantically flopping and flapping, it was such a sight that he burst out laughing. He laughed so hard, he lost control and released his grip on

Vulture. Vulture managed to pull his head out but when he did, he lost every feather on his head.

To this day, the vulture still has a naked head and you know, it still stinks (like you know what).

"And that's why, like your friends found out, when a vulture finds a dead animal now, he looks it over very, very carefully before he tries to eat it."

I realized that this was the Chippewa-Cree version of the "vulgar" story that Mooney referred to back in the 1800s.

I once watched a flock of black vultures feeding at a riverbank in south Georgia. They were eating mudfish that had been thrown up on the bank by so-called sport fishermen. The mudfish, also known as "grinnel" (or more properly, bowfin), is a thick-skinned, primitive-looking fish. They are good to eat, but because they are slightly more difficult to prepare than many other fish they are held in low regard and labeled a "trash fish" by sportfishing types, who are only satisfied with bass and other game fish. When these sportsmen caught the mudfish, rather than release them unharmed, they simply threw them on the bank to die and rot. Many sport fishermen feel that any fish they don't approve of has no right to live in waters they fish, especially if these fish keep taking their bait. For a day or two this pile of fish carcasses formed an odoriferous monument to the arrogance and snobbery of sport fishermen in America—until the vultures found them!

To the vultures, this was a divine gift. They were an excited and unruly mob as they descended upon this fragrant heap of rotting fish. Ravenously, they picked and tore

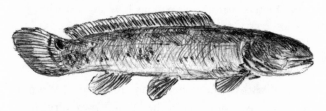

Mudfish or Bowfin

gobs of flesh from the carcasses while jostling and elbowing one another like bargain basement shoppers crowding around a table full of marked-down merchandise. Occasionally, some individuals would be forced out to the edges of the flock's feeding frenzy. When this happened, the ones on the outskirts had a unique strategy for regaining a good position at the center of the feast. One of these vultures would take a peculiar hopping leap and pounce right back into the center of the feeding area. This would startle and unsettle the central vultures, and the new arrival would get to feed there for a few moments before it would get pounced on by the next vulture that came leapfrogging in. It was hardly the most polite and orderly way of dining, but it seemed that everyone got something to eat.

Shortly after I watched these feeding vultures, I had the opportunity to visit Bessie Jones, an old black gospel singer who lived on one of Georgia's Sea Islands. Bessie was in her seventies and had a unique perspective on the history of the South. In her younger days, she had spent a lot of time with her grandparents, who had been slaves, so Bessie knew songs, stories, and games from slave times. Later, she was declared a national treasure and presented with a National Heritage Fellowship Award for her work as a singer of these old sacred songs and her role as a bearer and preserver of these traditions.

She told me of a children's game from the time of slavery called "the buzzard lope," where the children would gather in a circle and take turns jumping into the center. She told me, "The chil'runs gits in a circle and they lopes like a buzzard. You seen buzzards lope ain't you."

"Yeah, I have seen 'em lope," I said, feeling privy to an ancient body of knowledge.

As the children loped around in their circle they would sing this song:

> Throw me any where Lord, in that old field [repeat]
> You can bruise and break me, in that old field
> Jesus'll come and take me, in that old field …

"Yeah, dat song's from slavery times," Bessie explained. "They singin' about how the masta' can kill you and throw you out in the field for the buzzards to eat. It don't matter though, 'cause the spirit gon' sail on, jus' like them ol' buzzards."

❧

Under the Vulture-Tree

We have all seen them circling pastures,
have looked up from the mouth of a barn, a pine clearing,
the fences of our own backyards, and have stood amazed by the
one slow wing beat, the endless dihedral drift.
But I had never seen so many so close,
hundreds, every limb of the dead oak feathered black.

I cut the engine, let the river grab the boat and pull it toward
the tree.
The black leaves shined, the pale fruit blossomed red, ugly as a
human heart.
Then as I passed under their dream, I saw for the first time

its soft countenance, the raw fleshy jowls
wrinkled and generous, like the faces
of the very old who have
learned to empathize with everything.

And I drifted away from them, slow, on the pull of the river,
reluctant, looking back at their roost,
calling them what I'd never called them, what they are,
those dwarfed transfiguring angels,
who flock to the side of the poisoned fox, the mud turtle
crushed on the shoulder of the road,
who pray over the leaf graves of the anonymous lost,
with mercy enough to consume us all and give us wings.

"Under the Vulture-Tree," by David Bottoms, is taken
from *Under the Vulture-Tree* (New York: William Morrow,
1987) and reprinted by permission of the author.

7

The Root Doctor

DOCTOR BUZZARD AND THE SHERIFF

As I mentioned in the Introduction, I used to gather roots and herbs for a living. Traveling in an old Volkswagen van loaded with field guides, botany books, camping gear, and a canoe, I covered many miles of America's backcountry, driving rural roads, canoeing in swamps and rivers, and hiking through forests and other wild places. I observed wildlife, studied plants, gathered herbs, and enthusiastically questioned any local folks who would talk to me about the flora and fauna of their area.

To finance these activities I would stop at folk festivals and country fairs, where I set up a booth displaying herbs, teas, and old-time remedies. These events provided an ideal setting to sell the herbs I had gathered and to teach informally about the powers of the plant world, and also to learn a great deal myself. Many of the performers and attendees at the festivals were rich repositories of traditional knowledge, including plant lore and folk medicine. By the time a festival was over, I had usually talked with anyone who had experience with herbs.

Occasionally, I would see Bessie Jones at one of these gatherings. (You'll recall Bessie from the previous chapter.) She would perform with various members of her family and her church congregation from Georgia's Sea Islands. They would captivate the audience with their raw and powerful a cappella gospel singing.

Between performances, she often made the rounds of the craft booths. Her eyes would light up as she caught sight of all those jars of herbs I had on display. As she headed my way, I could hear her booming voice announce to her entourage, "Now here's somp'm I like. I always gets my medicine out' the woods and the fields....Yes, sir!" She would ask about different herbs that I had on display and tell me about different plants and remedies that she grew up with and still used. I hung on her every word, asking questions, comparing notes, and drinking in every drop of her special wisdom. In the meantime, my sales often came to a complete standstill; I could hear the grumblings of impatient customers. They wanted to make their purchases and quickly get back to the main events of the festival. They did not seem to understand that to me, this *was* the main event.

As we talked, I realized that she and I did not know the plants by the same names, and that there were many she knew of in south Georgia that were unfamiliar to me. So I asked her if I could come visit sometime so I could learn more about her local plants. She said that would be fine.

Shortly thereafter, I found myself sitting with her in her small frame house on Proctor Street in the old black settlement on Saint Simons Island. I brought a bag of various wild plants I had collected on the way. I pulled the plants out and asked her about them during lulls in the conversation—not that there were many lulls. She had plenty to say when it came to herbs and traditional medicine. She told me about making a tonic out of sassafras roots, life everlasting (*Gnaphalium obtusifolium*), wild cherry, and wild plum bark (*Prunus* sp.). She talked about her favorite bone-strengthening oyster-shell tonic (made by steeping parched oyster

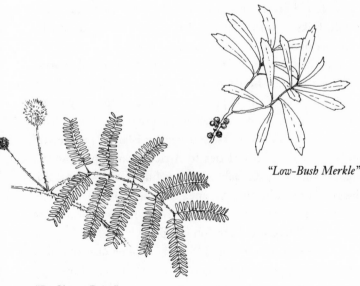

"Low-Bush Merkle"

"Be-Shame Brier"

shells in water), about doctoring ailing chickens with red oak bark and poke leaves, and about how as a young girl, she once used "low-bush merkle" (wax myrtle, *Myrica cerifera*) to heal the stomach ulcers of a white plantation owner.

Then we got to talking about the sensitive brier, a creeping, prickly mimosa (*Schrankia microphylla*). Because this plant's leaves fold up when it is touched, as if ashamed, she called it "be-shame." She said her mother used to put it into the chickens' water; it would purify the water and serve as a medicine for them. "People use it too," she added.

"What's it good for in people?" I asked.

"It's not for takin' but it's good to tote."

"To tote?"

She laughed and said, "Well, you won't hardly need it. You don't want to make nobody coward."

"It makes 'em into a coward?"

"I say 'coward' because they're submissive. You can touch 'em and tell 'em what to do and they do it; do what you want 'em to."

"...kinda like hexin' somebody?"

"Yeah, I call it ugly weed. It ain't ugly, but..."

"It can be used that way."

"Tha's right. Everything out there in the woods and anywhere else is just like a table set. Everything out there to eat but some of it will hurt you and some of it won't. You know dat. Ladies take be-shame [root] and tote it in their pocketbook and certain times and certain places they go, they chew it—pieces of it."

"Now, it will make the other person submissive?"

"Oh yeah, they had words they used with it, you know, and they'd chew it talking to you, like I'm talking to you now. And they could go a long way with that thing and do a heap a' conquering with it. It may not be be-shame [they're using]. It might be something else; I don't know, but I know conquering when I see it and somebody [else] come along after a while with somethin' to conquer the conqueror. You know that? You know that, don't ya! I don't care how bad or what it is, somebody else come along with somethin' else that's a little bit higher…a little stronger; that's all there is to it."

"So you just don't play with it."

"That's right—no kinda junk like that, 'cause I don't like it! A lot a' times I watch people when they chewin' and they might not be chewin' gum!" she said with a chuckle.

There began my education about root work, an occult world that was flourishing right beneath my nose. Being part of mainstream white culture, I had no idea that it even existed.

Bessie went on to tell me about other roots with names like "High John the Conqueror," "Little John the Conqueror," and "Devil's Shoestring."

She told about other ways that people used the roots to cast a spell on someone or to remove a hex, and how sometimes someone would use a root to "help them go forth" to turn aside aggression and calm a violent person. She didn't see "no harm in dat at all—but not the conquering—making people do what they don't want to do. But to conquer the devil, that ol' vile spirit that you had, that gonna make sin between you and me, I don't see where dat's wrong."

Bessie was a devout Christian, and yet I realized that she was telling me about the still-viable remnants of the old religion of her people, dating back to the times before the Christian slavers brought her ancestors in chains to this country.

The principal practitioners of these ancient arts are known as "root doctors" or "root workers." They tend to be, in various proportions, a combination of herbalists, hoodoo shamans, and faith healers. Roots, herbs, charms, and potions are the tools of their trade. Individual root doctors may "specialize." Some work primarily in psychic realms, placing and removing hexes, others may have the gift of taking the fire out of burns, while still others may use medicinal herbs in their practice.

I was particularly interested in the herbal aspects of this healing art and wanted to investigate further. Roots were a special interest of mine. I had even written a book about roots, yet I had never heard of root doctors.

Root doctoring is a difficult phenomenon to investigate, and in some ways it seemed foolish to even try. It is primarily based in rural black culture. People simply do not talk about it openly, especially to a white stranger. As I persisted in my search, I managed to glean tidbits of information here and there from conversations with both black and white folks in various parts of the Deep South. I heard a number of second- or third-hand accounts.

I learned that one of the central areas for root doctoring is known as the "Low Country" of coastal South Carolina. In this region of sun-dappled piney woods, shadowy moss-draped cypress swamps, extensive salt marshes, and isolated black communities on coastal barrier islands, people still have strong traditional ties to Africa. Some speak an old dialect known as "Gullah," which is full of Africanisms. It is largely unintelligible to speakers of modern English. Among these people, the word "root" means much more than the underground portion of a plant.

One time I was driving in South Carolina near the coast and I picked up a hitchhiker—a young black fellow who looked about my age (late twenties). He said his truck was broken down and he was waiting for a part to come in. That's why he was hitching, but things were going pretty well for him; he was working on a bricklaying job and he was just about to start his own business. Yeah, he was born and raised around these parts. I asked casually, "Many root workers around here?"

"Yeah, there's root workers around here," he replied. "Matter of fact, last year, I gave a guy twenty-five dollars. He made me up a little packet—a little root packet for good luck. And, man, I've had the best luck! Like I said, I'm 'bout to start my own bricklaying business. I tell you, when I get my business lined up, I'm gonna go to that root doctor again and get him to give me some more of that stuff."

"Sort of like an insurance policy?" I asked.

"Yeah, just like an insurance policy."

Later on that trip, one of my South Carolina friends showed me a book from his local public library. It was entitled, *Fifty Years as a Low Country Witch Doctor*, by J. E. McTeer. The author is a white man, born on a plantation just after the turn of the century, who became sheriff of Beaufort County, South Carolina. In the book he gives an account of how, as sheriff, he dealt with root doctors and occult practitioners and how he came to learn their techniques. He also discusses his current practice of what he calls "white witchcraft."

There was something about his writing that was very open and down to earth. It was not self-aggrandizing, nor did he claim to be the sole guardian of the secrets. His attitude seemed honest and charitable. He wrote about good and evil and about faith and discussed in depth the therapeutic and cultural value of his kind of work.

He paints an awesome picture of Beaufort County in the twenties and thirties. There were a number of practicing root doctors in the area and some of them were regarded as very powerful. People came from near and far for treatments and sent them orders to get roots and remedies by mail.

Root doctors were enlisted for more than the casting and breaking of hexes; their doctoring extended into all aspects of society. For example, if you had been arrested for a crime and were being brought to trial, you could hire a root doctor to help. Sometimes, he would sneak in before the trial and sprinkle certain magical powders around the courtroom. For serious offenses, the root man would actually come into court with you and he'd sit in the back and he would "chew de root on de judge" and you'd get off. If you didn't get off, you'd at least get a lighter sentence than you would have received. (Would you call that root litigation?) Roots were also used for romantic purposes, to increase one's attractiveness or ensure the fidelity of a spouse.

This is the way things were back in 1926 when twenty-two-year-old J. E. McTeer was sworn in as the youngest sheriff in the United States. McTeer was raised on a plantation there in the Low Country of South Carolina. The occult was a part of his own upbringing and he was certainly familiar with root doctors.

There was Dr. Crow, Dr. Bug, Dr. Snake, and Dr. Eagle to name a few. But the "king" of the root doctors, the most powerful of them all, the heaviest dude in the Low Country, was none other than the infamous Dr. Buzzard.

As sheriff, McTeer's job was protecting people and enforcing laws. He had no intention nor any desire to attack people's belief in the supernatural. However, prescribing medicine without a license was another issue entirely. He knew of charlatan root doctors looking for a quick dollar who were selling roots to victims of syphilis or cancer. They were charging desperate people hundreds of dollars and giving them nothing but false hope. Things had gotten out of hand and he was determined to put a stop to it. "A true witch doctor invokes the astral forces to do his bidding," McTeer proclaimed. "He does not administer medicine."

He figured that if he could catch and convict Dr. Buzzard, then the word would filter on down to other practitioners. So he tried every way he could to pin something on Dr. Buzzard. But Dr. Buzzard got wind of the plan and became very cautious and secretive. They might have called him "Buzzard," but he was sly as a fox. No matter how they tried, the sheriff and his deputies never could pin any concrete charges on him. Dr. Buzzard knew he was being watched.

People had been sending Dr. Buzzard mail orders for different kind of roots and remedies. According to one story, Dr. Buzzard once went to his post office in Frogmore, to cash a large wad of money orders. The postmaster showed him where to endorse them.

"I gotta sign for this?" he asked.

"Yes sir, sign right here and I'll cash them for you."

Dr. Buzzard sensed a trap. "I ain't gon' sign nothin,'" he said, and he tore those money orders into little pieces and walked out. Somebody looked in the trash after he left and saw there was over fifteen hundred dollars worth of money orders. He just let that fifteen hundred go rather than risk getting arrested.

Well, the sheriff's department finally got their chance when they apprehended a young man breaking into houses.

They took him into custody and when they searched his clothes, they found a root packet sewn into the waistband of his trousers. McTeer recognized it as one of Dr. Buzzard's. The young man, scared enough at being arrested, was even more terrified when they found his root. He had been told that it would turn on him if he let anyone else see it. They also found a small vial of yellow liquid in his pocket. This vial could be the evidence they were looking for. If they could connect this vial of medicine with Dr. Buzzard, they would finally have their case.

Sheriff McTeer had a talk with the young man. He told him, "We know Buzzard sold you that medicine and that root to protect you. Now look at where you are. His root's no good. I'm a witch doctor too, and my power is stronger than any root Doctor Buzzard can give you. We'll go a little easy on you if you'll testify in court against him."

The young guy was so scared that he agreed to testify and tell all. McTeer dispatched a deputy to arrest Dr. Buzzard and bring him to court. In the interim, they did all they could to bolster the young witness's courage. Dr. Buzzard was brought into the court. He was wearing dark purple glasses. As soon as Dr. Buzzard saw that young man, he fixed a stare on him. The doctor now knew why he had been arrested.

Before the court could be called to order, the witness started to groan and swat himself as if ants were biting him all over his body. Dr. Buzzard kept his eyes fixed on him and soon the witness fell over on the floor frothing at the mouth with his eyes rolled back. They were able to revive him later, but he was obviously incapable of testifying.

"Are you through with me?" the doctor asked.

"Yes, for now," McTeer said, "but let me tell you somethin, Buzzard. I don't care what you do as far as your root doctoring, but prescribing medicine without a license is illegal. If you keep that up I'll get you. My root's as powerful as your root. If you don't quit giving people medicine to take I'm gonna get ya."

"You do your job, I'll do mine," said the doctor and he strolled proudly out of the courtroom.

After that, Dr. Buzzard was even more careful, but he kept up an active practice. During one term of general-sessions court, he was seen sitting among the spectators, wearing his purple glasses, busily chewing the root. White powder was regularly found sprinkled on the judge's desk and on Sheriff McTeer's desk as well. They arrested him a couple more times, but one way or the other he always got off.

Finally, word came to McTeer that Dr. Buzzard was getting fed up with this harassment. The doctor was openly declaring that he "would bring McTeer down." McTeer sent word back to Buzzard that he did not like threats, that he was a witch doctor too, and that they would soon see whose root was stronger. Dr. Buzzard had better watch out "because trouble was coming his way."

The fates intervened shortly after this exchange of threats. Dr. Buzzard's son was driving late one rainy night when his car ran off a bridge and he drowned. The loss of his son saddened and demoralized him.

One day shortly thereafter, McTeer came home, drove up in his backyard and found Dr. Buzzard sitting in his car waiting. He had brought McTeer a peace offering—two fine chickens. He said, "Let's you and me be friends. I got power and so have you. I ain't gon' give out no more medicine. I just gon' deal with the spirit."

They did become friends, and over the years Dr. Buzzard taught the sheriff many things. As his acceptance of McTeer as a root doctor became known, the sheriff gained a level of respect in the county that he had never known before. McTeer said that as far as he knew, Dr. Buzzard kept his promise and never did prescribe medicine after that. Their friendship lasted for many years and they developed a strange alliance of power—the power of the law and the power of the spirit embodied in a white lawman and a black root doctor.

Dr. Buzzard outlived most of the other well-known root doctors of that era and his friendship with the sheriff lasted until he died in the late fifties. McTeer lived on and he soon realized that, along with his duties as sheriff, he now had another role to fulfill—that of a root doctor. He felt obligated to fill Dr. Buzzard's shoes. Being a white man raised on his family's plantation, he was obviously a member of the dominant white culture, but the community needed a root doctor. He was the person who retained Dr. Buzzard's legacy. And long after he stepped down as sheriff (a post he held for thirty-seven years), people still came from far and near for his root work, to have hexes removed and spells broken.[2]

I was fascinated by this story. My friend who had loaned me the book said that he heard McTeer was still alive. So I looked him up in the Beaufort phone book—and there it was—J. E. McTeer. I dialed the number and after several rings someone picked up the phone and said, "McTeah."

"Mr. McTeer, I'm interested in roots and herbs. I read your book, and I'd like to learn more about what you do. Could I come and talk to you?"

He said, "I'm in my office every day from nine in the mornin' till noon. I'm in semiretirement."

"Where's your office?"

"214 West Street, right in Beaufort."

"Can I come?"

"Anytime in the morning. Just come in."

Two days later, shortly after 9:00 A.M., I was in his office. He was a tall, thin, rather dignified elderly man dressed in a suit and tie. His head was bald and he wore thick, dark-rimmed glasses. He was in his seventies.

I told him that I was very interested in what he was doing. I told him of my interest in herbs and that I was especially interested in roots. When I showed him my roots book, he was somewhat impressed. "Well, I've written a couple of books, myself, Mr. Elliott, so I know you've done a lot of work there."

There was so much I wanted to ask. I wanted to learn about Low Country herbs. I was interested in what he had to say about his own root doctoring. I also hoped to do a little bit of botanical detective work; if I could get one of those chewing roots, I could perhaps identify the plant. I asked him if he had any chewing roots on hand.

He said, "Well, a lady on Saint Helena Island digs them for me, but I don't have any right now."

I asked what other herbs he used.

"It's not so much which plants you use, but where they come from. You mix certain things together, and you use certain kinds of dirt—from graves maybe, dirt from a bishop's grave or from a murderer's grave. It depends. Where the plants grow is as important as the kind of plant."

I asked him what kind of people come to him.

"All kinds of people from all walks of life come to me. I get at least one patient a week sent to me by medical doctors here in town. I usually get one a month from the Charleston Medical Center. They'll have a patient from one of the outer islands somewhere that believes they've had a bad root put on them and they won't respond to medical treatment. The medical center just sends 'em to me. I take the spell off; then the doctors can treat them. People that are really in distress come to me. Their lives are falling apart because they've been hexed. Some of them are suicidal. I'll break that hex on them and set 'em back on the right track.

"Now, somebody could come through the door anytime and if you're here, I don't mind if you want to witness what I do. I have no objection to that. Just kind of go along with what I say, and be quiet. I'll just tell 'em you're here helping me."

"When I saw Sheriff McTeer's back room, I realized that he was indeed living in two worlds…"

He had a rather ordinary office. There was a large oak desk, filing cabinets, and a number of plaques and certificates on the wall. After he retired from the sheriff's department, he started selling real estate. He got involved in developing some of those beautiful outer islands off the coast. He was still an influential man in the community.

He took me to a back room adjoining his office and when I saw this room, I realized that he was indeed living in two worlds. Here he had a large collection of occult paraphernalia arranged on tables. He had a large mask on the wall. It was made out of the shell of a giant horseshoe crab; eyes, teeth, and other facial designs were painted on it. There was a twisted, dried rat nailed to the wall above the mask and mythological pictures on the wall below. One table looked like an altar with its various accoutrements such as incense burners, aerosol sprays, bottles of essences, and black humanoid candles. There was a large gnarled root that Dr. Buzzard had given him, as well as what looked like a human-shaped piece of driftwood, with a head, arms, and legs, that was bound with a gold chain. He called it a "mondrake root," and he told me he had to keep it chained with gold or it would release its powers.

There was a little Aztec calendar, a tourist item from Mexico. He had a cobra with rhinestone eyeballs; its spread hood hovered above the rest of its body, which was coiled around an ashtray. He had a little porcelain vessel with bluebirds on it. There was a woven doll from Africa, a miniature totem pole, and an earthenware figurine of Mayan design. It was an extraordinary cross-cultural assemblage. These were both display tables and altars. He was simultaneously a collector and a practitioner.

After my tour of the back room, I asked, "If I gave you a self-addressed, stamped envelope, would you send me one of those chewing roots when you get some?"

"I'd be glad to do that to help your studies," he replied. So I went out to my van. In the few minutes it took me to find an envelope, address and stamp it, and return to his office, three black women had come in and were sitting on chairs right in front of his desk.

McTeer looked up and said, "Mr. Elliott, glad you're heah. You're just in time. Where's that book of yours? We need that book of yours."

"Oh... yeah... here." I handed him my book.

"This gentleman heah," he explained to the women, "he comes from up in North Carolina, and he does quite a lot of root doctorin' up in theah. He and I are workin' together. See, he wrote this book on roots."

He held my book up to show them. On the cover there is a big picture of a gnarly skunk cabbage root and the word "Roots" written in large letters across the front. (What more perfect credentials could I want?)

"Now, you wouldn't mind if he sits in and helps us heah today, would ya?"

Of course they didn't mind. So I just sat down.

"Now you were heah before," he said to this one woman.

"Yeah, I came to you 'cause I had a sore on my leg, and the doctor, he couldn't do nothin' about it. I came to you but it's still not getting better. I don't know what to do. And I brought my friend, too."

"Why'd you come heah?"

She explained that she had a drinking problem and just couldn't seem to break herself of it.

The third woman hadn't been feeling well, and it seemed that since her two friends were coming she decided to come along, for whatever good it would do.

Addressing the woman with the sore leg, he said, "Now, you say you've been to the doctor."

"Yes sir."

"You took all the medicine he told you to take?"

"Yes sir."

"'Cause if it's something the doctor can fix, I can't do anything about it. Now, I can only help you if the doctor's done all he can do. Then, maybe, I can help you."

She said, "No, I went to the doctor. I took all his medicine, and it's not getting better."

"All right," he said. "I gave you something last time, didn't I?"

She said, "Yeah," and reached into her purse and pulled out a little packet—a red flannel bag. He took the bag from her. He examined it and said, "There's a hole in this bag. How'd the hole get in there?"

She looked at it and said, "I don't know 'bout that hole. I don't know one thing about that."

He said, "There's a hole in this bag. No wonder it's not been working. We'll fix that."

He says to the other women, "Have you all been to any-body else—any other root doctors?"

They said they had.

"Well, did they give you anything?"

They nodded.

"Let me see what they gave you." One woman had to excuse herself, and she came back carrying a little cloth bag (I don't know where she kept it). The other woman pulled something similar out of her purse. Root packets! He took the two packets in his hand and studied them solemnly.

"Now, I bet you paid a lot for these, didn't you?" he said. "Now, what I'm gonna give you heah is free. It won't cost you a penny, but it's more powerful than anything you can pay for.

"Now you came to me because you believe, right? You believe that I can help you?"

They nodded affirmatively.

"Well, if you believe I can help you, I know I can."

With this statement he set up the terms—the conditions for the healing session. Then, directing his attention to the woman with the drinking problem, who was his main focus this session, he asked, "Now how old are you?"

"I'm forty-four."

He said, "I'm almost twice your age. Now, you've got your whole life to live ahead of you. Do you want to live hiding behind a bottle?"

"No sir."

"Now do you think somebody put something on you?"

"Yes sir."

"You know who did it?"

"No, I don't know, but it just made me weak."

He said, "Look what they've done to you. They've taken away your confidence in yourself. They made you say, 'No,' when you should have been saying, 'Yes.' They've taken away your belief in your own strength. Now, what

I'm gonna give you heah is gonna help you get your strength back and your belief in yourself back."

He warned them that they might not understand all of what they were about to witness, but he assured them that they would be able to feel the withdrawal of the evil that oppressed them. He also told them that he only practiced "white magic," that is, he used his power only to help people. "But woe is he" who tried to use evil forces against them once they were protected by an amulet imbued with his power. "Let's go into the other room, heah."

So we all went into the back room and seated ourselves on folding chairs facing his altar-display tables. He showed them three hex amulets—little red-flannel packets of roots, herbs, and other materials he had prepared in advance. He told them that these bundles had no power now, but after their session today they would be imbued with all of their combined strength and would be truly powerful.

One at a time, he placed his hand on the back of each woman's neck (at the base of the brain, where the spinal cord begins). In his other hand, he held a "chalice" (a glass of water). This allowed him and his clients to join forces.

He handed each one of them a black figurine candle and said, "Now what I want you to do is point that candle up there at the top of that mask and focus your concentration there, and we'll try to call forth the powers."

So they all held the candles up in the air, each sighting along their candle, focusing their energies at that mask. McTeer stepped back, and as he stepped back I noticed his hand deftly slip under the corner of the table—and suddenly, POOF!—a big cloud of smoke came out of the top of the mask, and we all jumped. He said, "Okay, I think we're ready to go on now." Then taking the glass of water, "the chalice," he had each of them put their hands in the water and wipe their foreheads, and he said, "Now, this next procedure is a test to see if we are ready to go on further."

He stood before them and held the glass of water up, put a piece of cardboard over the top, and then turned the glass upside down. He said, "All right. This will tell me if we're ready to go on further."

Slowly, he began to slide away the cardboard beneath the inverted glass. Some water leaked out.

He said, "Something's not right. I can't understand. Something's not right. That water shouldn't spill out. This is very difficult to do, but if everything's right, I can do it. Now, let me try again."

He started to slide the cardboard again, and once more, water dripped out onto the floor. He looked at us and said, "Something's not right. I can't understand what is wrong."

The woman with the drinking problem said, "I think I know what it is." Whereupon she reached into her purse and pulled out a pint flask of whiskey—and set it on the floor.

"I think that might be it," he said, then he pulled away that piece of cardboard and the water stayed in the inverted glass! He held it up, and we could all look up into it and see that there was water still in there, mysteriously suspended in that glass. Then he poured it out.

I later learned that this is a common trick known to many sleight-of-hand stage magicians as "the hydrostatic glass." However, what impressed me was not so much his execution of the trick but how he used it to gain an extra level of acceptance and commitment.

"Okay, I think we're ready to go on now," he said, giving them each a little red-flannel root packet. He said that this packet was a symbol of his power as a root doctor and that he was today joining forces with each of them and sealing their combined power into these amulets. Should they ever feel that they were getting weak or that somebody was trying to put any kind of a root on them, they could just hold that amulet in their hand and that would remind them of the power they have against any evil and would protect them. If anyone tried again to put a hex on them, or if they were ever again the target of black witchcraft, it would turn that hex right around. It would just bounce right off them and back on to the person who first tried to send it.

Then he took a piece of Kleenex, and he tore it into three pieces. He gave them each a piece of the tissue and had them wrap the tissue around the root packet and hold it there. Then he collected the packets back from them, unwrapped the three pieces of Kleenex and twisted them together, saying, "This represents any power that anybody could have had over you." Then he lit the tissues on fire and placed them to burn in an ashtray. They burned down for a moment, then went POOF!, and just disappeared, leaving only a dusting of ashes.

Then he held those root bags in the last wisps of smoke coming out of the ashtray. "There went the last of any power that anyone ever had over you," he said. "We have today joined our forces together and imbued these root bags with our collective invincible power. Now I'm going to call forth every positive healing power that has ever been known in this world. With this departing smoke, we cast away any powers that could ever be used against you."

He held the bags in front of each of the items in his collection, proclaiming, "And now we will call forth the power of the Aztec sun-god, the woven-grass spirit doll of Zaire, the Serpent God of India, the Mayan god of strength, the power of the mondrake root with its golden chain, and the power of the great staff of Dr. Buzzard." He held up the root packets to each one of these items as he called forth their powers, then returned their root packets to the women. He then went over to the little porcelain music box, which stood at the edge of the table. The painted porcelain bluebirds, perched on top with their wings raised, seemed ready to fly up and away from this jumble of black-arts paraphernalia.

He pushed the little lever on the side of the music box and it tinkled out a sweet refrain—"Somewhere over the rainbow, bluebirds fly..."

He escorted them out. I noticed a difference in their stature and a spring in their step; indeed, their whole demeanor seemed changed.

I was amazed at what I had just seen. As we came out of the back room a pair of white women were just coming into the office for some of the same treatment. As there was little time to talk, I thanked the sheriff and left. I visited him several more times and saw him go through almost the same process with a young man whose wife had left him.

It took me a while to sift through what I had witnessed, and once I had, one question remained in my mind. I went back one last time to ask it. I said, "Mr. McTeer, I feel like you are very honest in what you're doing. You help people take responsibility for their own healing and acknowledge their own beliefs when you say, 'You came here because you believe I can help you. If you believe I can help you, I know I can.' I've heard you begin every session saying this. I've heard you emphasize it several times, but I can't help wondering, sir, what do you believe?"

He looked me straight in the eye and said, "I was born and raised on a plantation right near hah, more than seventy years ago. I've seen a lot of things that I can't explain. I don't know what I believe. I just know I'm helping people."

I never did get a specimen of a "chewing root" from the sheriff but I realized that his type of healing had little to do with the medicinal properties of herbs. In fact, as an ex-lawman, he was philosophically opposed to the prescribing of any kind of physical medicine or herbs without a license. However, I did interview a young M.D. in town who had brought an occasional patient to Sheriff McTeer. He assured me that he and other members of the local medical establishment considered McTeer's cultural/psychic-healing services a valuable resource to the community.

Sheriff McTeer died in 1980. It was written up in a quarter-page obituary in the *Charlotte News and Observer*. Lately I have heard about recent incarnations of Dr. Buzzard—one Dr. Buzzard who is the leader of a rhythm and blues band and another who was a guest on the Cosby show. Dr. Buzzard and his tradition surely live on, but there will never be another Sheriff McTeer.

I went to the root man, fell way down on my knees,
I went to see the root man, fell down on my knees,
I said, "Mr. Root Man, please have mercy on me!"
(Here's what he told me:)
I got High John the Conqueror, Little John the Chew,
[But] I ain't got nothin' [to] take the jinx off a' you...

from "The Low-Down Dirty Blues"
by Howard Armstrong

[1] From a recorded interview April, 1978.

[2] J. E. McTeer, *Fifty Years as a Low Country Witch Doctor* (Beaufort, S.C.: Beaufort Book Co., 1976).

8

Two Ways to Choke an Owl

WITH A FEW WORDS ABOUT PARADISE, GOOD AND EVIL, BIRD-WATCHERS, AND A STRANGE ENCOUNTER ON THE JERSEY SHORE

One night I was camping alone deep in the woods, near the summit of one of my favorite mountains. I was sitting half in my sleeping bag with my back against the trunk of a large maple tree. Drowsily, I stared into the glowing coals of the waning camp fire. Then I heard the distant call of a barred owl. The barred owl is a large, brown-eyed creature with stripes or bars down its breast. (Hence the name "barred" owl.) Its head is rounded, without the hornlike feather tufts charac-

Barred Owl

teristic of the great horned, the screech, and the other "eared" owls. Although the barred owl has an amazing repertoire of shrieks, hoots, and cackles, its standard call is a distinctive series of eight hoots, as if it were saying, "Who cooks for you, who cooks for you-all?" Some old country folk say that sometimes these noises are not from owls but are actually the sounds of conjure-women deep in the forest, cooking up and tasting forbidden potions.

If you can imitate the owls' calls, sometimes you can fool them and entice them to answer and come closer. On various occasions I have been able to bring in not only barred owls but great horned and screech owls as well. (I have yet to call in a conjure-woman, however.)

Barred owls are often the easiest to call, so without even crawling from my sleeping bag I burst forth with a volley of my best owl hoots in the direction of that distant owl and waited for a response—but none was forthcoming. So, I finally slumped down, pulled the covers up, and dozed off—until suddenly, right above my head, an extremely loud, piercing "HOOOO-AH!" shattered the still night air. It startled me right out of my bag. As I stood there shivering in the blackness, I couldn't help but chuckle at how, rather than me fooling the owl, it seemed like this time the owl was having the last laugh.

When I was a youngster, my dad told me an interesting

Screech Owl

way to catch an owl. He said that if you were to see one up in a tree, all you had to do was walk slowly in a wide circle underneath the bird. The owl, being curious, would watch you, and as it watched, it would swivel its head around and around until it wrung its own neck.

I may have actually believed that story for a while, but no owl is about to fall for it. This story comes from the owl's ability to swivel its head more than 360 degrees and to remain perched comfortably even while looking over its own back. In fact, most birds can perform this feat but it seems more extraordinary in owls because their necks seem to be so short.

The spooky, eerie-sounding calls of these mysterious, wide-eyed night creatures have spawned a great deal of folklore, fear, and superstition. The eerie wavering whinny of the small but rather common screech owl was once believed to be an omen of misfortune and death by Appalachian mountain folk. If a screech owl's call is disturbing your sleep, the standard remedy is to tie your bed sheet (or shirttail) into a knot. As you pull the knot tighter, the calls will dissipate. Some say this will actually choke the owl.

Here, we have another story about owl choking. What do we humans have against owls? I think it might come down to this:

Great Horned Owl

Owls are night creatures and as a species we are scared of the dark. We can't see well in darkness, and since the beginnings of humanity, creatures of the night have always seemed the most dangerous and fearsome to us. It is a basic human trait to turn fear into animosity and to try to eliminate any creature that scares us. We'd much rather do battle with the object of our fear than deal with the fear itself. So we tell stories about choking owls.

I was surprised to learn that some native Americans are superstitious about owls. I have even heard of instances at powwows

Barred Owl looking over its back.

where a dance was stopped and owl feathers were removed from the bustle of a costumed dancer because these were believed to be an ill omen. When I asked my Chippewa-Cree friend about this, he said that his people love and respect owls. They consider owls to be medicine allies. They are guides into the darkness, not only into the physical darkness of the night but also metaphorically, into the deep, dark recesses of the psyche.

He thought that this fear of owls is more prevalent among Christianized Indians. Once they become Christians, they become afraid of the dark. They come to associate darkness and night creatures with evil.

He told me that in his language there are no words that mean evil or bad, nor any words that mean good. This seemed incredible to me—to have a language and a culture where nothing is good or bad! Surely, translations of his language must use the words good and bad, I insisted. He patiently explained that words translated into English as "good" are usually words that mean beautiful, beneficial, or uplifting. Words translated to mean bad are words like difficult or unfortunate. But he assured me that they have no words for the abstract concepts of good or evil.

After I heard this, it became an interesting exercise to try to think of my own world without good or evil. I thought about the poisonous brown recluse spiders in my bathtub, and the copperheads and disease-carrying ticks in the grass. "Are they bad?" I wondered. I thought about bluebirds, butterflies, and bouquets of flowers. "Are they good?"

I thought about satanic cults and the laughter of children; about deadly nuclear waste and pure spring water; about sin and redemption; about saints and murderers; about Mother Teresa and Saddam Hussein; and about Hitler... Hitler?!

"What about Hitler?" I asked my Indian friend the next time I saw him. "Wasn't Hitler an embodiment of evil?"

"The same fire that burned in Hitler burns in you and me," he replied.

I began to realize that, to the extent that I judge something, my ability to understand it is limited.

The Bible says that Adam and Eve were cast out of Paradise for eating "of the tree of the knowledge of good and evil" (Genesis 2:17). Paradise can be defined as the state of living in complete harmony with one's environment. When you are in total harmony with your environment, you are truly living in paradise.

As soon as Adam and Eve saw the world in terms of good and evil, they had to learn to differentiate between the two and make judgments. In order to judge something, whether we judge it as good or evil, we have to set ourselves apart from it. That which we are apart from we can no longer live in harmony with. So as soon as we judge, whether it be owls or people or anything else, we lose the potential for harmony, and paradise evaporates.

❦

It had been a severe, blustery winter all up and down the eastern seaboard. At the time I was living in southern New Jersey. One wintry Sunday I drove toward Brigantine National Wildlife Refuge on the coast. I knew the cold weather would likely bring a concentration of wintering waterfowl there. I expected to see flocks of ducks, as well as Canada and snow geese, but what I was most hoping to see was brant.

As a youthful birder, who was raised a few hundred miles south of there on the Chesapeake, I had spent hours observing almost every kind of waterfowl that frequents the Eastern Flyway, but I had never seen a brant. This small goose travels along the coast and is rarely seen even as far inland as the western shore of the Chesapeake. Even though I no longer maintain a careful list enumerating all the bird species I've seen, I still get a special thrill when I see a new bird—what is known as a life lister in birding circles.

I was slowly cruising the road that winds around the marshes at the refuge when I came to a turnout overlooking a large expanse of salt marsh and open water. There were hundreds of snow geese intermingled with Canada geese and ducks in the marsh, and yes, there in the open water, was a large flock of what had to be brant! I pulled my car over, grabbed my binoculars, and jumped out. A young couple was there already. They had a tripod set up with a spotting scope. It was pointing out at the marsh and they were taking turns looking through it. The air was filled with a cacophony of sounds: the cackling of the snow geese, the hollow honking of the Canadas, the bugling of tundra swans, all punc-

Brant

tuated by the whistling of wings and the raucous quacks of black ducks and mallards. The brant were congregated in a large "raft" (a tight flock) in the open water. When I trained my binoculars on them, I could see the distinctive white slash on their black necks. I asked the folks with the scope if they were looking at the brants. "We've got a black hawk here," he said. (Birders regularly use the word "got" for the word "see.")

I looked through their scope and could see the hawk. It was at rest on a small, ice-encrusted island at the far edge of the range of the 30X scope. She had the book out to the hawk pages and we decided it had to be the dark phase of the rough-legged hawk, an occasional winter visitor from the Arctic. I had now seen two life listers already. I asked my new acquaintances if they'd heard of any other special birds in the area. "Eiders at jetty number eight in Barnegat," he replied tersely, "and a snowy owl reported around Barnegat Light." These people were obviously a party on the Audubon hot line. They had the word on the birds.

Eiders.... I had watched rafts of these great northern sea ducks bobbing like black and white corks on stormy green seas one winter along the coast of Maine. It would indeed be a treat to see them again. But a snowy owl! The most magnificent of the owls— even larger than the great horned owl. I had often dreamed of seeing a snowy owl ever since looking at the one that stared out at me from the boxes of my dad's favorite cigars. This owl rarely strays south of its tundra home, where it hunts lemmings, ptarmigans, and arctic hares. I almost swooned with delight at the idea of seeing a majestic snowy owl! But before charging off on some wild owl chase, I concentrated on the majesty of the birds right in front of me. The brant stayed out in the open water. The snow geese were in the majority here. Many of them were feeding on spartina, a marsh grass. Like patrons at a lunch counter, they were lined up at the water's edge with their backs to me. Great blue herons stalked the tidal canals.

I left this area and as I drove on through the refuge I came to a mowed lawn. A bittern was stalking across the yard and was about to cross the road when I speeded up to get a closer look. The bittern, feeling threatened, did what a bittern does in the presence of danger: It stood very still and extended its beak straight up. This is a successful strategy in the bittern's natural habitat of cattails, tall reeds, and marsh grasses. In grassy marshes, with its long thin neck, pointed beak, and vertically striped body, the bittern is a masterpiece of camouflage, but here on this close-cropped lawn, it was like much other lawn statuary, a surreal showpiece of misplaced instinct. (I've felt like that before.) I wondered if it might look more in place if it were pink.

Soon I was on my way north to Barnegat to look for the eiders, hardly daring to dream of getting to witness the rare southern occurrence of the snowy owl!

I stopped, somewhat dutifully, at jetty number eight on Barnegat Beach. There were two birders there with their tripod and scope, peering out at the surf. As I approached, I realized that they were the same two I had met down at the refuge. I had unwittingly become part of a bird-watcher's Sunday circuit.

"Fancy meeting you here," I said in greeting. He was peering into the scope. "We've got a female king eider," he said, without looking up. His companion had the book open to the sea duck page. Through my binoculars, I could see a lone brown bird bobbing just beyond the surf line.

"So, would you call this a 'queen' eider?" I asked with a smile.

"King eider," he corrected. "You can differentiate it

Male and Female King Eider

from the female common eider by the facial profile—the shorter bill length."

When I looked through their scope I could see it much more clearly, and I saw that it did compare well with the picture in the book. The male of the species is a dramatic bird, black and white in color with a bright-orange bill shield. This female we were observing, however, was a uniform drab brown. I had never seen one before. Here was yet another life lister!

I asked directions to the lighthouse and bid them adieu. They said they would be there shortly. The town of Barnegat is at the northern end of a coastal barrier island, separated from Island Beach to the north by Barnegat Inlet, which flows between the ocean and Barnegat Bay. Island Beach is one of the only stretches of undeveloped seashore on New Jersey's coast.

I arrived at the lighthouse and found dozens of birders lined up along the beach. There were eleven tripods in a row with scopes of all kinds. The scopes were all pointed across the inlet to Island Beach a couple of hundred yards away.

"Have you seen the snowy owl?" I inquired of a kindly looking man sitting on a folding chair behind a huge Questar scope.

"Yes, he's over there across the channel, in that pile of rocks. You can see the top of his head and he's facing away from us. Here, look through my scope. It's right on him." I gratefully accepted, and sure enough, there before my very eyes, behind a large rock, was the top inch and a half of a majestic snowy owl. All I could see was the round white dome of its head.

"Keep watching," the man said. "Sometimes he turns his head this way and you can see his eyes."

The words were no sooner out of his mouth when the owl looked my way. I could barely make out the upper halves of those piercing yellow eyes. All too soon it turned its head back away, leaving me to watch nothing but a stolid white dome.

I heartily thanked the man and visited among the other birders. Everyone was waiting for the owl to move again. Many had been there all afternoon; some had been there all day. The owl had been spotted early that morning on this side of the inlet near the lighthouse. When disturbed by human activity, it had flown across to the quiet side of the inlet. Some of the birders were chatting among themselves, while others were scanning flocks of gulls, hoping to see an iceland gull or a black-legged kittiwake, which might have come south with the inclement weather.

As I drove home, I thought about the day. Four new birds in one day was not bad, in fact it was pretty special for a seasoned birder like myself. But somehow, seeing only an inch and a half of this regal snowy owl who stands more than two feet tall and has a wingspan of almost five feet, felt frustrating and left me wanting more. This mystical Arctic being rarely ventured this far south. No one knew when it would return north. All I knew was, while it was here, I wanted more of an experience with this owl.

I started working out a strategy. In its Arctic home, the owl lived in open, windswept tundra. It made sense that on this southern excursion, it had chosen the windswept dunes of the preserved part of the Jersey shore as a winter resting place. Tomorrow would be Monday. I figured that I would wait till afternoon. If the owl had been resting on the Barnegat side of the inlet, the daily human activities would probably force it back over to Island Beach, which would have little human traffic on a wintry weekday afternoon.

There, if anywhere, I would have the best chance of encountering the owl.

The next day I fidgeted all morning, and about noon I packed my binoculars and my camera bag with my telephoto lens and headed for the beach. I stopped at the ranger station on the way in and was assured that it was permissible to park at the end of the paved road and walk the last mile or so down to the point at the southern end of the island.

I walked along a soft sandy access road down between the dunes. This entire end of the island was deserted. I knew that the owl would probably choose a vantage point like a post or the crest of a high dune to rest on. Occasionally, I picked my way through the fragile dune plants up to a high spot from where I could scan the surrounding area for my quarry. The island was narrow enough so that with my binoculars I was able to scan its entire width. I felt sure that if the owl was out in the open and not hiding under a bayberry bush somewhere, I would be able to see it. I climbed the dunes several times and systematically scrutinized every ridge, crest, and high place, but no owl was to be seen. I neared the end of the island and walked down between some boarded-up summer cottages. There, at the tip of the island, on a spit of smooth sand about twenty yards away, was a vertical six-foot piling. On the top of that piling perched the owl!

Its sharp, one-and-a-half-inch long black talons emerged from its white-feathered feet and gripped the edge of that piling. Its breast and wings were a pristine white with black flecks, which contrasted magnificently with the gray overcast sky. The entire bird stiffened and became alert at my intrusion. It regarded me with intense, lucid, yellow eyes.

Ever so slowly, I reached into my camera bag, eased out

my camera, aimed, and focused. I was fairly close to the owl, and with my long lens, the image in the viewfinder looked good. I squeezed off a few shots. I slowly walked up a little closer and snapped a few more. The owl seemed agitated and ready to fly. It raised up on its perch slightly, but never broke its unearthly gaze.

The photographer in me wanted to slowly walk closer and closer while busily snapping away. It would be great to get a dramatic close-up, possibly even a picture of the owl with its wings spread as it finally flew away.

But as I looked into those deep eyes, something told me to stop and savor this special moment. I slowly sat down right there in the sand, and the owl and I locked our gazes. Those unblinking eyes met mine straight on. They looked at me, into me, and right through me. They were so deep and clear, so knowing. Folklore calls owls wise. Scientists call them stupid. Yet as we beheld each other on that wintry beach, each of us a finely tuned product of eons of evolution, I knew there was wisdom here all right, but it was a wisdom beyond intelligence, much more than can fit in an owl's brain (or a human brain, for that matter).

Amerindian wisdom teaches that the owl with whom I was consorting is only a shadowy manifestation of Real Owl. One might describe this as "owlness" or "owl essence."

I took a deep breath, straightened my spine, and relaxed my eyes. The owl, never breaking its gaze, fluffed out its feathers and settled itself on the post. Then one eyelid dropped in a slow-motion wink and opened again. I returned the wink, as slowly and owl-like as I could. We continued our stare again, until the owl slowly closed both eyes. I closed both of my eyes in response and breathed slow, shallow breaths. I felt owl essence surrounding me. Quiet. White. The still air was cold on my face. Then I felt a gentle, almost warm puff of wind touch me. I opened my eyes, and the owl was gone. This startled me, and I whirled around just in time to see it land on a tall flagpole near the summer cottages.

Something caught my eye beneath the piling where the owl had been sitting. I walked over, and there on the sand was an owl pellet. I'm not referring to an owl dropping (there was one of those on the sand, too), but rather a casting, expelled from the mouth and made up of all the bones, teeth, hair, feathers, and other indigestible parts of an owl's prey. After rolling around in the owl's gullet until all the nutrients are extracted, the pellet is simply burped up. Wildlife biologists who study owls and other raptors can analyze these pellets and learn a great deal about an owl's diet as well as about the rodent population in a certain area.

I was thrilled to find this token of our Arctic visitor. As I bent down to examine it, a fleck of color caught my eye. Next to the pellet on the sand was a beak from a small songbird. It was the size of a pencil point, with a tuft of tiny feathers attached. One of the feathers was white, another was black, and yet another was yellow. The owl had caught this bird and carried it back here to eat. In the process, this

Owl pellets, containing remains of a rail bird (left) and a vole (right).

piece had become detached and fallen to the ground. Because of these three colored feathers, I knew the owl had dined on a golden-crowned kinglet. Arctic owls are known to be day flyers, as any bird who lives in the Arctic in summer must be. And these bird remains confirmed that it was feeding during the day here, as well. I thought of that kinglet's death—of suddenly being engulfed by a puff of warmth from the Arctic, silent, white, impeccable, and merciless—the final snap as that great bird's beak sank home at the base of the kinglet's skull.

Golden Crowned Kinglet

I walked back over to the flagpole, but as I approached, the owl again flew off and landed on top of a nearby dune. I resolved then to disturb the owl no more, and paused for one last look. The owl was perched sideways on the crest of the dune, looking alert and magnificent. A gentle wind was moving the grasses. I silently offered blessings and thanks. I had turned and was walking down the sandy, rolling dune road heading for the beach, when I heard an engine roar. Over a rise ahead of me loomed a jeep with monstrous tractor-tread dune-buggy tires. In it were two men and there was a New Jersey State Parks emblem on the side. I assumed they were on a routine patrol, but I got an ominous feeling when the jeep's lights flashed like glaring pupil-less eyeballs and headed right for me. Still not quite believing they were looking for me, I nodded an uneasy greeting and started to walk past along the driver's side.

From the open window a voice growled, "Just a minute, Mac, lemme see your identification."

"Identification?" I asked weakly, and fumbled for my wallet. I felt a sinking feeling deep in my gut. My head was reeling from having been snatched so abruptly from one reality to the next. "Is something wrong, officer?"

I looked in to see two men in uniform. The driver was older and regarded me with a tired grimace through heavy, dark, bloodshot eyes. His companion was considerably brighter and younger; perhaps a rookie in training, I thought.

"You're damn right there's something wrong. You're in a restricted area."

"A restricted area?" I protested. "I asked at the ranger station when I came into the park and they told me I could walk down here."

"You're allowed on the beach only, not back here in the dunes." I nervously flipped through my wallet. "Will a driver's license do?" I asked. We were more than a mile from my car. He took my driver's license and examined it. All during this transaction his companion kept looking at me with clear blue eyes and a friendly, strangely excited expression, like he was bursting with something he wanted to tell me.

The officer in charge looked up from my license and said, "Mista Elliott, you were up on them dunes. We know you were 'cause we followed your tracks." Then he continued, "Let me ask you somethin', are you concerned about the environment?"

I assured him that I was.

"Well, then, for your information, when you climb on them dunes and step on them dune plants, it kills 'em *Instantly.* Without them dune plants, we wouldn't have no dunes, and without them dunes you wouldn't have no pretty beach to come to. Do you unnerstand, Mista Elliott?"

I was sure that I hadn't killed any dune plants, but this did not seem to be the place to debate the finer points of dune plant mortality (or to point out that he had been following me in a four-wheel-drive jeep). When I looked at the larger picture, I felt a strange sense of gratitude for this surly officer tirelessly executing the thankless job of protecting this seashore from the vast hordes of beach-hungry Jerseyites who flock to this last pristine strand every summer.

"I'm sorry sir," I said softly. "I stand corrected; I should have known better than to climb the dunes in a heavily used area like this."

He handed me back my license and said, "Now you can go right through there to the beach. You can walk back along the beach, but you stay offa them dunes!"

"And on your way…" his companion blurted out, "look on that dune over to your left. There's a snowy owl!"

Our eyes met. "Yeah, thanks," I said, "I saw."

The truck engine roared back to life and I turned and walked down to the beach. A soft flurry of snow began to fall and gentle waves lapped the shore as I headed home.

9

Observations of Social Parasitism

OF FEMINIST BEES, SLAVE-MAKING ANTS, RADICAL GARDENERS, AND SLEAZY ACADEMICS

"This is Greek oregano; smell it; it's good for cooking. This here is globe basil; it's great for pesto. This is lemon thyme; smell how it's different from the regular thyme over there. Here's southernwood; we use that for fragrant herb wreaths. And this is wormwood..." Carlson was giving Theron and me a tour of his extensive herb garden. As he led us between the beds, he rattled off the name of each clump of plants.

We must have looked like a strange procession as we slowly moved along, pinching leaves and sniffing the scent of each new herb. Carlson, a bearded, frizzy-headed, Detroit City radical relic of the sixties who had turned North Carolina gardener, was leading the parade, madly gesticulating and calling out the plant names. I was right behind Carlson, eagerly asking questions and making comments. Last in line, and several steps behind, came Theron, an older mountain man in blue jeans, a denim jacket, and a well-worn felt hat with a crow feather in the band. He was taking his time, closely examining and smelling each plant. Theron is both a good friend and a respected elder; he is

always willing to learn something new as well as share his vast knowledge and experience with us transplanted suburban bumpkins.

"This is variegated lemon balm," Carlson continued. "Here's coyote mint, and this is hoary mountain mint; it's much stronger than regular mint. It has sort of a camphor smell. This is pineapple sage and this here's bronze fennel..."

"What's this herb here that smells like mad piss ants, Carlson?" Theron interrupted.

Carlson looked around, "That's variegated lemon balm."

"Smells like mad piss ants to me," said Theron.

"Mad piss ants?" I asked.

"Yeah, you know, them little yeller ants. They smell just like that when you bust into a nest of 'em."

"Why do they call 'em 'piss ants'?" I asked.

"I don't know why they call 'em that," he replied, "but they'll sting the piss out of you if you let 'em get on you."

I went back to that lemon balm plant and smelled it again. It had a very pleasant lemony-citrus aroma. Lemon balm's scientific name is *Melissa*, the Greek word for honeybee, in reference to bees' fondness for the flowers. But what was this about angry ants?

"You say there's ants that smell like this?" I persisted.

"Yeah, there shore is," Theron declared. "I might even be able to find you some right around here." He went over to the edge of the garden and started turning over rocks. In a few minutes, he hollered triumphantly, "Here they are!"

There, beneath an upturned rock, Theron had exposed a cluster of small yellow ants.

"Now them's piss ants," he said with a grin, "and they're plenty mad. Now you smell of them."

I put my nose down and sniffed. Sure enough, that same lemony fragrance filled my nostrils—an ant and a plant with the same smell.

When I described the ants to an entomologist, he told me they belong to the genus, *Acanthomyops*. There are three common species of them in the East and they come in different sizes. He said they are known as the "larger yellow ant," the "smaller yellow ant" and the "just plain yellow ant."

The fragrance they give off when disturbed has been analyzed and found to contain several volatile chemicals. Two of the predominant ones bear the names citronellal and citral. These two aromatic compounds are also found in many fragrant lemon-scented plants, including citrus, bay leaves, lemon verbena, and lemon grass, as well as in

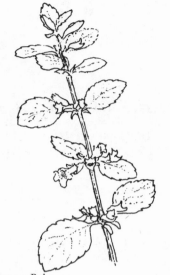

Lemon Balm

the lemon balm that Carlson grew in his garden. These chemicals serve as repellants, protecting the plant from leaf-eating insects and browsing animals who find the aromas disagreeable.

The ants, also, repel other species of invading insects as well as larger animals with these chemicals. We humans also use the same compounds, especially citronellal, as an insect repellant. We extract it commercially from a tropical grass *(Cymbopogon flexuosus)* as citronella oil.

In the ant colony, however, these aromas are more than a simple repellant. They also serve as a chemical alarm for other members of the colony. When a chemical is secreted to communicate or convey information (such as alarm, assembly, sexual readiness, etc.), it is known as a pheromone (pronounced "fair-o-moan"). Pheromones such as these play the central role in the organization of colonies of social insects. (Social insects include ants, termites, and many species of wasps and bees.)

When an ant colony is disturbed, either by other insects or larger animals (including us), the alarm pheromones are secreted. These substances, when sensed by the other worker ants in the colony, act as behavioral "releasers" and they elicit defensive behavior in the workers nearby who rush to fiercely defend their colony. "And they'll sting the piss out of ya," as Theron warned. Most of these individuals will be swatted to death for their trouble.

In a colony of social insects this kind of self-destructive behavior among the soldier and worker castes, in which they endanger themselves in defense of their nest or hive, is known among biologists as altruism.

Removed from the strict biological realm, altruism is also defined as unselfish devotion to the needs of others. In human society, altruism is a highly regarded ideal. However, occasionally this kind of unquestioning, fearless, insect-style altruism becomes the obsession of nationalistic and industrial leaders, who encourage their workers and soldiers to work, to fight, and to die if necessary to serve their queen (or other leader). Throughout history this behavior has been encouraged and idealized in symbols, in poetry, and by decree. The bees depicted on Napoleon's coat of arms symbolize this theme. Tennyson's famous poem "The Charge of the Light Brigade" celebrates it as heroism:

> Half a league, half a league,
> Half a league onward,...
> Into the valley of Death
>   Rode the six hundred.
> Theirs not to make reply
> Theirs not to reason why,
> Theirs but to do and die...
> Into the valley of Death
>   Rode the six hundred.

One of the legends concerning the origin of Valentine's Day says that back in Roman times, the emperor noticed the biological vulnerability of his troops, i.e., that once a soldier married and had a family, he lost his fighting spirit. He became a parent, responsible for his family, and his biological focus changed. He was much less willing to risk his life for vague nationalistic ideals. So the emperor prohibited soldiers from marrying. St. Valentine was an early Christian priest who married young soldiers against the emperor's decree. He was martyred and eventually canonized for his trouble.

In insects altruism is genetically programmed. This self-destructive behavior in the nonreproducing worker castes puzzled evolutionists for a while. They wondered how these fatal altruistic traits could have been selected and passed on to subsequent generations if the individuals leave no offspring. Charles Darwin himself, while composing his *Origin of Species*, found this a "special difficulty which at first appeared to me insuperable, and actually fatal to my whole theory." Then he realized that selection operates at the level of the family rather than the single organism. "Thus a well-flavoured vegetable is cooked, and the individual is destroyed; but the horticulturist sows seeds of the same stock, and confidently expects to get very nearly the same variety; breeders of cattle wish the flesh and fat to be well-marbled together; the animal has been slaughtered, but the breeder goes with confidence to the same family."[1]

These principles, which Darwin wrote about more than a century ago, are still the basis of any genetic breeding program today. A commercial beekeeper I talked to had a concise way of explaining it. He was intolerant of aggressiveness in his bees. If he was stung more than a few times while working a particular hive, he would requeen that hive with a queen of gentler stock. He told me, "We have a sayin' in our bee yards: 'You sting me and yo' momma dies.'"

In the early 1900s, due to the work of William Morton Wheeler, biologists began to realize that the entire hive or colony of social insects is not really analogous to a family of potentially equal individuals. A colony is more like one single organism (or "superorganism," as Wheeler called it) composed of interdependent parts. Since no individual ant, bee, or termite can survive (for long) independently of the colony, they saw the different castes of thousands of sterile workers and soldiers as extensions of its reproductive parts or "germ plasm" (namely the queen and the males).

The power of the genetic connection is a dominant theme in most biological organisms. However, many modern religions encourage their members to look beyond their particular biological kinship group, whether it be a family, a community, or a nation, and acknowledge the "human spiritual family" or the "brotherhood of man."

The "Gaia Hypothesis," recently brought forth by two scientists, James Lovelock and Lynn Margoulis, suggests that we need to look beyond the human family concept and realize the entire planet earth is one living organism. Lovelock once said, "The rocks, the air, the oceans, and all life are an inseparable system that functions to keep the planet livable. In fact, I now believe that life can exist *only* on a planetary scale. Can't have a planet with a sparse life anymore than you can have half a cat." Humanity is not the ultimate purpose of creation, according to the Gaia Hypothesis. We humans are merely a particularly successful and conspicuous part during this current, a few moments in the life cycle of this planetary organism.

As revolutionary and "wholistic" as the Gaia Hypothesis may seem to the modern scientific world, it is a relatively basic tenet of many native American and other ancient pagan religions, which have always viewed the earth as well as the entire universe as one interdependent whole—from the realm of the Star Maidens and Father Sky to the depths of the Mother Earth. Many native American religious ceremonies begin by acknowledging this universal kinship with the invocation "All my relations."

Insects are very different from us humans. Yet in many ways their complex societies, made up of thousands of individuals, have much in common with human society. The idea that there are creatures so different from us but who organize themselves in similar ways provides us with new perspectives on our own anthropocentric world.

As I write about various insect societies, and other animals, a scientist might accuse me of the sin of anthropomorphism—attributing human motivations and qualities to non-humans. I confess: I do see the world through human eyes. However, upon closer examination I think my approach is really the opposite. Rather than attempting to attribute "human-ness" to the animal world, I am learning to see the "animalness" in us humans. In this way, I have found other species can teach us about our own humanity.

Honeybees might be a good start. Honeybees are regarded as the most highly evolved of the social insects because they are able to communicate amazingly abstract information through pheromones and through certain behaviors.

The queen bee exerts a strange kind of authority over the hive. It's far from a monarchy. She runs a chemical kingdom—what might be called a "pheromonarchy." All the activities in the hive are determined, controlled, and coordinated through her pheromone production. She spends most of her time going from cell to cell laying eggs (about a thousand eggs per day) and oozing out pheromone-laden secretions known as queen substance.

Everywhere she goes, she is followed by a retinue of attendants who are constantly feeding her, carrying away her fecal material, and licking this luscious pheromone-laden queen substance from every millimeter of her tawny body. As long as the queen is in good health, pumping out plenty of pheromonal exudations, and there is enough space for the hive to grow, the workers, who are constantly "promiscuously" exchanging body fluids through a process called trophylaxis, distribute the queen substance throughout the hive so that each one of the sometimes eighty thousand or more bees in the hive "knows" how the queen is doing by the "taste" of her pheromones.

Should the queen become weak, she will produce less of the pheromone, or if the hive becomes crowded, this will interfere with the distribution of the substance. Whatever the cause, when the workers (who are underdeveloped infertile or sterile females) detect a deficit of queen substance, they automatically begin making a few large queen cells. Into each queen cell they place a recently laid egg. These eggs are regular worker eggs, but they develop into queens because they are treated differently. They are given more space in which to mature, and they are fed not only the regular honey-and-pollen "bee bread" that the worker brood are fed but this "princess" is given jelly—royal jelly—with her bread. This royal jelly will make her a queen. Royal jelly contains extra nutrients and hormones. It is even collected by beekeepers and sold to people, who take it as a dietary supplement.

When the old queen discovers these new queen cells and realizes what is going on, she puts out a few good squirts of swarm pheromone, which is her way of saying, "Come on girls! If that's what they think of me, let's go!" She assembles all the active field bees; they pour out of the hive and fly off, landing on a nearby bush or tree limb to plan their next move.

Scout bees fly off into the countryside to look for a new place to live. This could be a cavity in a tree, a rock crevice, the walls of a building, or even a beekeeper's vacant hive. As each scout bee returns, she dances a little recruitment waggle dance, which tells the rest of the bees how excited she is about the new place she found. Through this dance she tells the others the location of her find. This ability to communicate abstract information, such as the location of a distant tree cavity through a dance, is what sets bees apart from all other insects.

In response to the dancing worker, some of her sisters fly off to check out what she has found. When they come back they dance out their assessment of the place. Meanwhile, other scouts come back and dance about places they have found. Soon there are various waggle-dancing factions, each dancing their own recruitment dance, encouraging other bees to go and check out the place they found. Eventually, the faction that has the most dancers and the most vigorous displays will recruit the most bees, and through a process of elimination, they all end up dancing the same dance, indicating that a consensus has been reached. They all fly off to occupy this agreed-upon location.

Meanwhile, back at the hive, there remains only the developing brood with a number of young nurse bees attending them, and the male bees, known as drones. The drones do not bring in any nectar or pollen. They are stingless and cannot defend the hive (or themselves, for that matter). When they are not hanging around the hive, accosting the workers and demanding to be fed, the drones fly around outside with a horde of other drones and eagerly await the "nuptial emergence" of a virgin queen.

Inside the hive, the larval queens are developing and metamorphosing in their cells. When, at last, one of the queens matures, she chews off the cap of her cell and crawls out onto the comb. Her first activity will be to patrol the hive. She will approach each of the other queen cells and make a high-pitched vibration called piping. She sings this

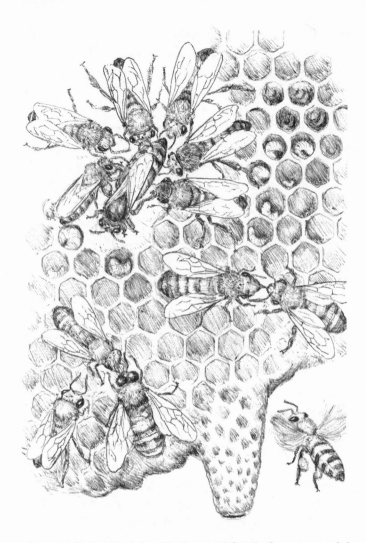

A portion of a honeybee colony. In the upper left is the Queen surrounded by her retinue of attendants. They rest on a section of capped cells that contain developing pupa. Moving in a clockwise direction, we see: cells containing honey and pollen as well as eggs and larva in various stages of development; two workers exchanging regurgitated nectar; a worker returning with a load of pollen on her hind legs; a queen cell; and a drone (with thick body and large eyes) begging for food from a worker.

piping song to her rapidly maturing sisters. If the sister is about to emerge, she will answer with her own piping from inside her cell. The already-emerged sibling will then sting her sister to death through the wall of the cell, and she will die without ever emerging. If one of the sisters emerges before the first queen can get to her, they will battle to the death.

When only one virgin queen remains in the hive, she prepares for her nuptial flight. The next calm sunny morning, she releases a cloud of pheromone that announces, "Young virgin, ready and willing—catch me if you can, boys!" Then she flies straight up, trailing an entourage of desperately willing suitors. High in the sky, the strongest of the drones will finally catch up to her and they will mate in the air. As he climaxes his genitalia actually explode within her and his reproductive organs separate from his body. He falls back to earth mortally wounded, and she returns to the hive trailing his entrails from her abdomen and carrying all his genetic material in her spermatheca.

She may leave the hive again for a few more of these flights, but when she returns, she will have accumulated enough sperm from those few drones who gave their all to fertilize a lifetime of eggs. After this moment of glory in the sky, she becomes a veritable egg-laying machine for the rest of her life, laying as many as two hundred thousand eggs a year for up to seven years. She will never leave the hive again, unless she swarms.

Since the drones eat a considerable amount of honey and contribute nothing but genetic material to the hive, there is little use for them in fall and winter, when there is no production of queens that need mating. In the late summer, as part of the preparations for winter, the workers turn the drones out of the hive. It takes several of the smaller female workers to drag a large, bumbly, defenseless male by his appendages out of the hive and heave him off the landing board. He often comes crawling back home, trying to get back into the hive, but these feisty little feminists don't need him, and they don't want him; they have changed the "locks on the doors." "Thus," writes Karl von Frisch, the great pioneer of honeybee study, "they find their inglorious end at the portals of the bee dwelling, driven out and starved, or stung to death, on a fine summer's day."[2]

For the winter, honeybee society is exclusively female. In the spring when they need a few males for sexual purposes, they will produce them. To do so, the queen will withhold sperm from a few eggs as she lays them. These infertile eggs, as strange as it seems, will develop into drones. Drones have grandfathers, but no fathers.

A behavioral phenomenon of bees that has amazing human parallels is the behavior known as robbing. Bees make honey by collecting watery nectar from flowers, adding enzymes to it and evaporating it by fanning with their wings until the sugar concentration is so high it will not ferment or spoil.

When there is a strong nectar flow with a profusion of flowers in bloom, the bees will work busily all day and very little will distract them; a mood of peaceful, industrious contentment pervades the bee yard. A beekeeper can open the hives and work with the bees, and they rarely become irritable.

Even if there is a dearth of nectar, the beekeeper can place containers of sugar water near the hive, and the bees will busily gather this syrup just like they gather nectar. But if open containers of honey are placed out near the hive, the bees seem to go crazy. An angry buzzing will be heard.

The bees will fly madly in all directions, swarm all over the honey and fight each other; numbers of them will get caught and even drown in the honey. If there is a group of hives together, the bees will raid each other's hives, rushing the entrances, trying to break through the guard bees and steal honey.

During peaceful times a bee can walk right into another hive with impunity. Sometimes, they even carry nectar into and contribute to neighboring hives. This happens frequently in large apiaries that have a number of similar hives all lined up and evenly spaced. On breezy days some bees will be blown off course and fly into a nearby hive, apparently by mistake. (This has happened to me in neighborhoods of identical suburban or urban row houses. Once I left a party and ran down the street to get something from my parked car. When I turned around to come back to the party I looked up and down the street and could not tell which house I had just come out of. I was lucky I wasn't arrested as I quietly crept up on to strange porches listening for the reassuring sounds of a party going on.)

A bee in a robbing mode moves in an agitated way, and probably releases a pheromone that makes her "look suspicious" to the guard bees, who rush to fend her off. If several robbers attack in a mob, like looters, some of them distract and occupy the guards while the others break through and run into the hive. There they find unguarded cells of stored honey and steal all they can carry. If the hive is weak, robbers from strong hives will sometimes strip the weaker hive of all its stores and leave it to starve and die.

The human analogies scream at me. I can envision an equally alarming scenario if you were to pour several bushel baskets full of hundred-dollar bills into a stock exchange or the orderly offices of a financial institution. You would likely incite these conservative, hardworking businesspeople into an angry robbing frenzy, too. The money, like the honey to the bees, represents the sweetness of wealth and security to these highly evolved social animals.

The honeybee, not being native to the Americas, was imported by white settlers from Europe. Native Americans regarded the bee as an ill omen and called it the "white man's fly" because when they saw honeybees, they knew white settlers were not far behind. John Burroughs pointed out that this was a good name for the honeybee: "In fact she was the epitome of the white man himself. She has the white man's craftiness, his industry, his architectural skill, his neatness and love of system, his foresight; and above all, his eager, miserly habits. The honey-bee's great ambition is to be rich, to lay up great stores, to possess the sweet of every flower that blooms. She is more than provident. Enough will not satisfy her; she must have all she can get."[3]

As you can see from Burroughs's writing from the late 1800's, I'm certainly not the first or the only one to find human societal traits modeled in insect societies (and vice versa). Along with altruism, feminism, nationalism, and division of labor, I was astounded to find not only robbing bees but also slave-making ants.

I first heard of this from my friend John Connors, a graduate student in wildlife biology, who had written a report on it. "Observations of Social Parasitism between the Ant Species..." began the dauntingly scholarly title of his scientific paper. But what a tale emerges! A martial drama of ruthless cruelty, fierce combat, heroic altruism, propaganda campaigns, and even chemical warfare unfolds when two societies—the red slave makers and their black slaves—meet their destiny. As if slavery among insects—"social parasitism" as John calls it—wasn't bizarre enough,

his observations revealed chains of insidious parasitic behavior beyond the scope of his paper, extending even into the upper echelons of human society.

John was working one summer as a naturalist at a local state park. One day, he saw an army of several thousand red ants traveling across the ground. He realized that this was a raiding foray by the local species of red slave-maker ants known as *Formica subintegra*. He followed them as they marched along. There were no leaders at the forefront of the phalanx; rather, they advanced as a constantly shifting amoebalike mass, with some ants dropping back while others moved forward to take their places. They were following a pheromonal scent trail that was laid out by scout ants earlier that day, marking the way to the nest of their slave species, a black ant known as *Formica subsericea*.

Slave-making behavior in ants is a curious type of social parasitism known to entomologists as dulosis. "In a dulotic relationship one species of ant initiates raids on the colonies of a closely related species, disperses or dispatches any resistance, penetrates the nest, and returns to its colony with the captured pupae of the other species." When these captured broods metamorphose into adult workers, they will become functional members of the colony as part of a slave caste destined for tasks of foraging, brood rearing, and nest building "while the captors generally perform none of these chores."[4]

There are six genera of dulotic ants. They have evolved a variety of different relationships with the "institution" of slavery. Some species can get along without slaves. They are known as facultative slaveholders, since their colonies are sometimes found to have no slaves and the workers are able to conduct all of the affairs of colony life in a competent fashion on their own.[5] Other ants, like those of the genus *Polyergus*, are totally dulotic. They are "obligate social parasites," completely dependent on slave-holding as a way of life. They are fierce warriors with large, sharp, sickle-shaped mandibles. These mandibles are only well-suited for the purpose of piercing the bodies of other adult ants. They cannot move soil or excavate their own nests. Their mandibles are so sharp, they cannot even handle their own young without injuring them. Slaves are necessary to care for their brood. They cannot obtain their own food or feed themselves; they have to be fed by their slaves. As they go through life, they display two contrasting sets of instincts: "When outside the nest on one of their predatory expeditions they display a dazzling courage and capacity for concerted action... while in the home nest, they sit in stolid idleness or pass the long hours begging the slaves for food or cleaning themselves and burnishing their ruddy armor."[6]

Another species of dulotic ant (*Formica wheeleri*) uses two different species of slaves in its colony. The ants of one species serve as an "infantry" force that not only defends the home colony but it also accompanies its captors on raids and assists them in plundering the victims' nests. Ants of the other slave species stay deep in their captors' home colony and perform "domestic" chores such as specializing in food storage and brood care.[7]

The target colony of the ants that John was following was about twenty yards away (though some forays of more than one hundred yards have been observed). The raiding behavior of this genus of ants has been well studied and documented. "When the first workers arrive at the nest to be pillaged, they do not enter it at once, but surround it and wait till the other detachments arrive. In the meantime the [ants that are about to be attacked]... scent their approaching foes and either prepare to defend their nest or seize their young and try to break through the cordon [of attackers] and escape. [Some] scramble up grass blades with their larvae and pupae in their jaws and [others] make off over the ground." Most of these would-be escapees are intercepted and their charges are snatched away, while the rest of the force swarms into the entrances of the nest, killing any of the defenders that offer hostile resistance.[8]

"The red, raiding ants grabbed the appendages of the black defender. Then the chemical warfare began..."

John saw a number of individual conflicts in the combat zone around the entrance to the colony. He reported that several combat strategies and kinds of warfare were used on this battlefield; not only was there plain and simple ganging up on an individual enemy defender, but there was chemical warfare and even a propaganda campaign of sorts. "Typically, three to four red *subintegra* raiders would simultaneously grab appendages of the defender, stretching them in all directions." Then the chemical warfare began. "The *subintegra* warriors would bend their thoraxes bringing the abdomen under [the rest of the body with the anal pore pointed forward] and shoot a stream of the pheromone [from the anal pore] and thus fumigate the defender."[9]

This chemical dousing causes temporary "discomfort and disorientation" and/or irritation, submission, and possibly exhaustion.[10] In most cases, the final fate of the victim was dismemberment, mutilation, and subsequent death.

However, these kinds of combat encounters were relatively scarce considering the large number of ants involved in this battle. Only those few defending ants that offered hostile resistance were attacked. What was more apparent was the great number of black *F. subsericea* ants "hiding" up on the grass blades and in the tops of bushes and saplings above the battleground. The red *F. subintegra* invaders were never seen climbing in pursuit of the vanquished defenders.

This makes sense, biologically. If one species is dependent on a slave species it is essential that it not destroy the source of its slaves.

The reason the invading ants met with so little active resistance is because when a large number of ants releases this mixture of powerful, chemically complex, acetate pheromones it overwhelms the colony and alters its behavior patterns, triggering a flight (rather than fight) response from the black *F. subsericea* workers. Because the pheromones evoke this kind of dispersal response, they are known as "propaganda substances."[11]

Once the colony has been conquered, the red *F. subintegra* workers remove the larvae and the pupae of the black *F. subsericea* colony and carry them back to their own colony, where they deposit them in their brood chambers to be attended and nurtured by slave workers captured on previous forays.

In the midst of watching this martial drama of nature unfold before his eyes, John suddenly noticed a tiny wasp hovering directly above one of the invading red ants. The ant was actively defending itself against this aerial adversary's advances until it was distracted by an oncoming black *F. subsericea* defender. As the invading ant turned to face its terrestrial opponent, the wasp quickly lit on the ant's abdomen, deposited an egg and fled, all in one split-second interval.

Once he saw this first wasp, John noticed twenty or thirty more hovering above the melee; each occasionally darting down to lay an egg on the abdomen of a battling red *F. subintegra* ant.

He captured some of the wasps and took them to an entomology professor at the university to be identified. He found out that it was a Braconid wasp in the subfamily Neonurinae, belonging to the genus *Elasmosoma*.

After an extensive literature search, John learned that this group of wasps is "exceedingly uncommon" and very little is known about them except that they "pass the larval period as internal parasites of ants."[12]

These tiny rare wasps are not only dependent on their parasitic relationship with these slave-maker ants but the only time the gravid female wasps have an opportunity to lay their eggs on their prospective hosts is during the heat of a slave raid, when the ants are too distracted to fend off the wasps.

These wasps are attracted to the battlefield by the same pheromonal substances the invaders use to "propagandize" and subdue their victims. "It is imaginative irony that conceives such insidious relationships," John comments rather philosophically.

The chain of parasitism, insidious relationships, and imaginative irony does not stop there, however. John never could get his specimens of the rare wasp back from that entomologist. The professor would not return John's calls and John never heard from him again. Shortly thereafter, the professor transferred to another institution. John was rather offended by this treatment and was quite perturbed when he was later told by a third party that the wasp he discovered was a species new to science and that the same entomology professor had published a description of the wasp, naming the species and thereby adding another publication to his résumé by parasitizing John's work. That would be called "academic parasitism," and it is quite common among higher primates in certain ivy-covered environments. The last link in this complex parasitic chain would be yours truly, the author parasite who tries to make a buck telling the story.

In the course of researching this story I made a number of phone calls in an attempt to track down the particulars of this case. I found that, although it's true that he was treated with complete disregard by that entomology professor, it seems that the rumor John heard about him publishing a description of that wasp as a new species was untrue.

This illustrates that sometimes the highly complex vocal communications of us advanced social primates is less effective at communicating direct information than one well-placed squirt from the anal pore of an ant. Ants and other social insects may squirt propaganda, alarm, and other messages, but they never excrete rumors.

[1] Charles Darwin, *The Origin of Species*, first edition (London: Murray, 1859), p. 237.

[2] Karl von Frisch, *The Dancing Bees* (London: Methuen & Company, Ltd., 1954).

[3] John Burroughs, "Bees," essay from *Best Book of Nature Stories*, Pauline Rush Evans, ed. (Garden City, N.Y.: Doubleday Inc., 1957).

[4] John Connors, "Observations of Social Parasitism Between the Ant Species *Formica subintegra* and *Formica subservicea* at Umstead Park, and the Concurrent Endoparasitism of *F. subintegra* by a Braconid Wasp During Dulotic Raids," 1976 (unpublished paper).

[5] E. O. Wilson, *Insect Societies* (Cambridge, Mass.: Harvard University Press, 1971), p. 364.

[6] W. M. Wheeler, *Ants: Their Structure, Development and Behavior* (New York, N.Y.: Columbia University Press, 1910).

[7] Wilson, *Insect Societies*, p. 366.

[8] Wheeler, *Ibid.*

[9] Connors, "Observations of Social Parasitism," *Ibid.*

[10] Connors, *Ibid.*

[11] F. F. Regnier, and E. O. Wilson, "Chemical Communication and 'Propaganda' in Slave-Maker Ants," *Science*, 172: 267–69.

[12] Connors, *Ibid.*

10

So Goes the Life of a Bat

The first day of spring was warm and bright, and this first breath of balmy weather had encouraged me to break my winter dormancy and spend the day outside. I had been pruning in the orchard, planting in the garden, cleaning out the bluebird boxes, and raking up the yard.

About sunset, I took a break and sat down beside the flowering plum tree. I was surprised and pleased to see my first bat of the season. It was a tawny-furred red bat. This warm spring weather must have roused it from hibernation, or possibly it had just migrated here. Its orange-tan fur was ablaze with the golden evening light. It was a hypnotic sight as it fluttered and swooped in silent, graceful arcs, not forty feet from where I sat. I had been watching it for about thirty seconds when out of the setting sun darted a small, grey, sharp-shinned hawk that snatched the bat (and me) from our aerial reverie. The bat emitted one sharp squeak on impact. I gasped. Then, for a split second, the world stood still as the mammal and the bird, this unlikely duo locked in a one-sided embrace, sailed off into the woods to fulfill their respective destinies as predator and prey.

So goes the life of a bat. A bat's list of enemies is long and varied and not only includes various species of hawks, but also owls, opossums, mink, weasels, raccoons, cats, and snakes. Fish, such as trout and bass, and even frogs have been known to eat bats. Of course, the worst enemies bats must face is human ignorance and fear.

I'll never forget a lecture I heard about bats. The speaker was an authority on these amazing flying mammals and was dazzling his audience with one fascinating piece of bat trivia after another. Every so often a wry smile would cross his face and he would affect an accent and say, "Now, ever' body knows, that bats get caught in yer hair, suck yer blood till you turn white and die, and give you rabies." He did this often enough that, before long, he had the audience merrily repeating it along with him as a chorus. What he was doing was encapsulating and summarizing the general public's fear and loathing of bats and turning it into humor.

The more we learn about bats, the more we realize how unfounded these fears are. Bats are one of the most misun-

derstood and yet one of the most valuable and fascinating of our native mammals.

They are the only mammals that are capable of sustained flight. Their front legs are like our arms and hands, with greatly elongated fingers connected by a very thin membrane of skin.

Bats are not blind. All species have eyes and some possess excellent vision. However, hearing is more important to bats than eyesight. They navigate in the dark, locate prey, and orient themselves in their environment by "listening to their own silent screams."[1] This is called echolocation. Echolocation is also used by whales, dolphins, shrews, and modern submarines. Bats echolocate by producing a series of short pulses of high frequency sound (from fifteen to two hundred squeaks per second). This sound is too high pitched to be heard by the human ear, which is fortunate because the loudness of some of these signals has been compared to that of jet engines. (If we could hear those sounds, think of what that would do to a quiet summer night in the country.) As the sound travels through the air it spreads out, and when it hits an object it is reflected back in the form of an echo. From these echoes a bat can tell the size, shape, texture, and distance of an object. If the object is moving, the bat can determine the speed and direction of the movement. With this information, a bat formulates a detailed sonic image of its surroundings. It is able to track and intercept flying insects as small as fruit flies, and it can maneuver to avoid obstacles as fine as a single human hair (which shows how unlikely it is that a bat might become entangled in a head of hair).

During the course of researching this chapter, I asked a number of chiroptologists (bat experts, not foot doctors), if they had ever heard of an instance where a bat became entangled in someone's hair. None of them had ever heard of such a case, but one told me that this story might have come from the habit that young big brown bats (*Eptesicus fuscus*) have of clinging tightly to their mother's fur when they are carried in flight. In fact, they have been known to fall out of the roost and be rescued by grabbing hold of their mother as she swoops by. Often, big brown bats roost in barns and attics. Thus, it is possible that if you were to walk under a bat's nursery colony and a young bat was to fall on your head, the terrified little creature might just instinctively cling to your hair, giving both you and the bat your own true-to-life horror stories.

The bats in our temperate climate eat insects exclusively—lots of them. Bats are the most important predators of night-flying insects. Studies have proven that a single little brown bat can catch six hundred mosquitoes in an hour. A single gray bat can eat three thousand or more insects a night. The large bat colony inhabiting Bracken Cave in Texas has been estimated to consume a quarter of a million pounds of insects in a single night. Bats usually capture and eat their insects on the wing. They either seize the insects directly in their jaws or they use their wings like tennis rackets to deflect and bounce the insects into their mouths. They commonly use the membrane that connects the tail with the hind legs (the uropatagium) as a scoop to capture prey. After trapping an insect in its curled tail the red bat tucks its head down into the pocket formed by the tail membrane and collects the insect in its mouth. In the process, it folds its wings and performs a complete split-second aerobatic somersault. It does this hundreds of times in the course of an evening feeding flight. To an observer, it looks like no more than an erratic flutter.

Most interactions between a bat and its insect prey are uncontested encounters where the insect rarely escapes, but recently, it was discovered that certain moths have built-in "fuzzbusters." These bat "radar detectors" are actually simple ears on either side of their thoraxes that are sensitive to the ultrasound range used by many bats. Upon detecting an approaching bat, they adopt a series of evasive flight patterns including loops, abrupt turns, and vertical dives into protective vegetation. Some moths can even generate a sequence of ultrasonic clicks that mimic the bat's signals and "jam" the bat's echolocating system, causing a pursuing bat to break off its attack. So goes the life of a bat.

Many bats in the tropics subsist on pollen, nectar, and fruits. They play important roles in the pollination and dispersal of the seeds of many tropical plants, including a number of crops. In fact, if you enjoy bananas, cashews, dates, figs, mangoes, avocados, or tequila, or if you have ever benefited from the security of a kapok-filled life preserver or found a piece of sisal baling twine handy, you can thank a bat because, through the course of evolution, bats have played an essential role in the survival of these valuable plants. Some tropical crops are still totally dependent on bats for pollination.

There are fish-eating bats and frog-eating bats and, yes, there are vampire bats. Vampires really do slurp fresh blood from living warm-blooded animals. They are small, New World tropical bats weighing less than two ounces. In their native habitat, they were originally rather rare, but with European colonization and the introduction of cattle, horses, and other livestock, their populations have grown, and now vampires can be a serious pest to domestic livestock, though they rarely bother humans. Vampire bats are not found in the United States, or Europe. Any vampire you might find in Europe is not a bat.

During warm weather, bats roost in a variety of locations including the branches or hollow trunks of trees, clumps of Spanish moss, rock crevices, caves, attics, barns, and the belfries of churches. In fact, chiroptologists maintain that the holy smell associated with many old churches is the direct product of bat colonies.

Some bats congregate in large summer roosts while others are solitary. Some species establish maternity colonies of females and their young, while the males form "bachelor" colonies elsewhere. Bats usually mate in the fall and the females carry the sperm with them into hibernation. The females give birth to one to five young, usually in May or June. The little ones are on their own by late summer. As winter approaches, temperatures drop, and insects become unavailable, bats of our temperate climate must either hibernate or migrate. Some bats do both. They may migrate long distances (not necessarily southward) to their hibernating caves. Caves with a stable cool temperature and high humidity are the ideal sites for most hibernating bats, though some hibernate in hollow trees or unheated buildings.

In the fall, as hibernating time nears, bats accumulate reserves of fat to sustain them through their winter torpor. When in the depths of hibernation, their heart rate and breathing are greatly reduced. Their metabolism slows down and the peripheral blood circulation to the wings and other extremities is shut down to reduce heat loss even further.

Occasionally bats may become wakeful during warm spells in the winter and they fly about drinking water and catching early emerging insects to supplement their dwindling fat reserves. For most hibernating bats, their fat stores are just barely enough to carry them through the hibernation period. If hibernating bats are aroused or disturbed in winter, even if they are not physically harmed, just arousing them can cause a fatal depletion of these reserves. Most responsible cavers and outdoor people know this and are careful not to molest bat colonies, especially when they are hibernating.

Many people are concerned that bats constitute a health hazard. It is true that, like most mammals, they can contract rabies. When they do, they die quickly and rarely become aggressive. No more than eight human deaths have been attributed to bats in the United States and Canada in the past thirty years. Most of these were from bites received while handling sick or dying bats. More people die each year from dog attacks, bee stings, and lawnmower accidents than this thirty-year total of deaths from bat rabies. Nevertheless, it would be foolish to handle sick bats that are lying on the ground.

Sometimes people are disturbed by bats roosting in the attics of their houses or outbuildings. Most of these colonies are small and pose no serious problems. They do not damage the paint work or structure of the buildings. Their droppings are usually dry and harmless, and these can sometimes be collected on a sheet of plastic spread beneath the roost and disposed of with less danger than emptying a cat box. (In fact bat guano has long been prized as a garden fertilizer.)

Because of their incredible efficiency at consuming large numbers of night-flying insects, some people are erecting bat-roosting boxes in their yards. Plans can be ordered from Bat Conservation International, P.O. Box 162603, Austin, Texas, 78716. Ask for their newest design plans for the "Macrobat Dwelling," the ultimate in bat condo living. As their brochure says, it's "enough shelter for 100 bats. Five fixed dividers allowing for different crevice widths [are] combined with an 'attic' feature above... for a greater diversity of species." Along with your bat-house plans, you will receive their color catalog of everything a bat lover could want, including bat books, bat puppets, bat bumper stickers, bat Christmas cards, bat jewelry, bat T-shirts, and even a bat nightgown. Yes, everything a bat lover could want.

So what do you do when late one summer night your kids, wife, husband, or houseguests come running out of a room with terror in their eyes, screaming, "*Bat!*"? There are two approaches you can take. One approach is that you gather yourselves together, arm everyone in the group with tennis rackets, baseball bats, and two-by-fours and march off to battle chanting, "Bats get caught in yer hair, suck yer blood till you turn white and die, and give you rabies!" Then, when you get in the vicinity of the bat, scream and flail those weapons with all your might. This is dangerous and may reduce your furniture to shambles, but this is war and war is hell! Another approach would be to open the windows and turn out the lights in that room. Then leave the room, closing the door to the rest of the house and allowing the bat to fly out on its own. This second approach is not so heroic but it does have its advantages.

❧

The most bizarre bat story I know comes from the annals of World War II. It seems that a Pennsylvania dental surgeon named Lytle S. Adams was driving home from a vacation visit to Carlsbad Caverns—where he had gazed in wide-eyed wonder at the millions of bats that darkened the twilight sky as they emerged from the caverns—when he learned of the Japanese attack on Pearl Harbor. Somehow, his first froth of patriotic outrage combined with his mental image of the multitudes of bats and produced a brainstorm of outlandish proportions. Soon a plan was hatched. Adams wanted to arm the bats with tiny incendiary bombs and have them and their payloads dropped from bombers over the paper cities of Japan!

Within two months he somehow got the ear of President Franklin Roosevelt and convinced him that the plan warranted investigation. Shortly thereafter, Dr. Donald Griffin, the eminent Harvard chiroptologist, was lured into the scheme and in July 1942, the two men returned to Carlsbad, covered the entrance to the cave with netting, and caught some five hundred Mexican free-tailed bats. They transferred the captured bats to cold-storage chests. They hoped the low temperatures would induce the bats to hibernate, making transportation easier, and feeding unnecessary. This plan did not work as well as they had hoped, but three hundred of the bats did survive the flight back to Harvard. There, Griffin found that the surviving bats could be kept in hibernation for a period of up to two weeks at a temperature of 10 degrees Centigrade. Tests showed that each bat could carry a weight of fifteen to eighteen grams.

Soon the National Defense Research Committee and the army's Chemical Warfare Service became involved in the "Adams Plan." Even the navy was drawn in when a top official suggested that the bats could be released from submarines as well as from bombers and that they would be very demoralizing, especially when used against a "superstitious people." (Flocks of invading napalm-bearing bats might be enough to make anyone superstitious.)

The bat-sized incendiary unit was designed with a celluloid case three-fourths inch in diameter and two and one-half inches long. The bomb was shaped so that it could be easily dragged into a small crevice by the bat. Each unit was to be filled with concentrated napalm gel, equipped with a fifteen-hour delay mechanism, and attached to the loose skin on the bat's chest with a surgical clip and a string. According to the Adams Plan, the bats, when dropped from a plane, would spread out over a city, seek refuge in hidden crevices in buildings, and then gnaw through the strings and leave the incendiary units behind.

This bat incendiary was calculated to be more effective than any other bomb in the arsenal; one estimate had it that a planeload of bat bombs would set between 3,625 and 4,748 fires as opposed to 167 to 400 with a planeload of standard, state-of-the-art incendiary bombs.

Not only was this considered more effective than a regular bomb, but it was considered more humane. A city could be leafleted and the inhabitants could be warned to evacuate before the fires started and their city was burned. Even the bats could escape once they had chewed through the string!

The first field tests at a remote airport in California on May 15, 1943, were an unequivocal disaster. The bats were difficult to handle—they could not be put into or brought out of hibernation as easily as expected. When the groggy bats armed with dummy bombs were tossed out of the plane, many of them broke their wings and a number of them hit the ground without ever waking up.

Then after these tests, when several officials recommended scrapping the project, Dr. Adams redoubled his vigorous promotional efforts and explained to every admiral or general who would grant him an interview that the bats were weak and intractable only in the spring, when they had conducted the tests. Any other time of the year, he assured them, the bats would prove to be very robust and manageable. Finally, in October 1943, Rear Admiral D.C. Ramsey, Chief of the navy's Bureau of Aeronautics, asked the Chemical Warfare Service and the NDRC to keep working on the Adams Plan.

But, as the work continued, more problems arose. The secrecy of the project was such that researchers working on various aspects of the incendiary device could not keep abreast of the findings of their coworkers. (Even today, the blueprints of the incendiary unit remain classified by the CIA.) Dr. Adams himself became a problem as well. All this uncertainty apparently became too much for him to bear and he soon proved to be even more "batty" than his little bombers. An NDRC consultant complained that he skipped appointments and could not be found at home. "Apparently, he just chases around from one part of south-ern California to another without staying put long enough for anyone to corner him," he commented. When Adams did occasionally surface he would get into furious confrontations with various military officers. By the middle of December 1943, Dr. Adams was squeezed out of the Adams Plan and the navy renamed it "Operation X ray." Further tests were conducted at the Dugway Proving Grounds in Utah on December 15, 1943, and these were quite promising.

However, the most noteworthy consequences of the project occurred when top military officials needed photo documentation. They wanted photographs of the bats armed with their incendiary capsules. The researchers pulled a few of the bats out of cold storage, armed them with the live napalm units, and placed them on a table in the sunlight while the photographers readied their cameras. Before the photographers could start shooting, however, the bats, warmed by the desert sun, revived and flew away toward the buildings of the air base dragging their napalm behind them. The bats crawled into crevices and disappeared—as they were supposed to do, though preferably in Japan. No amount of searching the grounds could produce the bats. A few hours later a few outlying buildings, some of the hangars, and the general's automobile burst into flames. They were the first and only victims of the American Bat Bomb.

In March 1944, twenty-seven months and two million dollars after its conception, Operation X ray came to an abrupt end because of what the chief of naval operations termed "uncertainties."[2] So goes the life of a bat.

1 David Quammen, "Wool of Bat," *Outside* V. 7, #5 (Aug/Sept 1982).
2 Joe Michael Feist, "Bats Away!" *American Heritage* V. 33, #3 (Apr/May 1982).

11

Appalachian Alchemy
OF GOATS AND BEES AND LOCUST TREES

One of the first times I went to visit my neighbor, Theron, I found him up on the gently sloping hillside pasture in back of his house. He was surrounded by a small herd of goats. The pasture was overgrown with a stand of young locust trees up to five inches in diameter. Some might say that this piece of ground had been neglected; that it hadn't been cared for since it had last been plowed several years before. These thorny, fast-growing trees had quickly sprouted all over the field, as locusts are wont to do. Because of their invasiveness locusts are often considered nuisance trees. They are notoriously difficult to clear out of a field. If you try to grub them out or plow over them, each small piece of root that remains in the ground can sprout and become a tree. The trees in this goat pasture had all been topped. All the branches and the trunks had been cut about six feet above the ground.

It was early spring. The buds on most trees were swelling but I could see that these trimmed locust trees were clearly dead. I asked Theron what he was doing with this piece of land. "Last spring I fenced this in and put my goats here. Then last summer, when the signs was in the heart, the moon was full, and the trees was all leafed out, I cut 'em back. The goats ate the bark, the leaves, and all the root sprouts that came up. And now," he said, grabbing one of the trunks with both hands at chest height, "all I have to do to clear them out is this." And he started rocking the upright tree trunk back and forth until the dead root snapped off underground and he pulled the tree up out of the earth. "Then I'll drag 'em to the house, saw 'em up, and I've got good dry wood for the stove. The field'll be cleared and I'll be able to put my garden in here."

I was charmed when I listened to his simple words, casually delivered in his characteristic down-home mountain drawl. I was intrigued when I saw how well his manipulations of this overgrown patch of ground and this handful of goats seemed to be working. But I was astounded when I realized the broad level of wholistic knowledge and attunement that was brought to bear in this process.

As I thought about what he told me, I realized that within these few sentences of simple, straightforward explanation was a veritable interdisciplinary discourse integrating several completely different systems of knowledge, including agriculture, astronomy, astrology, agronomy, forestry, and animal husbandry. These diverse systems were all tied together with a strong, cohesive thread of ancient folk wisdom, fine-tuned with intuition, and tempered by years of down-to-earth, hands-on, practical experience.

In first deciding to reclaim his "neglected" pasture, Theron turned his awareness to the heavens, especially to the lunar cycle. The moon affects the tides and certain life rhythms of animals. In a similar way, the phase of the moon is believed to affect the life energies in plants. As it waxes and becomes full, the moon is believed to exert a magnetism that draws a plant's growth energy into its upper parts. As the moon wanes, these energies are perceived as receding back down the plant and, in so doing, the roots and other underground portions are stimulated to grow. So, those who plant with the phase of the moon in mind usually try to plant root crops during the "going down" or the "dark" of the moon while above-ground crops are usually planted during the "coming up" or "light" of the moon.

This belief is carried through to more than just planting times. Apples and other fruits that are to be kept for a considerable length of time are gathered on the "down side" of the moon. When this precaution is taken, the bruises are said to dry up and not fester. However, fermented foods like home brew, wine, and kraut that have to "work" are best made during the moon's waxing. Firewood is said to dry better if it is cut on the dark of the moon.

Since he was trying to clear his pasture of these locusts, Theron waited for the full moon to draw the life energies up into the branches before he cut back the trees.

He also consulted an almanac to find out the moon's position in the zodiac. The zodiac is an invisible zone sixteen degrees wide encircling the heavens. Its center is the apparent yearly path of the sun (called the ecliptic) against the background of the constellations. The paths of the moon and all the principal planets also are included in this zone. Astrologers divide the zodiac into twelve "Nomes" of thirty degrees each. Each of these divisions is represented by a sign of the zodiac, which is named after the constella-

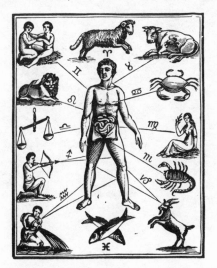

Each sign is believed to rule a part of the body.

tion that formerly appeared with it. According to the ancients, each of these signs rules a part of the body. Many traditional country folk refer to the various signs by their body parts rather than by the classical names of the constellations. So, whereas Theron spoke of "the signs in the heart," an astrologer would say that the moon was in Leo. From the observer's perspective here on earth, the sun appears to travel completely through the twelve signs of the

The Zodiac is the path on which the sun, moon, and planets appear to travel, from an earthbound observer's perspective. It is divided into twelve "signs of the zodiac" that formerly corresponded to the constellations bearing the same names.

zodiac every year. The moon also passes through the zodiac as it orbits the earth, but it replicates the sun's journey every month, spending about two days in each of the signs. Half of the signs are considered barren and half are considered at least somewhat fruitful. The barren signs are best for weeding, plowing, cutting brush, and harvesting, while it is best to plant and graft during the fruitful signs. Any given activity is best conducted on a day that falls both during a good phase of the moon AND under an ideal sign. This is what Theron did by cutting the trees on the full moon under the barren fire sign, Leo.

Animal husbandry comes into the picture with his management of the goat herd. Goats thrive when they can regularly move to fresh pasture and vary their diet. Free-ranging goats naturally browse on a variety of plants, including grasses, shrubs, shoots, and herbs, instinctively balancing their own diet and medicating themselves. They are masters at handling thorns. They are almost the only way to nonchemically eradicate the tenacious bristling multiflora rose. Providing confined goats with fresh shoots and branches is good animal husbandry.

As always, there are many facets to everything in nature. Much of a nuisance as locust trees can be, they not only nourished those goats but they nourished the soil as well. Their vigorous roots pull minerals and other nutrients from deep in the earth. Locusts are legumes, like peas, beans, and most other pod-bearing plants. Agronomists tell us that legumes "fix" nitrogen. Nitrogen is essential to plants. It is the element they need in the largest amounts and it is the one most quickly depleted in the soil. Nitrogen is abundant as the stable N_2 gas in the air, but it is available to plants only when fixed in another form. No plant can fix its own nitrogen, but legumes and a few other plants form symbiotic relationships with microorganisms like *Rhizobium*, bacteria that form nodules on the roots and bring the freefloating, ethereal, yet atomically stable nitrogen "down to earth." The agricultural benefits of interplanting or alternating legumes with grain and other crops has been known for centuries.

By letting his field grow up in locusts, Theron was actually practicing a laid-back form of long-term cover cropping, increasing the soil's fertility by inoculating it with nitrogen. Pasturing the goats there cleared the field, plus it added some manure, which is, of course, another source of nitrogen. The wood he cleared from the field gave him a good start on the next winter's pile of stove wood. The following year, when he plowed and tilled the land, his garden produced well and continued to do so for a number of years.

I asked him if he might use some of those locust trees for fence posts.

"Naw, these are white locusts," he said. "They ain't no good for fence posts. A fence post made of white locust won't last any longer than one made out of poplar. It's the yaller locust that makes good, long-lasting fence posts. A yaller locust post'll last as long as you will."

Now, I knew from my botany studies that the only tree-sized locust that botanists recognize in our region (other than the honey locust, which is uncommon in that part of the mountains) is *Robinia pseudoacacia*, known as "black locust" in the tree books.

"What's the difference between a white locust and a yellow locust?" I asked.

He explained that white locusts grow out in fields. They have white wood and are small and weak and wormy. Yellow locusts, on the other hand, are large trees that usually grow in the woods and have thick, deeply furrowed bark and dense yellow wood. They both have the same kind of flower and leaf.

When I asked a local lumberman-logger what the difference was between a white and a yellow locust, he replied, "'Bout forty years."

Botanists classify plants by their reproductive organs. They examine the flowers and seeds and attempt to arrange them in an evolutionary order. They see the black locust as one species. Traditional mountain people don't care much about evolution. They tend to classify each plant in their lives based on their intimate working relationship with that plant. People who work with locust trees can clearly see two kinds of locusts where a botanist sees only one. I tend to agree with Thoreau when he said, "I love best the unscientific man's knowledge; there is so much more humanity in it."

Locusts are one of the first of the woody pioneer-tree species that invade fields and turn them back into forests. Ecologists call this "forest succession." When locusts sprout in a field, they grow rapidly. For the first few years, they may more than double in size every year. As they grow they create shade, which discourages growth of open meadow and pasture plants while creating conditions suitable for the seeds of shade-tolerant hardwoods to sprout and grow. Stands of locusts in a forest tell a tale of cleared fields several decades ago. Forest locusts grow slowly and can attain large size. The wood produced is dense, deep yellow in color, and rot resistant. This is the wood that is so prized for fence posts. The best fence posts are split out of a large yellow locust log that is cut in the winter when the sap is down. The bark must be scraped off and then the post is best driven into the ground and well tamped. A mound of soil is left around the base of the post to facilitate drainage away from the wood. A well-set locust post, it is said, will "last a hundred years and then turn to stone." I call that Appalachian alchemy.

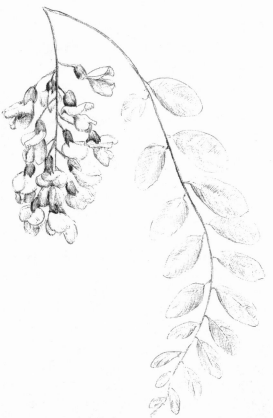

"In spring fragrant clusters of white pealike flowers cover the locust tree…"

The young locust saplings that first colonize a field are well armored with sharp thorns. This protects them from deer and other native browsing animals. As bristly as they are, the thorns do not protect the trees from their worst enemy, the locust borers *(Megacyllene robiniae)* that dine on the wood. The damage is perpetrated by the larval stage of the beetle. This is a white, segmented grub worm that hatches from eggs laid in pits cut into the bark. It eats its way into the young white sapwood. As it grows larger it can eat into the heartwood and make a tunnel that is almost one quarter inch in diameter. The larva overwinters in its tunnel in the wood. When just about to pupate, it burrows to the edge of the wood and pupates under the bark.

When they emerge in late summer, the adult beetles are about three-quarters of an inch long and are strikingly marked with black-and-yellow zebra stripes. They are known as long-horned beetles because of their long antennae. As adults, wood is no longer a part of their diet. At this stage of their life they spend most of their time on goldenrod flowers "innocently" sipping nectar, eating pollen, and mating. Maybe that long dark year crunching through North America's toughest wood does have its rewards.

Goldenrods are usually common in the same overgrown fields the locusts are invading.

Flowering time for locusts is usually in April or May. These fragrant, dangling clusters of white pealike flowers often cover the tree. Some years, they produce copious amounts of nectar during their brief two-week bloom. Occasionally, this provides nearby beekeepers with a bumper crop of heavy-bodied, water-white, elegant-flavored honey. In some parts of the Appalachians, locust honey is often called "the beekeeper's honey" because the locust bloom is very unpredictable, and on the few occa-

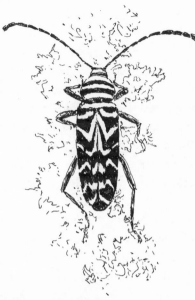

Adult Locust Borer Beetle

sions when beekeepers harvest a crop of this special honey, it rarely makes it to the market because beekeepers usually squirrel it away for their own use.

Locust blossom cordial is the most elegant use I know for the flowers. To make it you must have freshly opened locust blossoms; they are best gathered in the morning, before the bees and butterflies have sipped away their nectar. Loosely fill a container (ideally, a glass pitcher) with the flowers and then cover them with cool spring water and stir gently. Set the pitcher in a refrigerator or other cool place for about an hour, and serve in wine glasses. Allow a few flowers to spill into each glass as you pour. The drink has a delicate bouquet and the nectar imparts a subtle but distinctive sweetness. One of the benefits of this beverage is that you can drink glass after glass of this cordial and still drive home safely.

The locust tree first came to Europe in the early 1600s, when it was introduced to France by Henry IV's herbalist, Jean Robin (hence the generic name *Robinia*).

By the early 1800s, the planting of locust trees in England and other parts of Europe became a craze. The sudden surge in the popularity of this foreign tree was largely due to the efforts of the flamboyant English journalist and political reformer, William Cobbett. Few trees have ever had a greater champion, before or since, than Cobbett. Cobbett's brash political commentary managed to offend and outrage well-placed officials in both the United States and England. When one country got too hot for him he would flee across the Atlantic to the other until things cooled off. On one of his exiles in America, he took to growing locust trees on his farm on Long Island.

He called the locust "the tree of trees." In his book *Woodlands*, published in 1825, he claimed, "The durability of the wood is such, that no man in America will pretend to say that he ever saw a bit of it in a decayed state." And he admitted "this seems hyperbolic, but every American of experience in country affairs will… confirm what I say. It is absolutely indestructible by the powers of earth, air, and water."

He discussed its strategic importance for those days when England's military strength was dependent on the wooden ships of its navy. Because of locust's toughness and rot resistance, it was the wood of choice for ship construction.

Whenever possible, locust was used for the ribs of ships, as well as the tiller, rails, and stanchions around the deck. Locust was also the best wood from which to make treenails, or trunnels, the pegs that held the ship together. The American victory in the War of 1812 has been attributed in part to the superiority of the American ships, which were built largely of locust. "Without Locust, it is impossible to match [the Americans]," Cobbett wrote.

"But as important as these matters are," he continued, "they are by no means to be compared to the various uses about buildings and fences. How many thousands of houses are rendered useless in England, every year, by... dry rot, proceeding solely from those villainous soft woods, which impatient people take such delight in planting, and which carpenters of delicate constitution take such delight in sawing and planing." He added, "Endless are the uses to which [locust] might be put," mentioning everything from bottle racks, wagon axles, and grindstone stands, to rafters, joists, door sills, and posts for cart sheds.

"Use locust timber and it will wear out the stone walls of the building," he claimed and went on to tell how locust could be used for fences, gates, and "everlasting hop poles" (the tall poles used for trellising hop vines). On and on he went for almost forty pages, enumerating its virtues, detailing the methods and the economics of its cultivation, and minutely describing the condition of certain posts he had seen in America that had remained in the ground for decades (particularly an eighty-year-old, Long Island "hog-gallows post"). "They were all as sound as they had been the first day they had been cut down; and even the little axe chops were sound.... But how to persuade English people

to believe this, and to believe... that there was a timber about a hundred times as good as their heart of Oak!

"I dare say that every reader who delights in rural concerns, and who duly considers the vast importance of this matter will lament that he, also, could not see these posts," Cobbett wrote sadly. However, in the very next sentence, he assuaged the laments of his readership by announcing (in capital letters) that they "MAY SEE THEM NOW" if they were to stop by the office of his Political Register on Fleet Street in London, where he had those very posts on display (along with a locust windowsill). He also offered to give away or send blocks of locust wood to any interested parties. "There is nothing like seeing in cases like this."[1]

When he returned to England in 1819 from his exile in America, along with parcels of locust seeds he actually brought these two old locust posts with him. He was a true English patriot who had a deep love for his homeland and he felt that the introduction of locusts was as much a part of his patriotic duty as was his strong opposition to government corruption. He felt that bringing locusts to plant in England was an investment in the future strength of the British navy as well as in the betterment of the lives of the English country people.

Locust trees or not, the oppressive British regime was not exactly ready to welcome the return of this raucous, radical, rabble-rousing reformer.

"The Manchester Magistrates brought out horse and foot to prevent me from passing through their town. The Bolton Magistrates put John Hayes [the town crier] in prison, for ten weeks, for announcing that I had arrived... in good health. But my Locust posts came safely to London, and I came soon after them, with the following memorandums in my pocket." Whereupon Cobbett published, in their entirety, various letters from judges, doctors, and other reputable Americans (including Richard Smith, founding father of Smithtown on Long Island) testifying to the veracity of his statements about the length of time these locust posts had remained in the ground.

Along with these old locust posts and sacks of locust seeds, he also brought with him one other unusual piece of luggage. It was a long, weathered, wooden box. This box, though not made of locust, had been in the earth ten years.

When the box was opened at the customs house, Cobbett declared, "There, gentlemen, are the mortal remains of the immortal Thomas Paine."

He had dug up Paine's body from its neglected grave in New Rochelle, intending to reinter it in a splendid monument to atone for his former attacks on the author of *The Rights of Man*. The monument was never erected, and after Cobbett's death in 1835, the auctioneer in charge of selling his personal effects refused to offer for sale a box "found to contain human bones." Whatever happened to the box and its contents after that is lost to history.

But Cobbett, even though he failed to inter Paine nobly, did wonders to keep alive the popularity of the locust tree. By 1825 he had sold more than a million young locusts, though he never realized a significant profit from the venture. He was far more interested in promoting the planting of locusts than he was in making money from them. He even offered strawberry plants at cost to those who bought trees.

To this day, locust trees bloom throughout England every spring. Locust-blossom honey is an important honey crop for beekeepers in England and it's the principal honey crop in parts of Eastern Europe. As Cobbett predicted in *Woodlands*, there will be those who think that "Locust-trees have always been… in England; and some curious writer of a century or two hence, will tell his readers that, wonderful as it may seem, 'the Locust was hardly known in England until about the year 1823, when the nation was introduced to a knowledge of it by William Cobbett.' What he will say of me besides, I do not know; but I know that he will say this…. I enter upon this account, therefore, knowing that I am writing for centuries and centuries to come."[2]

And so he was.

How strange it seems that, because of my interest in the locust tree, I now read about myself, that "curious writer of a century or two hence," in the writings of a man who lived two hundred years before me, and I find myself playing a part in fulfilling his posthumous destiny.

The locust tree has taken us on quite a journey. Talking about locust trees with an earthy mountain farmer sent us sailing heavenward into celestial realms, touring the zodiac, and learning about lunar influences. This celestial excursion gave us a new perspective on the cyclical nature of life here on earth. Following the locust's roots into the soil revealed the underground union of earth and air through nitrogen-fixing bacteria. The locust shoots nourished the goats. The fence posts demonstrated the locust's toughness; the borers showed its vulnerability. Cobbett brought us to Europe with his cargo of locust seeds. Theron's traditional rural wisdom showed us how it is all connected, and the bees brought home the sweetness of it all.

[1] William Cobbett, *Woodlands* (London: 1825). Printed and published by William Cobbett, 183 Fleet Street, p. 362.

[2] *Ibid*, p. 351.

12

Stalking the Old-time Apples

CROW'S EGG PIE AND SHEEP NOSE SAUCE

It's early March as I write this—long past apple time—but on my desk are several Winter John apples. Crimson flecks show through their greenish-yellow base color, and there is a little blush of lavender here and there. Their skin is wrinkled, but the white flesh is predictably firm and delightfully tart. Their tangy flavor has mellowed considerably during the four months since that brisk, breezy day last fall when I picked them.

Just about anyone who spends time in a rural area with an apple-growing history will come across old and almost forgotten varieties of apples like Winter Johns.

Until recently, an apple was just an apple for me. That was before I started ranging the hills and hollows with my friend Theron, who was raised in the mountain tradition of self-sufficiency, and who is still in touch with much of the old-time wisdom and ways. After a couple of seasons of seeing apples through Theron's eyes, I felt like someone who had been shown a rainbow in full color after seeing only black and white.

The fact is, there's an incredible variety of apples in this country and by biting into a few of these old-time apples, we can tap the richness of a rapidly disappearing culture and lifestyle.

When I asked Theron how many types of apples he knew, he rattled off a list of more than twenty varieties. Just the names of these almost-forgotten breeds left my mind reeling with delight. Some were named for what they resembled, like the elongated, lopsided Sheep's Nose apple, the oval Crow's Egg, and the yellow Bellflower. Others took people's names, presumably the ones who developed the variety or who first brought it into the area. So there's Stark Apples, Betsy Deatons, Black Hoovers, Striped Ben Davises, and Ducketts. Still others, like the Winesap, Sweet Russet, Stripey, and Spice apples are named for their distinctive tastes or color patterns or both. The Spitzbergen and the Virginia Beauty refer to their places of origin; the Horse apple is so big and sour that it is considered fit only as feed for horses; the Limbertwig was named for the distinctive shape and flexible limbs of the parent tree. And who knows how the Leatherman, the Milam, the

Democrat, and the Knotley Pea got their names. Many of the apple varieties I mention here are found only in a particular area, perhaps as small as a portion of a county. And some names might be local names for a widespread variety. For example, Theron showed me what he called a Northern Spice Apple, which looked suspiciously like a common New England variety called Northern Spy.

One of the great proponents of preserving the many varieties of apples was L. H. Bailey. His book *The Apple Tree*, published in 1922, lamented that of the more than eight hundred varieties listed in the nurseryman's catalogs in 1892, not more than a hundred were available at the time of his writing.

"Why do we need so many kinds of apples?" Mr. Bailey asked. "Because there are so many folks," he said. "A person has a right to gratify his legitimate tastes. If he wants twenty or forty kinds of apples for his personal use, running from Early Harvest to Roxbury Russet, he should be accorded the privilege. There is merit in variety itself. It provides more contacts with life, and leads away from uniformity and monotony."[1]

I'm afraid Mr. Bailey would be less than pleased with our present state of affairs, where monotony and uniformity are encouraged in our corporate society and "shelf life" has more priority than "contacts with life."

In 1920 he complained of having to choose from only a hundred varieties of apples. Seventy years later, some school children don't even know that apples grow on trees and the North Carolina Agricultural Extension Service boasts that 90 percent of the state's commercial apple crop is made up of only three varieties: Red Delicious, Golden Delicious, and Rome Beauty. We've come a long way, Mr. Bailey. Welcome to corporate America!

In traditional rural communities, people developed an appreciation for a variety of apples because apples were used in so many ways. In the old days, apples were more than an occasional treat; they were a staple food. From the planning of the home orchard to the drying of apple slices, every way possible was used to extend the apple season and preserve the fruit. In the absence of modern refrigeration, various kinds of apples came to be known not only for their taste but also for their rate of ripening and their capacity for preservation. Each apple had, and still has, its specific season and purpose. Some apples are early apples and some are better late in the season. Some are for drying, some are best suited for sauce, while others are best for canning. There are juicy ones for cider and hard ones for storing and, of course, there are good old eating apples.

During the season, some of the local favorite old-time eating apples are Crow's Eggs, Bellflowers, Black Hoovers, and Virginia Beauties. The small yellow Spice-Apples actually have a distinctive wintergreen-mint flavor. Some eating apples will keep for months, while others might be right for eating only for a few weeks of the season. Theron showed me a little apple called a Stripey. Early in the season the apple has a crisp, tangy, white flesh, but if it gets too ripe, or if you let it sit around the house for even a few days, its crispness turns mealy. "It'll almost choke you," says Theron of its sawdust-like texture. As delicious as this short-lived morsel is fresh from the tree, you'll never find it in the supermarket.

Sauce apples and canning apples each have different properties; they aren't just labeled as cooking apples. Good canning apples are firm-fruited and won't turn brown while a whole pan full is being peeled and sliced. The slices hold their shape as they are exposed to the rigors of home canning. Some good canning apples are Winter Johns, Pippins, Milams, Sweet Russets, Knotley Peas, and Spitzbergens. Although it is possible to make sauce out of almost any apple, the best have a soft texture that will break down with little cooking; Bellflowers and Stripeys are ideal for sauce making. Juicy apples like Winesaps and Sheep's Nose lend themselves well to cider making. Pippins and Crow's Eggs are favorite pie apples. The large Striped Ben Davis is a favorite baking apple.

Good canning apples are also good drying apples because of their firm flesh. Apple drying was an important home industry in many parts of the southern Appalachians. Itinerant merchants traveled the backcountry buying or trading dried apples. Theron tells of peeling and slicing basket after basket of apples, which were dried on racks over the cookstove. In some areas, the apples were cored and sliced into rings, which were dried by stringing the slices on a pole.

Drying is one of the simplest and, if you have a wood stove, one of the most efficient ways to preserve apples. Just slice the apples thinly and spread them on window screens (preferably nylon) suspended a few feet above your wood stove or other heat source. The drying usually takes three days to a week. During warm, dry weather apples can be sun-dried, but they must be taken inside every night to protect them from the dew. Traditionally, people who were preparing apples for the market peeled them to make a more refined product. However, this is not necessary, especially if the apples have not been sprayed.

The art of preserving fresh eating apples nowadays has been relegated to the realm of horticultural science and refrigeration engineering. Modern storage houses are vapor sealed and have massive refrigeration systems that maintain a constant temperature of 31 degrees Fahrenheit and a relative humidity of at least 85 percent. However, the old-time methods of storing apples are still worth knowing, not only because they may be useful to those who might like to store a few bushels of apples for home use, but also because they demonstrate a creative relationship with the environment and a sensitivity to nature that is disappearing from our modern world.

The person versed in the art of storing fresh apples takes into consideration a variety of things, from the moon in the sky to the cellar in the earth.

First, they consider the phase of the moon. As Theron tells it, "keeping" apples are best picked on the "down side" of the moon (when it is waning). During this phase, any bruises that occur will more likely dry up and not ruin the apple. However, if you make hard cider or home brew, Theron says you'd best make it during the "comin' up" of the moon, since things "work," or ferment, better as the moon is waxing.

Next, a good keeping apple must be chosen. Winter Johns and Hardenings are the favorites in our area. The apples are picked carefully, each apple lifted upward to snap it off with the stem. If it is pulled so that the stem rips out of the apple, decay can soon ruin it. In colonial days two men, a picker and a packer, harvested each tree with gloved hands. The picker handed two apples at a time down to the packer, who carefully laid the apples in straw on a sled. (A sled jiggled and bumped less than a wagon or a wheelbarrow.) When loaded, the sled was skidded over hay to the packing cellar.

The apples were then stored in the cellars. In Vermont and Connecticut, where there was ready access to quarries, some apple cellars actually had marble shelves to keep the fruit cold and dry. Sometimes, these even had windmills that operated fans inside that kept the air moving. Noah Webster recommended packing apples in heat-dried sand. Others used grain or dry straw. Sometimes, really special apples were hung "by their tails" (stems) from the cellar's rafters. I have heard a number of older southern mountain folks talk about using a hollow chestnut stump to store apples. It is cleaned out, lined with dry leaves, filled with apples, and covered with more dry leaves and some slabs of bark to shed the rain. Theron has also piled apples on the ground and then covered them with a thick layer of "loose blade fodder" (dried corn leaves) tied in bundles. This insulates the apples from severe cold, yet allows plenty of air circulation. "They'll keep all winter," Theron says. (He did warn me that the ones on the bottom might acquire an earthy taste by spring.)

The apple tree, like most of us who call ourselves American, is not native to America (with the exception of some types of crab apples). Apples actually originated in Persia. The expression "as American as apple pie" has an ironic twist to it because nothing in an apple pie is native to the Americas. The wheat flour for pie crust originated in the Middle East, the butter comes from cows whose ancestry is in north-central Europe. Cinnamon comes from Southeast Asia and cane sugar is originally from India. Apples were cultivated in Europe for at least two thousand years before the first seeds and trees reached the New World, when they were brought to the Massachusetts Bay Colony around 1629.

Despite its foreign origins, no tree has contributed more to America than the apple tree. Besides the vinegars and tonics, its given us apple jack, apple brandy, apple wine, and apple cider. There's apple jelly, apple sauce, apple butter, apple cake and apple pie; don't forget apple leather (dried apple sauce), candy apples, baked apples, scalloped apples, apple grunter, and apple crisp. There are apple toys like apple-faced dolls and apple games like bobbing for apples. Apple wood is prized wherever a hard, fine-grained wood is needed. In colonial days, it was used for machinery, particularly cogs, wheels, and shuttles. Even the apple tree's bark can be used as a vegetable dye; it gives vivid golds and yellows.

Jonathan Chapman, better known as Johnny Appleseed, said, "Nothing gives more yet asks less in return than a tree, particularly the apple."

Whenever you roam the brushy hills and the hollows of old farm country and come upon an apple tree, stop and look around. You will probably see other apple trees as well as some ancient rose bushes, lilacs, or other cultivated plants. Nearby, you may see ruins of an old cabin, or perhaps just the fallen chimney. There may be no more than a depression in the ground that marks the cellar where many

To make an apple face doll, carve facial features into a carefully peeled, firm apple. Then hang it in a warm place. As it dries the face will wrinkle and "age."

Mount the apple face on a form made of pipecleaners or wire dressed with doll clothes. Wool or cotton can be used for hair and beads can be used for the eyes.

an apple was stored. This is the remains of an old homestead where, far from the road, people's lives unfolded, close to the land, close to their source.

It was in just such a high mountain pasture, known locally as Don's Mountain, where Theron introduced me to a pair of beautiful old Winter John apple trees. It was a steep mile-long hike up to these trees. Because they grew so high on the mountain, they were above the late spring and early fall frosts that sometimes freeze the blossoms and ruin the fruits on trees in the valleys. For a number of years a pilgrimage to these trees was a regular autumn ritual for us. Donning backpacks or pack baskets, we would set forth on day-long, epic forays. We would often take a circuitous route up the mountain, exploring favorite ridges and hollows, ranging through mountain pastures and secluded clearings, drinking from favorite springs, and being ever watchful for whatever the countryside might offer. Sometimes we'd find tangy fox grapes, sometimes October peaches, or maybe butternuts, black walnuts, or hazelnuts. Other times, we would gather herbs like pennyroyal, mint, catnip, horehound, angelico, mullein, and ginseng, or wild greens like creasies, crow's foot *(Dentaria)*, and wild turnips. Occasionally, we'd even find mushrooms, like puffballs, oysters, or meadow mushrooms.

Before heading back, we would always stop at our two favorite Winter John trees. I would usually climb the tree and shake out enough to half fill our packs. Then, on top of these, we would fill a gunny sack with "keepers" for storing. These we would try to handle more carefully by picking them from the lower branches while standing on the ground, or I would climb the tree and throw them one at a time to Theron. Once our packs were loaded as full as we could bear, we would head on down the mountain. We would walk as gently as possible, so as not to jostle and bruise the apples, while trying hard to keep our knees from buckling from the weight.

Whenever possible we would try to make a few trips to the trees each fall, so we could each have a bushel or two to store. Autumn is a busy time in the country, and sometimes it was hard to make time for a couple of trips up the mountain during the two or three weeks that the apples were prime. So one year I suggested to Theron that we try to find a large hollow chestnut stump up near the trees to store the apples in, like people used to do in the old days. If we could store a couple of loads of apples somewhere up there on the mountain where they would be safe and protected from freezing, then we could come up and get them later that winter when it would be more convenient. Theron considered this a great idea.

So when we got into the vicinity of the apple trees, we combed the woods searching for the perfect upright chestnut stump. They are a fairly common sight in the woods around there and we did not think we would have any trouble locating one near the apple trees, but there were none to be found. There were a number of fallen logs but no intact hollow stumps where we could store apples. I was pretty discouraged as we approached the trees, especially when I saw how many apples were on them. They were so full of fruit that they glowed golden in the clear autumn air. No one would use these apples if we didn't, but it was late October already. A hard freeze would be coming soon. How many could we carry down in the next week or so? I had a lot of other things to do that fall and so did Theron.

Then Theron said, "Look, one of them apple trees is hollow."

Sure enough, its trunk was almost as big around as a bushel basket. It was about five feet to where the trunk forked and there, at the fork, was a large hole. Theron stuck his walking stick into the hole and probed around. "This tree's hollow all the way to the ground," he said, "and it gets bigger down there at the bottom. Dig around down there and see if you can get up into the hollow part here." I started digging at the base of the trunk between two major roots. The tree was situated on the hill so that the uphill side of the trunk, where Theron was standing, was at least two feet above where I was digging at the base of the downhill side of the tree.

By using a short, stout digging stick, I worked my way up between the roots and into the trunk, and soon I met the end of Theron's walking stick. Theron kept stabbing his stick down into the hollow of the trunk, dislodging clods of dirt and crumbly decayed wood. I pulled the dirt out with my hands and soon I had a large pile out in front of the base of the tree. It looked like a busy groundhog had been working there. When we had it pretty well cleaned out, Theron tested it by dropping a couple of apples into the hole at the top. Sure enough, they rolled right out between those two roots like candy out of a gum ball machine.

We collected armloads of dry grass. I stuffed some of the grass up into the bottom of the hole and Theron put some in from the top. We were trying to create a soft, dry, insulated bed for the apples. Then I climbed the tree and gave it a good shaking. Apples thundered to the ground. We collected the apples and poured them into the trunk, a few at a time, while trying to pack the grass around them.

As I scurried about collecting the apples, Theron continued to pour them in. As the trunk was filling up, Theron said, "If you want to see somethin' purty, just look in here."

I looked down into the hollow trunk and there was the top of the pile of apples nestled in the darkened, grass-lined cavity, like a cluster of speckled golden eggs in a nest.

When we finally filled up the trunk, we stuffed more grass on top and put a large, flat rock over the hole to shed water. We estimated that the tree held between three and five bushels. We loaded up our packs with the remaining apples and headed on down the mountain.

One time in mid-November, we were up on the mountain scouting for deer signs and we stopped by the tree. We pulled out some apples and we were delighted to see they were keeping well. We filled our pockets to snack on but since we each still had several bushels at home, we left the rest in the tree.

It was a crisp, cool morning the following March when we finally returned to check on our apples. With bated, frosty breath I pulled the grass out from between those roots and the apples started rolling out of the hole like a slot machine on a big payoff. I raked them out of the way, then I reached up into the hole and dislodged some more. More and more apples kept rolling out and soon we had a great heap of them in front of the opening of the tree.

"Apples started rolling out of the hole like a slot machine on a big payoff..."

Some of them had turned soft and brown and some had large blemishes but most of them were still good—delicious, in fact. We ate a number of them right there on the spot, savoring their cold tangy crispness and marveling to each other about how strange it seemed to be eating fresh wild apples this time of year. After we had our packs loaded and were heading down the mountain, Theron said, "You know, if you was to tell someone that you knew of an apple tree that kept its apples till March and those apples were still good, they wouldn't believe you, would they?"

When you crush an apple with your teeth,
Say to it in your heart,
Your seeds shall live in my body
And the buds of your tomorrow shall blossom in my heart
And your fragrance shall be my breath
And together we shall rejoice through all the seasons.

Kahlil Gibran

[1] L. H. Bailey, *The Apple Tree* (New York: Macmillan Co., 1922), p. 68.

On Christmas and other special occasions, Theron's grandmother would make what she called "Dried apple stack cake." In order to experience this cake firsthand, I presented Theron's wife Doris with three cups of dried apples and asked if I could watch her make it. First she assembled the ingredients:

6–8 cups of sifted self-rising flour
in a large bowl
3/4 cup shortening
2 eggs
1/2 cup buttermilk
1 cup sorghum molasses
1 cup brown sugar
1 tsp. salt
1 tsp. ginger
1/2 tsp. cinnamon, nutmeg, and allspice

She warmed the molasses, added the brown sugar, the buttermilk, salt, ginger, and beaten eggs and blended them together. She poured this well-mixed liquid into the center of the bowl of flour. She then mixed these together with her hands, using a circular kneading motion, the way she usually makes biscuits. Next she rolled the dough out until it was one-quarter inch thick, and cut it to fit the bottom of a nine- or ten-inch frying pan, then baked it for about ten minutes at 375 degrees. Out of the oven, it was lightly browned and had risen to a thickness of approximately three-quarters of an inch. This was to be one of the layers of the cake. She baked four of these.

While the cakes were in the oven, she cooked the dried apples with a little water, cinnamon, allspice, and nutmeg, mashing them until they were the consistency of lumpy applesauce. She spread the cooled sauce between the layers of the cake and placed a generous ladleful on top. The only fault I could find with this traditional cake was that it didn't last long enough!

13

Poplar Appeal

AN ODE TO THE TULIP TREE

When I tell northerners that I built my house almost entirely of poplar, including the framing, rafters, interior paneling, and exterior siding, they seem confused. When I go on to say that there are a lot of old log cabins in the southern mountains built from large poplar logs, they look at me like I'm crazy.

I soon discovered that to a northerner, the word poplar refers to aspens and other related trees whose wood is light, soft, and virtually useless for house construction. After a bit more discussion, we would finally get our terminology straightened out and I'd get the response, "Oh, you mean tulip tree."

Yes, this magnificent tree has many names and even more uses. It is not a true poplar but was so named because its leaves are attached to its branches by long petioles, or leaf stems, that allow the leaves to move in the breeze in a manner not unlike that of a quaking aspen.

The tulip poplar is actually in the magnolia family. Its scientific name, *Liriodendron tulipifera*, translates as something like "tulip-bearing lily tree." This is a perfect name

for the tree because its flowers look like a combination of a tulip and a lily. They are a light greenish-yellow and each of its six petals has a blaze of orange at its base.

> Out of a giant tulip tree
> a great gay blossom falls on me;
> Old gold and fire its petals are,
> It flashes like a falling star.'
> Maurice Thomas

A large tulip poplar ablaze with hundreds of large cup-like blooms in spring is a magnificent sight indeed. The flowering of these trees is very important to beekeepers, for it is one of the most dependable sources of nectar in the Southeast. The yield of nectar per bloom is possibly the highest of any plant on the continent and has been calculated at an average of 1.64 grams per flower (that's about one third of a teaspoon). During a favorable season, the nectar is secreted so abundantly that it appears faster than honeybees and other insects carry it away. Sometimes, you can stand under a blooming tulip tree in a light breeze and feel

Tulip Poplar Flower

the nectar dripping down like a gentle sticky rain. Those who park their shiny new cars under tulip trees use less kind words to describe this phenomenon. Because the bloom comes early in the season, many honeybee colonies are not strong enough to fully utilize the abundance. For strong hives, however, harvests of a hundred pounds of honey per hive have been recorded during just the three-week poplar bloom. The honey is dark in color and is sometimes called black poplar honey. If you hold it up to the light, however, you'll see that it is actually a deep amber-red in color. Though it is not as light as locust honey or as sought-after as sourwood honey, it has a rich full-bodied flavor that can be used to sweeten fruit salads, yogurt, tea, and other beverages. It goes great on pancakes, waffles, cereal, biscuits, cornbread, and other baked goods. Rarely a day goes by that I don't enjoy a dollop or two. If you want the ultimate tulip poplar nectar-tasting experience, you can sip it straight from the flower like the bees do. To do this, you need to find a freshly opened blossom within reach. Pick or lower the blossom carefully without jostling it. Then lick the droplets on the inside of the petals and taste that ambrosia! Sometimes the nectar collects in a puddle on one of the lower sepals. If the air has been warm and dry, that nectar will often be thick, like syrup. After one taste, you will know you have imbibed the nectar of the gods!

The tulip poplar is the king of the magnolia family and the tallest hardwood tree in North America. In the old forests of the southern Appalachians, it has been found to attain a height of two hundred feet, with a straight trunk ten feet in diameter and clear of branches for eighty or a hundred feet. The largest tulip poplar of which we have a record is the "Reems Creek Poplar" in Buncombe County, North Carolina. It was 198 feet tall, with a trunk measuring 10-feet, 11-inches in diameter at 4 feet above the ground. When it was burned in April 1935, it was believed to be the largest tulip poplar in the world, possibly over a thousand years old.

"Each tulip poplar cone can produce a hundred or more seeds...."

But despite the splendor of its dimensions, there is nothing overwhelming about the Tuliptree, but rather something joyous in its springing straightness, in the candle-like blaze of its sunlit flowers, in the fresh green of its leaves, which being more or less pendulous on long slender stalks, are forever turning and rustling in the slightest breeze; this gives the tree an air of liveliness, lightening its grandeur. So even a very ancient tulip tree has no look of eld about it, for not only does it make a swift growth in youth, but in maturity it maintains itself marvelously free of decay.

This look of vitality comes partly from the vivid palette from which the Tuliptree is colored. The flowers which give it this name are yellow or orange at base, a light greenish shade above. Almost as brilliant are the leaves when they first appear, a glossy, sunshiny pale green; they deepen in tint in summer, and in autumn turn a rich, rejoicing gold. Even in winter the tree is still not unadorned, for the... cone remains, candelabrum fashion, erect on the bare twig... [until] all the seeds have fallen.[2]

Donald Culross Peattie

Each tulip poplar cone can produce one hundred or more seeds. Attached to each seed is a blade-shaped wing, called a samara, which keeps it airborne. On windy days these seeds whirl like tiny helicopters and are dispersed over great distances. Because they are released gradually all through the winter, the seeds are as important to wildlife as the nectar is to bees. They are eaten by many kinds of birds, as well as by squirrels, chipmunks, and other small rodents. On a bright snowy day two friends were cross-country skiing in Pisgah National Forest and were surprised to see a white-footed mouse scampering all over the snow, so busy collecting and devouring freshly shed tulip poplar seeds that it seemed completely unaware of their presence.

Indians had many uses for tulip poplar. Using fire and stone tools, they carved dugout canoes out of large straight sections of the trunks and taught pioneer settlers the art. One of the first accounts of this was in 1590, in Thomas Harriot's *Briefe and true report of the new found land of Virginia*. "[T]he inhabitants that were neere to us doe commonly make their boats or Canoes of the form of trowes, [troughs] only with the helpe of fire, harchets of stones and shels; we have known some being so great... that they have carried well XX men at once besides much baggage: the timber being great, tall, streight, soft, light, & yet tough." Cap. John Smith, in 1612, reported canoes large enough to hold forty men.

Daniel Boone made such a canoe that was sixty feet long and capable of carrying five tons. Into it he loaded his family and all their possessions and, in 1799, they floated from

Kentucky down the Ohio River and on into what was then Spanish territory. The tree is still known as "canoewood" in some areas.

In spring and early summer, when the tree is growing rapidly and the cambium layer between the bark and the sapwood is still soft, the bark can be removed relatively easily. The bark has been used in many ways. Large sheets of it were used by Indians as coverings for wigwams, wickiups, lodges, and other living quarters. In the North Carolina mountains, poplar bark has been used as siding on frame houses. When I first discovered it on some homes near Burnsville, in Yancey County, I was struck by its rustic, yet elegant beauty. As I was building my own house at the time, I wanted to find out how it was done and how long it would last. When I asked around, however, it seemed that most of the builders of these houses had long ago passed on, but they had left a legacy of poplar bark siding that was still holding up well after seventy years or more.

I finally found one older man who was a poplar bark craftsman, and he described the process to me. In early summer, when the "sap's running" (the new cambium layer is forming), large sheets of the bark are removed from medium-sized trees. The bark is carefully pried off the trunk with a tool known as a tan-bark spud. This tool harkens back to the days when the collecting of oak, chestnut, and hemlock bark was a part of every timber-cutting operation.

Tan Bark Spud

The bark was sold to tanneries, because it is a source of tannic acid. A spud could be improvised out of a stout curved stick with a chisel-like edge carved on one end. Those made by blacksmiths look somewhat like small spades.

After it is removed, the bark is cut into large rectangular sheets, taken to a barn or other dry place, and "stacked and stickered" like green lumber with narrow strips of wood placed between each sheet of bark to allow the air to circulate. Rocks or other weights piled on top of the stack of bark ensure that the sheets stay flat and do not curl up as they dry. After a month or two of drying, they can be cut to length and nailed like shingles on to the building.

Armed with these minimal instructions, and a lifelong love of tulip poplar, I knew that I had to attempt collecting bark to cover at least part of my house. A friend who was building his own house was about to cut some poplars on his land to use as support beams. He told me that if I'd help him cut them and haul them down to the building site, he'd help me get the bark. The first tree we felled was about a foot in diameter and it fell uphill. We trimmed off the upper branches until we had a length of clear trunk about thirty feet long. With the chainsaw, we made one long cut through the bark down the entire length of the log. Then, starting from the bottom, with one of us on each side of the log, we went at it with the bark spuds, our fingers, hatchet blades, and whatever else we could improvise to gently pry the bark from the log. The newly forming cambium layer between the bark and the sapwood was soft, slippery, and very juicy. As the bark gave way to our efforts and separated from the trunk it made a slurpy hissing noise. We gradually worked our way up the log, and the bark was coming off beautifully. When we finally reached the upper end of the log, the remaining section of bark separated with a resounding hollow "pop." We stood up and congratulated each other on a job well done, and as we did, we heard a noise and looked down just in time to see that newly skinned log sliding down the hill! Its freshly removed bark created a trough that was slicker than any bobsled run, and by the time that log left that piece of bark, it had picked up a terrific amount of speed and momentum. It went careening down the mountainside and all we could do was watch in astonishment as that log leapt over rock ledges and crashed through thickets. It was finally stopped about fifty yards down the hill when it crashed into a stump right above the house foundation. We breathed a sigh of relief. If it had not been stopped by the stump, that slippery battering ram could have damaged the foundation, or it might have kept right on going and ended up well below the

Poplar Bark Basket

house site, down in the creek! After this incident, we secured a rope to each log before we removed its bark. I found out later that mountain loggers have a word for this phenomenon. It's called "ball-hooting" and is recognized as a serious danger in logging steep mountain slopes during spring and summer. As one old logger told me, "Them poplar logs is bad for that. When the sap's up, that bark can slip off a log you're dragging, and if that log gets loose and goes a ball-hootin' down that mountain, buddy, hit can kill a man!"

The bark of small trees can be scored and folded to make carrying vessels of all sizes—from berry baskets to backpacks. Indians daubed the seams with pine pitch and used them as water buckets.

I was first introduced to bark basketry by my mountain neighbor and friend Paul Geouge, who has been making baskets for years. I was enchanted by the way he explained their simple practicality. "So, you've been out fishing all morning, following the creek up into the mountains. You're catching some of them native speckled trout, but after a while the stream gets too small. So you call it quits and head up on to the ridge for the long walk home. There you run onto the biggest patch of ripe huckleberries you have ever seen! You'd love to take some of them berries home, but you ain't got nothing to carry 'em in. What could you do?" Paul asks with a twinkle in his eye. "Well, if you knew how to make a berry basket, you'd just find you a young poplar tree, make you a poplar bark basket, and tote them berries home. Now they'd taste mighty good after a fish dinner!"

Between the outer layer of the bark and the sapwood is a layer rich in fibrous vascular material known as bast. When rotted under controlled conditions, it can be used to make ropes, twine, and other cordage. It was highly valued by native Americans for this.

The bark has also been used medicinally as a tonic and as a remedy for fevers, stomach ailments, dysentery, rheumatism, and gout. It is a source of tulipiferine, an alkaloid that acts as a heart stimulant.

In European gardens, tulip poplar is one of the favorite "exotic" American ornamental shade trees and it has been so for more than three hundred years. In fact, the tulip poplar was botanically described first in 1687, from a specimen that had been brought from the New World and was being grown in an English garden.

In the early part of the eighteenth century, John Lawson, Surveyor-General of North Carolina, reported a hollow tulip poplar "wherein a lusty Man had his Bed and Household Furniture, and lived in it till his labor got him a more fashionable Mansion." Of course, the settler's "more fashionable mansion" would probably have been no more than a log cabin made of tulip poplar logs. There is many an old tulip poplar log cabin still standing today, and new ones are still being built.

The first significant cutting of poplars in the New World was by settlers who were clearing ground for farming. They knew that the soil was the richest where the tulip poplars grew. Today, this still tends to be true. Ginseng hunters look for stands of tulip poplars when scanning distant mountainsides in search of the moist rich soil that characterizes a good ginseng habitat.

It wasn't till two decades after the Civil War, in the late eighteen hundreds, when the railroads began to penetrate the rugged mountainous areas of the southern Appalachians, that the huge poplars and other southern hardwoods were harvested. In those days, only trees over thirty inches in diameter, yielding a couple thousand board feet, were accepted at the mills. In some areas, tulip poplar still grows in almost pure stands. In 1912, a tract of land near Looking Glass Rock in Transylvania County, North Carolina, yielded forty thousand board feet of tulip poplar lumber per acre. Nowadays, loggers are pleased to get four thousand board feet per acre.

Foresters call tulip poplar a hardwood because it is a broad-leafed tree, like oaks and maples. Pine, fir, and other conifers are called softwoods. The wood of tulip poplar, however, is as soft and easily workable as white pine. Because its extensive heartwood is yellowish-tan in color, it is known as yellow poplar in the lumber business. The sapwood is creamy white and has been used as interior paneling. When used in this capacity, it has been called "whitewood." Because of its lightness and strength, it is used for boxes and crates. Yokes for oxen were often made from tulip poplar because it is carved easily. It was one of the favorite woods for aircraft in the days when wood was used in airplanes. If compressed, the wood retains the ability to return to its normal shape when the pressure is released. This property accounts for its having long been a favorite material for barrel bungs. Its porosity and ability to take glue makes it an ideal core upon which to glue veneers of other wood, and because it takes a polish better than any other native wood, it is often used as a veneer itself.

Yellow poplar makes a good framing lumber for house construction. It is moderately lightweight yet stronger than spruce, fir, and white pine. Unlike the whole poplar logs used in cabin construction, milled, dry poplar lumber has little tendency to split when nailed. In recent years, it has been little used because of the abundance of low-cost softwood timber such as Douglas fir and spruce from western states. The North Carolina Building Code accepts its use as a framing lumber when graded. As the supply of these western softwoods decreases, tulip poplar may become popular again.

Tulip poplar is valuable even when dead and rotting. The stumps rot quickly and provide an ideal habitat for various wood-boring beetles. These beetles and their larvae

Oyster Mushrooms

are one of the favorite foods of the majestic pileated woodpecker. It is North America's largest woodpecker, almost as big as a crow. These and other woodpeckers regularly visit decaying tulip poplar and some people purposely cut poplar stumps high or use the logs in garden beds near the house in order to attract them.

Dead tulip poplar is also the favorite growing medium for certain fungi, most notably the delectable oyster mushroom *Pleurotus ostreatus*. Oyster mushrooms are one of my favorite wild mushrooms. I learned to identify them by carefully studying them in mushroom field guides. They are fairly easy to recognize, hence one of the safest of the edible wild mushrooms. They grow in clusters, usually out of the sides of logs or stumps. They vary from a creamy, "oystery" white to tan or gray in color and are distinctive because the gills run down the entire length of the stem. They are delicious in soups, on pasta, and can be sautéed and gently stewed to make an elegant side dish. Once I ate them fried in fritter batter, and they actually tasted like oyster fritters.

It was always a rare and special occasion when I found them—that is, until I started roaming the hills with my older mountaineer buddy Theron. Theron learned about gathering roots and herbs at his grandmother's knee. He knows the woods well, but he has always been wisely hesitant about sampling unidentified wild mushrooms. The first few times in our wanderings, when we found some oyster mushrooms Theron would help me gather them and he would carefully examine them, but he always declined to share the harvest and take some home to eat. However, after a few times of hearing me talk about how good they were (and seeing that I was still thriving), he finally tried some. He and his wife really enjoyed them, and from then on it seemed that, with Theron's help I was hardly ever without oyster mushrooms. From him, I learned to visit areas that had been logged a few years previously and to look on tulip poplar stumps after a spell of rainy weather. In these areas we found many pounds of the mushrooms, in all seasons of the year. We often find enough to dry and store for times when the fresh ones are scarce. When we sit down and share a meal of oyster mushrooms and other wild edibles I think we must make a strange pair: me, a naturalist from the flatland with a university education, and he, a traditional mountain woodsman and farmer who barely finished eighth grade. Yet, we both realize that if we hadn't met and been open and receptive to each other's knowledge, neither of us would be eating this delicious wild mushroom supper. Traditional knowledge and book learning can go well together.

[1] Charlotte Hilton Green, *Trees of the South* (Chapel Hill, N.C.: University of North Carolina Press, 1939), p. 225.

[2] Donald Culross Peattie, *Natural History of Trees of Eastern and Central North America*, 2nd edition (Boston: Houghton Mifflin, 1966), p. 268.

14

I Wouldn't Take Nothing for My Woodpeckers

OF YELLOWHAMMERS, WOOD HENS, AND WHITE-ASSED NANNIES

Chips of wood sprinkled down on us as the little downy woodpecker pecked away on the dead poplar limb high above our heads.

"Now I take care a' my woodpeckers," Theron was saying. "They're good to have around. I've seen them little jobbers like that 'un—they'll hang on to an ear of corn and they'll work away on the top of that ear and they'll eat them worms right out of that ear of corn. They'll go right down the row and clean every worm out of the whole corn patch. No sir, buddy, I wouldn't take nothing for my woodpeckers!"

"What kind of woodpeckers are there around here?" I asked.

"We got a wood hen, a red head, a sapsucker, that little downy jobber, a white-assed

Downy Woodpecker

nanny and a yallerhammer. Oh, yeah, and twice I've seen a Dominecker woodpecker."

"A Dominecker woodpecker?"

"Yeah, the back of his head is red but the rest of him is colored like a Dominecker chicken."

I realized that to understand his description of this bird one has to know breeds of chickens as well as woodpecker species. The Dominecker chicken is one of the old favorite chickens that has been in this country since colonial times. Originally known as Dominique, the name has evolved over the years and it is now called Dominecker by most country folks. The chickens are marked with characteristic, fine black-and-white zebra stripes. These same black-and-white stripes on the body of the woodpecker and the red patch on the back of the head are the identifying field marks of what is known to birders as the red-bellied woodpecker. Although "red-bellied woodpecker" is the standardized name, officially recognized by the American Ornithologist's Union, any birder can tell you that there is no red visible on this woodpecker's belly—so much for standardized names.

The rest of Theron's list of woodpeckers was as complete—and as nonstandard—as any checklist of local woodpeckers could be. His "wood hen" is the pileated woodpecker. It is named "pileated" because of the brilliant red crest covering the pileus, or crown, of the head. It is called a wood hen because it's almost as big as a chicken; its piercing call sometimes sounds like a chicken, and in the old days, one of these woodpeckers would occasionally make it to the stew pot, and it's reputed to taste as good as chicken. "Hit makes good gravy" I'm told.

The red-headed, the downy, and the sapsucker are names recognizable to any birder. When I produced a bird book, Theron showed me the "white-assed nanny"; it is the hairy woodpecker. Its country name comes from its white back,

d-Bellied "Dominecker" Woodpecker

leated "Wood hen"

which is clearly visible when it's flying away.

"Yellowhammer" is the southern country name for the yellow-shafted flicker. The state bird of Alabama is called the yellowhammer, not the flicker. Once, at a flea market, I got to talking to an old man about birds. He told me he had recently obtained a bird book and when he looked through it, he had "learnt something mighty sad..."

When I asked him what that was, he said, "When I was a boy around here we used to have a bird called a yellowhammer. Well, I looked for it in that book and it weren't even there. Hit's a damn extinct species." He shook his head in sad disbelief. "Ain't even in the book," he repeated.

Dominecker Chicken

I told him that yellowhammers were still around. It was just that the books call them "flickers" nowadays.

"Sho 'nuff?" he asked, with a glimmer of hope in his eye.

I had seen one recently, I assured him.

"Son," he said with a relieved smile, "I reckon you made my day."

In coastal regions of the Carolinas, hunters used to erect tall "yellowhammer poles" in open areas at the edge of salt marshes. The poles would attract flickers as they migrated along the coast. They were considered to be gamebirds, and they were shot and eaten as food.

Woodpeckers often puzzle home owners by drumming on metal gutters, chimney flashing, or garbage cans. When I first saw a flicker do this, I too was astounded. I couldn't

Yellow-Bellied Sapsucker

"Redhead"

"Yellowhammer"

Hairy "White-Assed Nanny"

believe a bird that makes its living pecking into dead trees in search of insects could be foolish enough to hammer on an empty metal trash can. But when I learned about the drumming behavior of woodpeckers I realized that it isn't the birds who are foolish. A loud, rapid burst of drumming is used by a woodpecker to make its presence known, to attract a mate, and/or to claim a territory.

These drumming posts are carefully chosen for their acoustics, not for the insects they contain. In nature, the birds choose hollow trees with hard, dry wood that resonates loudly. Around civilization, in small towns and wooded suburbs, woodpeckers have come to appreciate the industrial age as much as the rest of us, especially once they discovered how resonant certain metals are. The loud, rapid drumming display is easy to distinguish from the irregular and quieter tapping of a woodpecker that is feeding or chipping out a nest cavity.

In a number of species of woodpeckers, both the males and the females engage in this drumming display. They both mark out a territory and search for an appropriate nesting place. The nesting hole is excavated in dead wood, often in the broken stub of a tree. The wood must be soft enough to peck into and excavate but strong enough to last for the season. Both the male and the female may start nesting holes in various locations; however, both must agree on a good tree and work together on the nesting cavity in order to establish a strong bond—and a successful breeding relationship. If they do not agree, or no suitable tree is found, they are likely to separate.

Woodpeckers have evolved with amazing adaptations to their way of making a living. Their feet are zygodactyl, that is, two toes point forward and two point back. Their claws are sharp and curved for clinging to the bark of trees. Their stiff, spiny tail feathers act as props for vertical tree climbing. The woodpeckers' brains are protected by special padding in the skull and their tongues are long and barbed in order to be able to spear and extract wood-boring insects.

The abilities of some woodpeckers to drill through solid wood amazes me. I have seen the distinctive oblong excavations where a pileated has pecked through three inches of solid oak to gain access to a carpenter ant colony in the decayed heart of a tree. The bird must also have sensitive hearing to be able to know that the colony is in there in the first place.

Because woodpeckers depend on the insects and nesting spaces provided by dead and decaying trees, they often find themselves on the losing end of modern forestry practices, whereby timber interests and tree farmers eliminate all dying or "overmature" trees from large tracts of land. This has been one of the major factors in the probable extinction of the ivory-billed woodpecker and the precarious state of the endangered red-cockaded woodpecker in the Deep South.

Some woodpeckers, like the downy, lay as few as four eggs per clutch, while the flicker may lay as many as nine. They usually have one brood per season (though it's sometimes two in the South).

By early fall the young woodpeckers have left their nests. Most of the drumming and other breeding displays have ceased. However, through much of their range most woodpeckers are permanent residents, and they can still be seen and heard in winter.

It seems astonishing that these hardy birds can manage to peck out a living in a bleak, blustery winter woodland. On a number of occasions, while walking through the drab browns and grays of a dormant forest, I have been dazzled by the brilliant flash of a woodpecker's crimson crest. Like a glowing ember in a bed of ashes, it reminds me that even in the frigid depths of a dormant forest, the fire of life is burning.

15

The Ginseng Hunt

"THE STILL HOG GETS THE SLOP"

In many parts of the Appalachian Mountains, the old-growth forests are the scene of the annual ginseng harvest. In the fall of the year, mountain folk prowl the wooded hills and hollows in search of this uncommon and valuable medicinal plant. For some root gatherers, this autumnal ritual of 'seng hunting seems to be an almost mythic quest, where the root hunter tunes into a realm of subtle interrelationships among plants, animals, and the land. Most ginseng hunters, whether consciously or not, are constantly receiving and evaluating myriad cues from the environment. They note the texture of the soil and the types of trees, as well as the kinds of low-growing understory plants around them as they move through the woods. Some even pay attention to the birds.

One old ginseng hunter I know asked me if I knew about the ginseng bird.

"The ginseng bird?" I asked.

"Yeah. It hangs out with the ginseng. It has a special relationship with the plant. It's sorta like a guardian spirit."

"What's it look like?" I asked.

"It's a big bird," he said. "It has some of the same colors as the ginseng."

"You mean it's green?" I asked, more puzzled than ever.

"No, it's mostly black, but it's got red on its head like the red of them ginseng berries and it's got white like the root. It has ginseng medicine. It drums and sings."

"Drums and sings?"

"Yeah, it's like a big woodpecker. When he gets to drumming and singing, you can hear him all over the woods. You'll almost always hear him making a fuss when you are digging up a root. If'n your mind's set right, sometimes he'll call you right on over to a patch of 'seng."

Quite a few questions later, I realized he was talking about the pileated woodpecker. I had often seen them in the woods but I had never thought about the bird in relation to the ginseng plant. Yet, what he was saying made sense; in the mountains, this bird does inhabit the same rich coves and backwoods areas as ginseng. The ginseng plant, like the bird, does best in large tracts of old-growth forest.

So the next time I was in the woods looking for ginseng, I watched for the woodpecker. I had found quite a few plants, and every time I got near a patch of ginseng, or whenever I dug one, sure enough, I heard the pileated's call. I realized that there might be something to what the old man had said.

I was walking across a slope, when I came to the mouth of a hollow where a small stream trickled out. I was wondering if I should turn up that hollow or keep on in the direction I was going, when I heard the bird call loudly and repeatedly from up at the head of that hollow. This was what the old ginseng hunter was talking about. Could this be the ginseng bird guiding me to more plants? I started up that stream and soon came into a beautiful hollow that looked like good ginseng habitat. I heard the bird call again. The soil was rich and dark and all the plants growing there were indicators of a rich "cove hardwood" forest of the type where ginseng is often found. The trees were mostly tulip poplars mixed with basswoods, some sugar maples, and buckeyes. The understory plants looked right, too. There was wild ginger (*Asarum canadensis*) in the moist areas. There were maidenhair ferns (*Adiantum pedatum*) and even a few rattlesnake fern (*Bortrichium sp.*), which the local folks call "'seng-sign" or "'seng-pointer." I combed the slopes of that hollow back and forth and up and down, and the bird kept calling all around me. When I heard it call from one area, I would change direction and head toward the call. I combed the entire hollow, but I never found so much as one ginseng plant.

I went back to the old ginseng hunter to ask him what he thought about this. I complained that I had been finding lots of ginseng until I followed the bird; then I didn't find any.

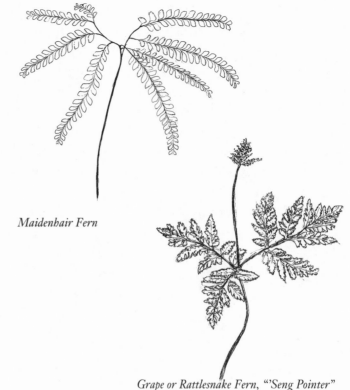

Maidenhair Fern

Grape or Rattlesnake Fern, "'Seng Pointer"

"I told you that the bird is a guardian of the ginseng plant, didn't I?"

Indeed, he had said just that.

"Well, it seems like maybe you had found enough for one day and that ol' ginseng bird wanted to get you off somewhere where you wouldn't dig any more. Them birds are like that sometimes. If that holler looked so good for ginseng and you didn't find any, maybe you ought to go back up there and scatter some seed. Somebody probably dug it all out years ago. Maybe that's what that bird was trying to tell you."

Ginseng Plant

I took the old man's (and the bird's) advice. I bought a couple of ounces of ginseng seed, returned to that hollow, and scattered them all over the woods.

The ginseng plant itself is not nearly as flamboyant as its price and reputation would have you believe. It is inconspicuous, rarely exceeding two feet in height. It has a perennial, slow-growing rootstock that produces a new top each year. Two to five "prongs," or leaf stems, radiate from its central stalk. Each leaf stem ends in a palmate cluster of five (occasionally, three) leaflets. Arising from the center of the whorl of leaves is a cluster of five to twenty tiny greenish-yellow flowers, which blossom in May or June, fol-lowed by a clump of two- or three-seeded berries, which turn a bright, shining red between August and October.

However, it is not the crimson berries or the five-fingered leaves that are so valued. The ginseng's treasure lies in its strange, tuberous root. This root is white, fleshy, and it is usually branched in one or more places. In recent years, gatherers have been able to sell the root for more than $200 a pound to exporters.

This unusual herb has created a unique link between North America and the Orient. Orientals are the world's principal connoisseurs and consumers of ginseng. For more than three thousand years, the Chinese have used ginseng as a rejuvenating tonic and attribute almost magical healing properties to the root. On rare occasions, the root may be branched in such a way that it takes a human shape. When this occurs, single roots are said to be worth immense sums of money. In fact the name ginseng is derived from the Chinese "jen-seng," meaning "man-shaped." From its long-standing reputation as a kind of panacea comes its botanical name *Panax*. There are essentially two species of commercial ginseng: *Panax ginseng*, which grows in the Orient, and *Panax quinquefolius* (five-leaved), which is our American ginseng.

Although ginseng is one of the most highly regarded medicinal herbs in Asia, the western medical world has only recently given it a glimmer of recognition. Scientists in Europe and the United States have found compounds that they call ginsenosides, which are beneficial to and stimulate the endocrine glands (particularly the pituitary-adrenal axis). This increases the body's resistance to stress and enhances skin and muscle tone as well as hormone balance. It is probably this property that gives ginseng its highly publicized and exaggerated reputation as an aphrodisiac.

In recent years ginseng has gained popularity in America. Practically every health-food store in the country now sells it in one form or another. You can find everything from imported whole roots to ginseng extract and instant ginseng tea—even ginseng chewing gum! Paradoxically, it is rare to find wild American ginseng for sale in these stores. Almost the entire harvest of our best quality wild ginseng is exported to Hong Kong—fifty tons in 1986. The Far East, in turn, ships its cheaper grades of cultivated ginseng back to us.

Before the white man reached America, virtually every Indian tribe that had access to ginseng held it in high esteem. The Cherokee name for it means "plant of life," and from what is known, it appears that ginseng was used by the Indians in many of the same ways as Oriental people use it.

The ginseng commerce between East and West owes its beginnings to a French Jesuit missionary, Father Jartoux, who traveled through Manchuria. In 1714, Jartoux published an article entitled, "The Description of the Tartarian Plant Ginseng." That same year the publication reached another Jesuit, François Lafiteau, in Montreal, Canada. Father Lafiteau showed one of Jartoux's drawings of the plant to a group of Mohawk Indians. They immediately recognized it and took him to a place where the root was abundant. He unearthed a few roots and sent them back to France, where their identity was verified. Soon, a small shipment was on its way to China to test for a potential market. In Peking, the roots were found to be of excellent quality and were sold for their weight in gold. The news of this sale spread rapidly and precipitated what has been called the Canadian Ginseng Rush of 1715. A great deal of frenzied trading ensued, as practically every able-bodied woodsman, trapper, and Indian scoured the forests for the newly-treasured resource. However, by the 1750s, ginseng was becoming so scarce that it was no longer profitable to gather, and the market more or less folded.

Farther south in the new colonies, however, the ginseng trade was just beginning. By 1775, one sloop had sailed from Boston to China with 110,000 pounds on board. Other ships loaded with ginseng were sailing from New York and Philadelphia. Large amounts of ginseng were being hauled out of various parts of the Appalachians on the backs of mountain traders and their animals. In 1784, on a trip to his lands on the Kanawha River, in what is now West Virginia, George Washington wrote in his journal: "I meet with many mules and packs laden with ginseng going east over the Forbes-Braddock Road." Even Daniel Boone got into the ginseng business for a while, though with uneven success. He managed to ruin several tons of it when his ginseng-laden keel boat swamped in the Ohio River on an island between Gallipolis, Ohio, and Point Pleasant, West Virginia, in the spring of 1788.

In the late 1800s, the successful cultivation of American ginseng launched a new boom and by the turn of the century, hundreds of plantations were started. But in 1904, most of them were wiped out by a leaf blight. A spray mixture containing copper sulfate and quicklime, called the Bordeaux Mixture, was finally developed as a deterrent to the leaf disease. Unfortunately, it was too late for many growers whose plants had already gone beyond the point of no return.

In the years following the blight disaster of 1904, ginseng trade with the Orient steadily increased; and in recent years it has proven to be a fairly dependable business. American ginseng is still cultivated and gathered wild from

Canada to the southern Appalachians. Because of its seasonal nature, however, the ginseng merchant must deal in other materials as well. It is not unusual to see signs in front of mountain junkyards reading, "We buy scrap metal, iron, copper, radiators, batteries, wool, fur, herbs, and ginseng. Top prices paid!"

Ginseng collection has been accompanied by various beliefs and rituals in many of the parts of the world where it is gathered. This is especially true in the Orient where some of these rituals may persist today. In times past, the diggers often wore special clothing and carried traditional accessories. The unearthing of the roots was often attended by priests, who had determined the most astrologically propitious time. Prayers and offerings were made and a sacred staghorn was used for the actual digging. There are even legends from Manchuria about the mystical and brightly colored ginseng bird who attended the plant.

In the Appalachian Mountains, the ritual of 'senging, as ginseng gathering is called, is not as formalized as in the Orient, but it is still a special autumn event for many folks. Usually, priests are not consulted to determine the proper time to gather it, but most ginseng diggers know enough to wait until the berries ripen in the fall. As far as astrology goes, some old-timers will tell you that the roots will dry better and will weigh more if they are gathered on the down side, or waning of the moon. Sacred staghorns are rarely used in North America for digging, but the local 'seng digger does have his favorite 'senging stick. Usually it's a hardwood sapling with a chisel point on one end, and it doubles as a walking staff.

I once spoke with my herb-hunting mentor, Theron, about my developing ginseng intuition. After a few seasons of ginseng hunting, I started to notice that while out in the woods I could almost "feel" its presence in a certain place. And sure enough, when I searched in that area I would often find it.

"And sometimes you don't find it, too," said Theron who often helps me keep my perspective. Theron has been hunting ginseng and other wild plants since he was a boy. Over the last decade or so, I have learned a great deal just from tagging along after him. Not only have I learned about plant lore and natural history from Theron but also about being in the woods—about moving slowly and observing thoroughly.

One bright sunny morning in late September, Theron and a mutual friend, whom I'll call Kenneth, showed up on my doorstep. They were going 'seng hunting. Did I want to come? I dropped what I was doing, grabbed a day pack,

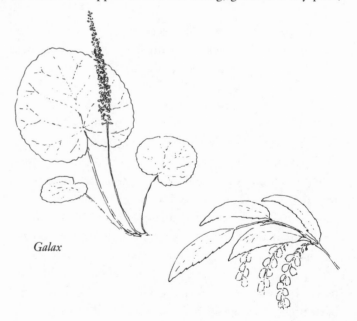

Galax

Dog Hobble

'Seng hunter shows off a prize.

and climbed into the pickup truck with them. Kenneth lived on the other side of the county and was as much a full-time "wild-crafter" as anyone I know. At that time, he was making most of his living out of the woods. He cut firewood to sell. He gathered galax *(Galax aphylla)*, dog hobble *(Leucotaoe axillaris)*, log moss, and shelf fungus for the florist trade. He and his wife made pine roping and wreaths during the holiday season. He split locust logs to sell for fence posts and he sometimes went into the high mountains to gather long-dead chesnut logs, which he split into rustic fence rails for suburban homes. This fall he had been 'senging almost every day, and so far he had gathered about twelve pounds, dried. Then the going rate was $165 per pound; he was making a good wage. He knew that if he could get Theron, who was older and more experienced, to go with him, Theron would take him to areas he hadn't been. I was only too glad to tag along, not only for the adventure, but also to see if I could learn some more ways of the woods from these two.

Theron and I had been in the woods together regularly, and we shared a similar approach. He was moderate in his gathering and collected a wide variety of herbs every year for medicinal use, as well as some ginseng to sell. Kenneth had a young family and needed to maintain a cash flow, so he was primarily interested in gathering what he could sell, rather than a variety of herb teas and remedies.

As soon as we got into the woods I could see that each of these men had a very different pace. Theron moved along slowly, pausing regularly to lean on his walking stick. Kenneth hiked along rapidly. Before long, Theron said, "I think I'm gonna head up in that little holler up in thar."

Kenneth said that he would keep on in the direction he was going. I decided to go with Kenneth, just to see how a "professional" operates. I was amazed at how fast he could move through the woods and still spot ginseng. He seemed almost to sprint along the slope, pausing briefly here and there when he found a plant. With a jab of his digging stick and a deft twist, that ginseng root was out of the ground and into his bag and he was moving on to the next plant, almost before I realized he had found one.

He kept up that pace all day, and his bag kept getting fuller. I managed to keep up with him, but I sure couldn't find ginseng while moving so fast. By the end of the afternoon I had found only two plants, and neither of them were big enough to dig. Kenneth opened his bag and showed me his harvest. It was a tangled mass of roots.

Heading back to find Theron, we wandered all around the area where we'd split up. We hooted and hollered and whistled. But no answer. I was starting to get concerned; then we heard him answer. Theron came hobbling down the hill with a big grin on his face. "Where'd you fellers go?" he asked.

"This guy 'bout ran me to death, Theron, and then he dug all my ginseng," I jokingly complained, trying to make light of being completely outclassed.

"I been in this same holler all day," Theron said. "You fellers do any good?"

Kenneth opened his bag, obviously proud of all the roots he had found, and then he asked Theron if he had found any. When Theron opened his bag, Kenneth's eyes got big. Theron had twice as many as Kenneth and all of them were large roots. (Theron leaves the small ones to grow.)

"Yessir, buddy," said Theron with a twinkle in his eye, "the still hog gets the slop!"

I later asked Theron what he meant by that expression. He told me that when you are slopping the hogs and they are all lined up at the trough, sometimes one will keep moving around trying to push into different places to get a better position. "But the hog who spends all his time trying to get to a better place doesn't get as much as the one who stays still," he explained. "It's the still hog that gets the slop."

In the wilds, it is possible to roughly estimate the age of a ginseng plant by the number of its leafstalks or "prongs." The first year or two after a seed germinates, it produces only three leaflets, which somewhat resemble delicate strawberry leaves. As the plant gets older, it will develop a main stem with two sets of leaves (two prongs) with perhaps a flower stem between them. Usually by the fourth or fifth year, the plant develops into a three-pronged "bunch of 'seng" and starts producing berries. ("Bunch" is a mountain term referring to one single plant, and it probably came into use because each plant is comprised of a bunch of prongs or leaf clusters). After six or eight years, if the plant is doing well, it may develop its fourth leaf prong, and it is usually producing a good crop of berries. I have heard stories of ginseng plants with as many as eight prongs, but personally, I have never found a bunch with more than five.

Ginseng is becoming scarce in some areas. The high prices being paid for it are causing it to be dug with ruthless shortsightedness by some. The experienced mountain ginseng hunters are often the most conscientious about their gathering. Theron has taken me to patches of ginseng where he harvests roots every year and has done so for decades. He always waits till fall when the berries are ripe, and then he only takes the larger plants.

Many people plant the berries in likely places in the woods. They feel that if the seeds are scattered, they have a better chance of surviving than if left undisturbed in an obvious cluster, vulnerable to the predations of foraging birds and rodents. I have often seen the shells of devoured ginseng seeds left by rodents under a large, fertile plant.

I still like to gather a few ginseng roots every year, but I try to gather them from larger plants that have young plants growing around them. Another point in favor of gathering the older plants is that as the ginseng root ages it gets larger and more complex, and it often puts out a newer auxiliary root—a sort of spare that serves to maintain and nourish the plant in case of damage to the main root system. Since harvesting the root usually destroys the plant, the conscientious ginseng digger can save the plant by protecting this auxiliary root. By digging carefully around the plant to expose the roots, the larger root can be twisted or cut off while the auxiliary root is left attached to the plant. This entire process can often be done without even removing the secondary root from the ground. This way, you can harvest the ginseng and still leave it growing in the woods.

Many traditional ginseng diggers take a few seeds and young plants home and set them out in the woods near their houses. If asked why, they will usually claim that a patch of ginseng is like money in the bank. But there is more to it than that. These folks have a lifelong fondness for the plant. For generations, not only has it been a source of medicine but it has been also a means of trade with the world outside their often isolated communities.

Many have depended on it for their livelihood; and although few people depend on ginseng for their entire support today, there are some folks who would have a lean Christmas without it. Besides, as one old-timer succinctly put it, "I just like to watch 'em grow!"

1 Andrew Kimmens, ed., *Tales of the Ginseng* (New York: William Morrow and Co., Inc., 1975), p. 62–63).

16

Jack-in-the-pulpit

GINSENG, BEARS, INDIAN TURNIPS, AND THE LITTLE PEOPLE

One time I was out 'sengin with Theron and his older cousin Lee. All three of us were traversing a steep, forested slope at the base of Bald Mountain in Yancey County, North Carolina. We had been slowly walking along, scanning the thick growth of understory plants for the telltale red berries or yellowish leaves of a coveted ginseng plant. We had spaced ourselves about twenty or thirty yards apart as we walked across the hill. Theron was the highest up on the slope. I was the lowest, and Lee was between us.

We had not been finding much ginseng when I came upon a large fallen log that had been broken apart. All around it were rocks that had been overturned. There was a distinct trail leading off that was marked by beaten-down plants, over-

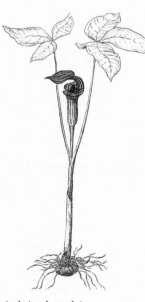

jack-in-the-pulpit

turned rocks, and recently disturbed dirt. This was the fresh trail of a bear.

I quickly forgot about ginseng—I wanted to see what that bear had been doing. There was some fresh dirt where it had dug a hole. I looked in the hole and saw the remains of the papery walls of a yellow jackets' nest. The bear had dug up and eaten an entire colony of yellow jackets. I was glad the bear had gotten there first. If I had stumbled into the nest, those yellow jackets might have devoured me!

I could see another place where the bear had clawed a tree trunk and where it had been digging roots. As near as I could tell, the trail seemed fresh. I hollered up the mountain to my companions. I told them that I had found fresh signs of bear and that they ought to come down and look. They replied that they were hunting ginseng and, being quite a ways up the slope, they didn't want to come all the way down to look at bear signs. So I followed the bear's path alone.

Because of the thick growth of the herbaceous plants that had been trampled, the bear's trail was quite clear and easy to follow. The bear had been feeding by turning over rocks in search of insects and digging up roots as it traveled. I looked more carefully at the holes where it had been rooting and found the tops of jack-in-the-pulpits lying beside holes where the bulbous corms (the roots) had been

"I watched a bear eating skunk cabbage fruits…"

bitten off. Could it be that this bear was eating jack-in-the-pulpit? I followed on. Yes, there were more holes and more tops lying beside with their roots bitten off. This was amazing. Jack-in-the-pulpit, sometimes known as Indian turnip, has an incredibly firey, irritating taste. In fact, it is a favorite trick of meanspirited country pranksters to try to get some naive person to taste it. Like many other members of the arum family, the plant contains calcium oxalate crystals. When you first put it in your mouth it tastes mild and pleasant, until the calcium oxalate crystals embed in your mucous membranes act as an irritant—not only chemically, but physically as well. To me, the sensation is like slivers of hot, broken glass in the throat—not a fun prank at all.

Apparently, this bear was not bothered by the calcium oxalate because it had eaten one jack-in-the-pulpit root after another; in fact, jack-in-the pulpit roots were its major

plant food that day. (Since that time I have seen several other instances where a bear had been eating jack-in-the-pulpit; this was in upstate New York. On another occasion, in early July in central West Virginia, I witnessed a bear feeding on the fruits of skunk cabbage, another calcium-oxalate-containing member of the arum family.)

The bear's trail turned uphill, and I followed. Soon, I met Lee and Theron. I was excited. I was finally going to be able to show them what this bear had been doing.

I pointed out the trail and showed them a jack-in-the-pulpit with its root chewed off. They both studied it. Finally, Lee said, "That ain't no bear been through here digging them Indian turnips. Hit was somebody."

"It was a bear," I protested. "People don't dig up Indian turnip roots."

"Yeah, they sell them."

"Naw, it was a bear," I maintained. "I saw where he busted up a log down there."

"Maybe down there," Lee said. "But up here, this is where somebody's been digging roots."

"Let's just follow along here for a while," I suggested. "Maybe we can figure this out."

The three of us followed the trail and found more uprooted jack-in-the-pulpits. Then, right beside one of the uprooted jacks we saw a large ginseng plant with red berries.

"Now, there ain't nobody who's digging Indian turnip to sell that's gonna pass up a ginseng with red berries," I said triumphantly.

"Well, what about that," Lee conceded.

We followed that bear's trail around the ridge. On the other side, we found a place where it had dug up several jacks. The tops lay there on the ground; the leaves were not even wilted, and a number of the roots had been bitten off. There was one the bear had started on, but it had been dropped, unfinished. From that point, the trail seemed to dwindle and disappear.

It wasn't till later that we realized that the bear had been prowling the slope hunting roots, just like we were. It was just ahead of us and when it heard us arguing, it dropped the root it was eating and slipped away.

After that day in the woods, I wood-burned a drawing of a woodland scene on an artist's conk (a shelf mushroom with a white underside). I drew a bear and a jack-in-the-pulpit and three tiny human figures up on the ridge in the background. I gave it to Theron for a Christmas present.

He looked at the scene I had drawn and said, "Well, that's about the way it was, wasn't it. That ol' bear was around the ridge thar, eatin' them Indian turnips and just a listening to us argue about whether it was a bear or not."

Jack-in-the-pulpit is one of the most well known and loved of our woodland plants. It is found in moist woodlands throughout the eastern half of the continent. The plant can sometimes attain a height of more than two feet.

Each plant has at least one compound leaf, each leaf being divided into three or four leaflets that shade the flowering portion. The flower is made up of a leaflike spathe, folded over like a hood to form the "pulpit," which shelters the tubelike spadix popularly known as the "Jack." The color of the spathe and spadix may be anywhere from a pale, washed-out green, to dark purple. At the base of the spadix, tucked well out of sight, are the actual flowers.

If you peek carefully into the flower spathe you can tell whether you have a male or a female plant. The male has pollen-bearing anthers on the shaft of his spadix. The pollen is carried to the female by fungus flies and other small insects. After he has shed his pollen, the male flower becomes flaccid and withers away. His one (or sometimes two) leaf remains to collect what it can of the sun's energy as it filters down through the forest canopy. If the plant can store enough of that sunlight in the form of starch in its rootstock over the course of the summer, then next year, perhaps, he will have enough strength to become female. The female plant is larger than the male and has two leaves. Her flower has a tight cluster of ovaries along the spadix. These ovaries swell into round green berries, which turn bright red in autumn. If the female expends a great deal of energy producing fruit and can't sufficiently recoup her stores, she will "take it easy" for a year or two and change back to being male.

In spite of the irritating crystals, early records indicate that jack-in-the-pulpit corms were often used as food by native Americans.

Peter Kalm, an eighteenth-century writer, tells in his *Travels in North America* how the Indians not only cooked the corm but whole plants by placing them in a pit in the ground and building a long-lasting fire over them. "How can men have learned," he remarked, "that plants so extremely opposite to our nature are eatable and that this poison which burns on the tongue can be conquered by fire?"

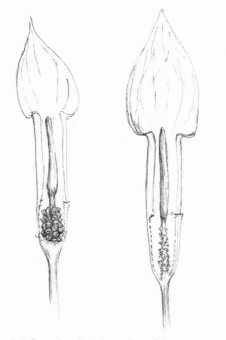

Female (left) and male jack-in-the-pulpit.

It seems that prolonged heat and/or prolonged drying will break down those irritating crystals and make jack-in-the-pulpit edible. I heard this years ago, and I decided to try Euell Gibbons's recipe for "Indian-Turnip Chips." He recommended slicing the root into very thin chips and placing them in a warm, dry place for as long as five months to dispel the acridity. After sufficient time has passed, the chips should be tasted cautiously. If there is no hot, acrid, or prickly sensation on the tongue or back of the throat, Gibbons tells us, they can be roasted, salted, and served like potato chips, crumbled and made into a cooked cereal, or ground and used as a flour or as a flavorful addition to other flours.[1]

I emphasize caution in the first tasting of the jack-in-the-pulpit because of my initial experience. After waiting five months for the "jack chips" to ready themselves, I took them down from the attic and toasted them with a little salt. After the first nibble, I promptly pronounced them delicious and started gobbling them as if I had fasted for the entire drying period. After I had eaten about twenty or thirty of the chips, the acrid, burning sensation from the first chip hit me. Whereupon I realized that I would have to stomach the acidity of the rest of the chips. I am thankful that this acidity had been somewhat dispelled, so that the only consequence was a few tormented but enlightening hours spent experiencing another aspect of the awesome power of Mother Nature. Somehow, after that experience, it's been hard to get back to nibbling Indian turnips.

Medicinally, the corm of the jack-in-the-pulpit was, from 1820 to 1850, officially listed in the United States *Pharmacopea*, where it was described as a stimulant, expectorant, diaphoretic, and irritant. I can certainly verify these qualities.

My friend Clyde tells me that jack-in-the-pulpits are important tools for the Little People. The Little People, he explains, are the guardians of the forest. They orchestrate the wildflower bloom in the spring and they monitor the goings-on in the woods. The reason you hardly ever see the Little People is that they live underground. They rarely ever have to show themselves because they use the plants and a. 'mals as sensory devices. All the ⊦lants are connected by their roots ı⌐ Command Central, an underground intelligence and communications networking center, where teams of highly trained Little People professionals interpret and evaluate the data as it comes in.

Every bush you brush against or tree branch you touch sends impulses deep into the earth through substrata processing units into the Little Peoples' data banks. This gives them essential information on any traveler in their domain. It tells them your location, as well as your height and the speed at which you are traveling. They also have weighing rocks set up in various places that tip and move when you step on them. These tell them your approximate weight. If they want to know what you look like, they will throw up a

spider web in your path. This gives them a facial imprint or an image of your body type. Sometimes they send out mosquitoes to obtain blood samples. In certain areas they also have listening posts, so they can hear what's being said. This is where the jack-in-the-pulpit comes in. These flowers are highly sophisticated microphones with directional hoods and the Little People usually locate these right near trails so that they can hear everything that's being said. If you ever have any special message that you want to convey to the Little People, all you need to do is speak clearly into one of their jack-in-the-pulpit microphones. You will be heard.

1 Euell Gibbons, *Stalking the Healthful Herbs* (New York: David McKay Co., Inc., 1966), p. 250.

17

Raccoon Discipline and Opossum Lessons

Once I had to discipline a coon. A couple of summers ago, I was working as a guide. I had backpacked for several miles into a prime wilderness area with a group of folks for a week of backcountry camping. We created a base camp and shared a central cooking fire. At night we suspended our group food between two trees to keep it out of reach of animal scavengers. Because there is some hunting and trapping in the area, I didn't anticipate trouble from the camp-raiding four-leggeds that are so common in parks where they are protected, and therefore, used to raiding campsites. Yet, I felt that this was an important procedure for new campers to learn, so I instructed my fellow campers to do the same with their personal food supplies as well. Most of them put their food in nylon stuff bags and hung them in trees near their tents, which were pitched here and there in the surrounding woods. I did not

check to see how each person had hung his or her cache, because I did not really expect any animal visitors.

Well, sometimes you get what you don't expect. It's true in the woods and it's true in life. That first night, not long after everyone had settled down, I was startled out of my first few minutes of dozing by the unmistakable clatter of pots, pans, bowls, and sierra cups. I bolted upright and flicked my flashlight in the direction of the noise. The flashlight beam was met by the bright, shining eyes and black mask of a handsome young raccoon. It was busily exploring the kitchen area, upsetting, overturning, and walking around in all our carefully cleaned and stacked dishes and utensils. I stormed out of the tent and shooed that coon out of camp chasing it into the bushes until it disappeared into the darkness. I checked the kitchen area again to be sure that we really had cleared up all the food.

We had; the cooking area was neat and clean (except for the now-scattered pots and pans). The coon didn't come back that night. The next night, however, it was back, as hopeful as ever, rummaging around through all our dishes, again. I charged out of the tent like I had the night before. And the coon scrambled off into the bushes like it had the night before; but half an hour later it was back. We had been hiking and exploring most of the day and we had stayed up late singing and telling tales around the camp fire. It had been a busy day and I was not looking forward to working third shift as camp coon chaser. So I gave up, pulled the covers over my head, and tried to ignore the racket. Soon the coon realized that, as good as it smelled, there was indeed no food here. It wandered off into the night and all was quiet—till later on, that is, when a new noise—a strident, ripping sound—tore me from my peaceful slumber. It was coming from a new direction. So, once again, I crawled out of my bag to investigate.

I followed the sound to one of the nearby tent sites. There was the coon up in the tree industriously ripping into someone's food bag. The bag was about six feet up, tied securely to the trunk of the tree. The coon leapt from the tree and disappeared. While the owner of the food snored away, I untied the tattered bag and took it back to my tent for safekeeping. I crawled back into my sleeping bag and soon was sound asleep…only to be awakened some time later by what was becoming a familiar wilderness sound—the sound of coon teeth ripping nylon—this time from a new direction. I headed off to investigate and, sure enough, there was that masked bandit merrily ravaging another happy camper's food cache. This bag was hung from a line on an overhanging branch, but the owner had pulled the bag up too close to the branch and the coon had

simply climbed out on the branch, reached down, and hauled the bag in. At my approach the coon beat a hasty retreat, scampering away with a granola bar hanging from its mouth like a big, flat cigar. I untied that bag as well and brought it back to my tent. Twice more that night I was awakened by that same sound and had to rescue two more improperly hung food bags. This coon was making the rounds and it was learning fast. So was I.

By the time I returned from my last rescue mission, the first rosy fingers of dawn were brightening the eastern edge of the woods. I was trying once more to get back to sleep, when I heard the sound of coon claws on tree bark right behind my tent. I looked out the rear window and there was that ring-tailed rascal climbing up after yet another food bag. This bag was hung by a rope and dangled several feet down from a high limb, well away from the trunk and several feet off the ground. I watched that coon attempt to reach down from above, then climb halfway down the trunk, and try unsuccessfully to reach out from the trunk and grab the bag. Finally, it slid down the tree and stood on its hind legs under the bag, trying to reach the bag from below.

About that time, I realized that I had had about enough coon for one night. It was daylight, and that coon would not be able to slip off into the darkness like it had all night long. I was going to give that coon a run for its money (or its granola bars)! That coon needed discipline. I quickly slipped my sneakers on and leaped out of the tent with a heartfelt, furious roar. The coon and I started a mad dash through the woods, over rocks, and through underbrush. I was keeping up quite well when the coon shinnied up a tall hemlock tree. It climbed out on a branch about twenty feet above my head and gazed back down at me with nothing but complacent smugness in its beady little black eyes. I shook my fist up at that coon. "This ain't no old hobbled-up coon dog you're messing with this time, you ring-tailed fuzz ball. I'm gonna learn you a few things!" I hollered. I cut a hickory switch and started for the tree. That coon's eyeballs about popped out of its head when it realized that I was coming up that tree after it. Slowly I climbed, growling ominously, the hickory switch clenched between my teeth. That coon turned tail and moved on higher up the tree. I kept right on climbing, growling malevolently, and showing my teeth at the coon. (It's hard not to show your teeth when you are using them to carry a stick.) I wanted to make an impression on this coon, for the good of our food supply as well as for its own future. I wanted that coon to know humans as we really are.

To the raccoon, we had seemed like harmless, noisy, bumbling creatures, whose sole purpose on earth was to bring delicious food into the woods to feed bright, young, opportunistic raccoons. I wanted to teach that coon the truth about humans: that we really are the most dangerous creatures on the face of the earth, that we are insatiable, and that we destroy large parts of the natural world every day—and that includes coons. And like my forefathers, I believed that in certain instances truth and discipline can be most effectively conveyed with the sting of a hickory switch.

Soon the coon was near the top of the tree, nervously climbing back and forth in the upper branches. I just kept climbing and growling.

The coon knew it was trapped—and I was closing in fast. So, it climbed out on the longest branch it could find, but because we were almost at the top of the tree, that limb was only about five feet long and, by the time I got there,

the coon was desperately hanging on to the flexible outer branches at the very end of the limb.

Looking out from the tree top into the fear-filled eyes of that pitiful coon, as it cowered there frantically clutching the green boughs with its delicately fingered front feet, was enough to melt my heart. All I wanted to do was comfort the little rascal and stroke its lush lovely fur. But I knew that the best thing I could do for this beautiful, wild, free-spirited animal was to teach it to associate humans with fear, pain, and danger. So I drew forth my hickory cane and switched the dickens out of that critter!

The coon turned and took a flying leap. It grabbed a few branches on the way down to slow its descent, then for a twenty-five-foot free-fall it fell spread-eagle, with its feet and tail stretched out so that it looked like a giant flying squirrel or a miniature bearskin rug. A few seconds later, it hit the ground running. And as far as I know, that coon is still running...running wild and running free. It never came back to our camp that week. I've been to that campsite several times since and have never had any more trouble with raccoons.

Occasionally, I think of my tree-top session disciplining that coon. That coon might still be traveling along that creek that runs by our campsite. When it gets a whiff of human scent I hope that it understands the dangerous unpredictability of the human species. Some are harmless campers, others are hunters and trappers, and other rare individuals might be like the deranged, snarling beast with the stinging hickory switch. I hope that memory has kept it out of trouble, running free and wild.

The raccoon is a New World animal. It was first described in English in the 1600s by none other than Capt. John Smith, who wrote: "There is a beast they [the Indians]

call Aroughcun, much like a badger, but useth to live in trees as squirrels doe." It did not take long for the Indian word to be corrupted by the king's English to "a raccoon," as we know the critter today. The Algonquian word for raccoon translates loosely as "shoreline wanderer."

In the same way that coon created chaos in my camp, the raccoon created chaos among the early naturalists and taxonomists who tried to figure out and classify the beast. Capt. Smith thought it was a badger. Linnaeus thought it was a bear. Other taxonomists thought it was related to Old World viverrid civet cats and mongooses. Others thought it was sort of like a dog. They finally realized that it was "nothing but a coon." It was classified as the ring-tailed leader of its own family, *Procyonidae*, which also includes the coatimundi and the ring-tail of the southwest. It is now known among scientists as *Procyon lotor*. The generic name *Procyon* is the name of the Little Dog star; *lotor* means "one who washes."

We have all heard about raccoons washing their food. I have known a few captive raccoons and I have observed this washing behavior. A coon will take a piece of food and rub it between its front paws while tasting and smelling it, then take it to the water dish and dunk it in the water, continuing to rub it back and forth, mushing it around in the water and feeling every detail of its texture and form. Raccoons are sensual beings with sharp eyesight, excellent hearing, and a sensitive nose, but what is unique about raccoons is their highly developed sense of touch. Most of what these intelligent beings know about their world they learn through touch. They love to feel things. The tough skin on the raccoon's front feet is softened by soaking, and this makes the skin more sensitive.

A large part of a coon's diet comes from the water—frogs, fish, salamanders, crustaceans, shellfish, turtles, snakes, insects, and worms. Coons often feed in shallow water by walking along a creek, lake, marsh, or tide pool, exploring the bottom with their front feet, turning over rocks, feeling for various animals, and gobbling them up as they are caught. A raccoon, while its "hands" are busy probing the bottom, often appears to be staring off into space, lost in a tactile reverie. This allows the animal while it is feeding to keep its eyes, ears, and nose above the water, ever alert for danger. Of course, when a raccoon finds food away from water it does not indulge in washing either its hands or the food. Raccoons are also fond of fruit, berries, corn, eggs, honey, insects, fresh meat, and poultry—when they can get it.

There is hardly a stream or shore anywhere in the lower forty-eight states, for that matter, that isn't occasionally patrolled by a raccoon. They range from Canada south into Mexico and Central and South America. Because of their omnivorous eating habits, raccoons are very adaptable and are found in practically every habitat except the driest deserts and the tallest of the Rocky Mountains. This includes cities and towns as well as the backcountry. Raccoons are as numerous as squirrels in some suburbs, where they enjoy a relaxed suburban lifestyle, denning in the chimneys, attics, and garages of expensive houses and dining on opulent garbage and pet food left by overfed dogs and cats. One of the first accounts of raccoons adapting to human food came from John Lawson who, in 1718, wrote in his *History of North Carolina* that the raccoon was "the drunkenest Creature living, if he can get any Liquor that is sweet and strong." I know a few people like that.

Raccoons prefer to use large hollow den trees for shelter and refuge, but with the demise of much of the old-growth forest, they often have to settle for abandoned groundhog burrows, rocky crevices, and sometimes even culverts and chimneys. Raccoons usually breed between January and March, depending on the climate. The female frequently gives birth to three or four (but sometimes as many as seven) young after a gestation period of about sixty-three days. The young stay with the mother at least until fall.

As they get older, the mother coon takes her young on nightly foraging expeditions. A curious and disorderly troop they are, as they range through the woods and along creeks, climbing in the bushes, splashing in the water, catching frogs, turning over rocks, digging in the mud, wrestling and fighting with each other—acting very much

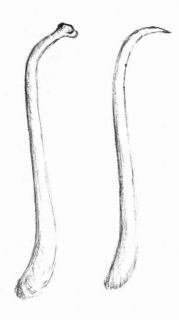

The "business end" of a raccoon's baculum is filed down to make a "mountain toothpick."

like a rowdy bunch of school. They communicate and express themselves vocally with a collection of sounds. The most common is a birdlike churring sound or a whistling trill. (Thoreau called it "whinnering.") When angered or threatened, they emit growls, snarls, and coarse squalls.

Raccoons do not hibernate, but during winter cold spells, when the temperature gets well below freezing, raccoons will hole up, staying in their dens in a drowsy state until the weather moderates. Sometimes, several families will den together.

For several centuries coon hunting and trapping have been important activities. In early colonial days the hides were so prized that they were sometimes used in place of money as a trade item. The meat was considered to be fine food. The fur is warm and ladies' shoes were made from the soft, durable leather. The oil rendered from the fat was used as a dressing for leather and even as a lubricant for machinery. Eighteenth-century writer Peter Kalm noted in his *Travels in North America* that "the bone of its male parts is used as a pipe cleaner." Nowadays, this peculiarly shaped bone (called the baculum) is known as a "mountain toothpick." Some native Americans value this bone to make a heavy duty sewing needle for lacing thick hides.

Today, coon hunting is still a popular sport. The greatest pleasure in coon hunting is getting out and roaming the woods on a frosty night and following the deep bellows of bugle-voiced hounds that are on a hot trail. A wise old coon is as clever as a fox and uses many tricks to hide its scent and fool the dogs. It runs along the tops of fences, wades down creeks, backtracks along its own trail, and walks fallen logs to break its scent. Sometimes, a coon will "tap a tree"; that is, it will climb a short distance up a tree, then leap to the ground and continue running, often leaving the hounds quite literally barking up the wrong tree. Sometimes, a coon will lead a pursuing dog out into deep water and then climb on to the dog's head and drown it.

The aim of the hunting pack is to chase the coon up into a tree. This is the first place an inexperienced coon will go. When the hounds have the coon treed they will change the tempo and tone in their voices. This is known among hunters as "barking treed." The hunters will then find their way to the dogs and shine their lights up into the tree. No matter how scared it is, a coon can seldom resist looking down at the hunters, and when it does, its eyes shine brightly and provide an easy target. If the coon doesn't show itself, some coon hunters have a special call known as a "coon squaller" that sounds like a coon crying out in anger or distress. At the sound of the squaller, most coons will look, and some will come down the tree to fight or begin running again.

There are some modern coon hunters who have little respect for their quarry and either throw the body of the coon away or let the dogs tear it up. However, most coon hunters are true sportsmen and realize that this animal is a noble beast and a precious resource. They work hard to preserve its numbers and its habitat. They kill only a small percentage of the coons they tree, and when they do kill one, they save its hide and use its meat. The sport of coon hunting is about much more than just coons. It is about the music of the hounds, the adventure of getting out in the woods at night, and the unpredictability of where you may go and what you may find. It is about fellowship with other hunters and about the stories that are told after the hunt.

When I was a small boy, my dad told me that once when he was out coon hunting, the dogs chased a coon into a tall hollow tree. He said the hunters saw it run into a hole at the bottom of the tree, and it seemed that no sooner did that coon get into the hole than it popped out of the top of the tree and ran back down the outside of the trunk to the hole at the bottom. Again, it squeezed into the hole in the bottom and, as soon as it did, out came a coon at the top, which ran back down to the bottom hole again. As this continued the hunters became amazed. They had never seen a coon act so strangely, and they wanted to investigate. They got an ax and chopped the tree down. When they did, they saw an amazing sight.

"That tree was plumb full of coons," he told me. "So full, in fact, that there wasn't even room for one more. As soon as that coon squeezed in at the bottom of the pile, there was no room for the one at the top of the heap, and down out of the tree it came, trying to get a place at the bottom of the pile."

"How many coons were there?" I asked, wide-eyed with wonder.

"There were forty-seven," he told me, "as near as we could count…"

That's true. It's true that my dad told me that story. It's also true that he sometimes told tall tales.

One bright "moon-shiny" night in late October, I got in on a coon hunt with Theron and a couple of neighbors. In our group there were two fellows whom I'll call Mike and

Jerry. Mike was in his mid-twenties. Jerry was in his mid-forties, and Jerry's two young teenage boys came along as well. I was in my mid-thirties at the time and with Theron in his fifties, the age of the group spanned five decades.

Jerry had been an avid coon hunter for years. He was an auto mechanic by trade but a coon hunter at heart. He had a repair shop at the local roadside general store. During raccoon season he worked what he called "coon hunters' hours." That meant that because he was out coon hunting every night, he didn't come to work till around ten or eleven o'clock in the morning. This man was clear on his priorities. That year he had a new redbone hound and had been doing well with it. He wanted to try hunting on some land near Theron's place.

Mike had just gotten a coon dog and wanted to train it by letting it run with Jerry's hound. Jerry consented once Mike assured him that his dog wasn't "ill" (mean tempered).

We met at Theron's place, about an hour or two after dark. We headed on up into the woods and turned the dogs loose. We then hiked up onto a ridge and waited and listened. Waiting and listening is a lot of what hunting with dogs is about—waiting to hear when the dogs first strike a trail, listening to the voices of the hounds, monitoring the chase, and interpreting the inflections in the voice of each dog.

We were five shadowy figures standing on that ridge top in the dappled moonlight. We were together as a group, yet each man was alone, listening, enveloped in the stillness, ears tuned to the quiet, listening to the immense silence of the mountains on this calm, frosty night. At moments like this I sometimes hear a faint roar at the back edge of my hearing. It feels like the silence is ringing in my ears. Is this the throb of my own metabolism—the blood coursing through my veins—or might this be the very "thrumming" of the universe that Thoreau writes about? Perhaps it is the cosmic pulse, the crackling of life's fire, the gurgling of the vital stream, that connects and flows through us all—through the dogs, the coons, the trees, and through the mountain itself. There is a lot to be heard on a silent, moonlit mountaintop.

Then, out of the south, carried on that still mountain air came the barely discernible but distinct, distant roar of a mufflerless motorcycle winding out on the Asheville highway. It was a good twelve miles away as the crow flies. The sound was faint, but clear. I looked over at Mike, who is an excellent backyard "shade tree" mechanic and loves motorcycles.

Mike listened as the sound faded off into the distance and said "Will you listen to that ol' boy gittin' gone."

I asked Mike if he could tell what kind of motorcycle that was.

"I can't tell you what brand it is, but that engine's a two cycle."

Coon hunters hear music in the baying of the hounds. Mike hears it in the roar of a motorcycle.

Then, out of the hollow below us burst the coarse, roaring bellow of Jerry's dog. Shortly thereafter we heard the higher-toned yelp of Mike's dog.

"They're heading up that ridge," someone said. "Sounds like a 'possum," said Jerry, disgustedly. "Yep, see thar', he's treed already," he said as the tempo of the dogs' barks changed.

We hiked around the slope toward the sound of the dogs and we found them barking and leaping beneath a small tree. There, on a limb about thirty feet up, was a 'possum, hunkered up against the trunk of the tree, gazing passively down at this curious assemblage of boisterous, hysterically baying hounds and taciturn mountain men who were gathered below in its honor. In the glare of the flashlights, its eyes shone like diamonds.

"A damn 'possum, I knew it," Jerry muttered as he snapped a lead on the collar of his hound. Mike caught his dog and they started off around the hillside with their dogs. I hung back from the rest of the group for a moment to admire the 'possum. Being rather fond of 'possums, this hunt was starting out well as far as I was concerned; we had treed one 'possum already and the best part was no one wanted to shoot it. This was my kind of hunt!

Jerry's experience of the same events was quite different from mine. As a modern coon hunter, he has no fondness for 'possums. In fact, he is disgusted by them.

'Possums are not a challenge for the dog or the hunter. There is little sport in running a 'possum. They are considered slow and stupid and they never run far before they tree. To make matters worse, if a 'possum is out in a field away from trees when it is overtaken by the hounds, it will keel over in its tracks and play 'possum, providing an irresistible distraction for most dogs. This makes it very difficult to break a hound from chasing them.

Even the dog itself would

"About thirty feet up was a 'possum…"

rather run a coon. It is much more energized when chasing one. Jerry could tell by the excitement in its bark when his dog had struck a coon's trail. But in the absence of coons, the dog simply could not resist a 'possum, and through the course of that night as we climbed all over those mountains following the dogs, they treed seven 'possums. I was amazed and delighted. I had never seen so many 'possums in one night. Jerry was getting more and more frustrated. To make matters worse, his two boys, dressed as they were in their new warm camouflage coveralls, would lie down in the dry leaves and they would both fall sound asleep while we were waiting for the dogs to strike another trail. Jerry didn't like this either. He wanted his boys to share his enthusiasm for the sport. The boys both liked to hunt, but the slow parts of these late-night coon hunts made them drowsy. Every time we would get ready to move, Jerry would have to wake the boys up.

"You boys shore ain't acting much like coon hunters," he would say, trying to instill in them the alertness, intensity, and steadfastness of a true coon hunter.

In each of his roles as father and as trainer of hunting dogs, Jerry faced a similar dilemma. The hunting spirit in both a dog and a boy is a delicate thing. It is

"We found the dogs barking and leaping beneath a tree…"

a deep, primal, instinctive behavior that must be cultivated, nurtured, and encouraged. Stern commands and canine obedience-training methods are used primarily to suppress natural urges. They cannot be used to cultivate them. If Jerry were to beat his dog to break him of chasing 'possums, he would likely intimidate the dog and destroy its hunting spirit, and it would probably lose its desire to chase anything. The same would be true of his sons.

Then we heard the dog's bellow coming from down in the next hollow near Theron's old family homestead, about a quarter of a mile away. Jerry paused and said, "Now, listen, he's running a coon this time!" He listened for a moment more, and then asked, "Theron, has there been timber cut down in there lately?"

Theron said, "No, I don't think so."

Jerry said, "It sounds like he's running in tree laps." (Laps are branches left on the ground after a logging job.)

Theron said, "No, there ain't been no timber cut in there."

Before long the dog's barks became more rapid and the barking continued from the exact same position.

"He's treed," said Jerry, and we started off in the direction of the noise. We hiked down the hill along an overgrown pasture into a wooded creek bottom. As we approached the barking dogs, we came to a strip where some trees had been cut for a power line right-of-way. As we clambered through the fallen trees, Jerry said, "Here's them tree laps I was talking about."

Theron said, "I forgot about them cutting these trees for the power line. I knew there hadn't been no timber cut in here, but I forgot about this power cut."

I later asked Jerry how he was able to tell from the bark of the dog that it was running in tree laps. He said, "He barks like he's barking treed, but he keeps moving." Perhaps just the smell of the coon in association with tree trunks was all the stimulus necessary for his dog to bark treed. With this hound, it didn't seem to matter whether the trees were vertical or not.

We finally got to the dogs. They were in a thicket of fallen tree branches. Jerry's dog was barking into a hole— an old groundhog burrow where the coon had taken refuge. Jerry was peeved again. Even if his dog did run a coon, he didn't want the dog barking treed when the coon was in a hole. Whether it is boys or dogs, it is not easy to get other beings to live up to your ideals and expectations.

I finally asked, "Now really, Jerry, if there's not any coons to be found, aren't you glad that your dog at least trees a few 'possums rather than nothing at all?"

"I'd rather that dog not open [start barking] all night as to have him tree a 'possum," Jerry said sternly.

Wanting to probe this dislike of 'possums further, I offhandedly mentioned to the group that I had eaten 'possum a few times and it had tasted all right to me. That comment was all it took to get the conversation rolling.

Jerry said, "I don't eat no damn 'possum."

Mike said, "That boar 'possum breeds the sow in her nose. And that's downright disgustin,'" he concluded. (More on this in the next chapter.)

These men's disdain for 'possums is a reaction I've noticed from a lot of folks, not just coon hunters. When people talk about 'possum they are talking about a lot more than a greasy little marsupial. The opossum is an embodiment of what we modern humans do not like or have trouble accepting about ourselves. This humble mammal mirrors those slow, drooling, dim-witted, fumbly, funky, gamey-smelling, perversely enigmatic parts we all have.

If you hold a mirror up to those aspects of a species as prideful and arrogant as modern, twentieth-century *Homo sapiens*, you can't expect much respect or appreciation in return. Kinship with 'possums is something modern folks hate to admit.

Whether we want to admit it or not, we modern humans do have a lot in common with 'possums. Even though we are at opposite ends of the evolutionary chain, humans and opossums are the only North American mammals with opposable thumbs. 'Possums have them on their hind feet and we humans have them on our forefeet—our hands. We use ours to manipulate the world, while 'possums use theirs simply to hold on to where they are—and they have been holding on for quite some time.

"Little stars and tiny monkey feet" are how 'possum tracks are sometimes described. The widely spaced five toes on their front feet make the stars, while the monkey-like prints are made by the hind feet with the distinctive opposing thumbs.

I was talking with a hunter friend about following 'possum tracks in the snow and he said, "Yeah, they look like they're drunk." He is right. I have followed 'possum tracks on numerous occasions and, from what I have seen, their way of traveling through the woods is sometimes amazingly erratic. Their tracks weave here and there, and sometimes even double back on themselves. Some people say 'possums occasionally bump into trees. As they amble along, 'possums certainly do seem to be marching to the sound of a very different drummer. Whether they are following vague odors that come wafting from different directions or if they are just bumbling about in a daze, no one (perhaps not even the 'possum) knows for sure. A 'possum leaves a trail very much like a disoriented human who is lost in the woods.

Once, during a cold snowy time in the North Carolina mountains, I followed a set of 'possum tracks for three days. Each day the 'possum would hole up in the base of a different hollow tree, and each night the 'possum would rouse itself and wander about. It never traveled more than about a hundred yards each night. I never saw evidence that the animal found anything to eat. On the third day, when I came to where the tracks ended at the hollow base of a tree, I reached a gloved hand into the hole, felt around and pulled the 'possum out. As I held this grinning, drooling beast up by the tail, I realized that it did not have much to grin about. A pitiful sight this critter was, its drool freezing at the end of its nose. The margins of its ears were shriveled from frostbite, and the tip of its tail was frozen. It appeared that some of its frost injury was a result of the recent frigid weather as the end of its tail was still somewhat raw and bloody.

The cold snowy weather had been rough on this 'possum. When I thought about those tender pink bare feet walking around on the ice and snow, I could understand why it had not traveled far each night. Given the same situation I admit that I would not have done much better. As I released the 'possum and watched it crawl weakly back into its hole, I could not help but feel sorry for it. I came back later that day and left a handful of cat food at the mouth of the den as an offering—maybe that would help tide the critter over till warmer weather.

As I think about it, a human (without equipment) and a 'possum are on fairly equal terms when it comes to survival in the woods. Neither can run fast. To escape enemies, they both can climb trees, but not very well. They both have an omnivorous diet—generally eating whatever is available to them, including fruits, grains, seeds, insects, meat, poultry, garbage, and junk food. The 'possum prefers its meat fresh, but it will eat meat that is more spoiled than most modern humans would consider acceptable. Theron told me of the time he came across the well-rotted carcass of a cow that had died in a pasture. When he kicked the carcass, two 'possums ran out from the inside of the body cavity. This experience made him lose his taste for eating 'possum. Those 'possums, once they had found a dependable food source, simply "moved in." Had they not been disturbed, they might have stayed there for weeks continually eating, sleeping, and enjoying the fragrance of their edible lodging. This is not unlike the behavior of humans who create boomtowns in order to "feed" off of a nearby natural resource until it is depleted.

The 'possum has a certain primal toughness. Humans are somewhat frailer than 'possums, but they have brain power which, combined with the opposable thumb, gives them the ability to improvise upon the environment and to make and use tools and weapons. Because of this, humans have become a very successful mammal species in the brief seven hundred thousand or so years that we have been inhabiting the earth, and we will likely remain so until we deplete or despoil the natural resources upon which we depend. 'Possums have been fairly successful, too. They have been around for many millions of years. They were here long before we humans appeared, and they just might remain here long after we're gone—sniffing and drooling and shuffling along.

18

Advanced 'Possumology

One bright May morning I was walking down a wooded road listening to birdcalls, when I heard a raspy clicking sound I could not identify. It had a distressed and urgent quality to it, but as much as I scanned the trees, I could not locate it. Then I looked down and my eye caught some movement. On the ground in front of me was a very distraught baby opossum. It was about four inches long with sooty gray fur, "shoe-button" eyes and tiny pink hands and feet. Its delicate ears and naked tail were black on the parts close to the body and pink on the extremities. As I watched, it backed away on wobbly legs, giving me that characteristic toothy grimace known as the "'possum grin."

I gingerly picked it up by the tail and looked underneath—a little girl 'possum. She must have fallen off her mother's back the night before, and she was very upset about it. I didn't know

"On the ground in front of me was a baby 'possum…"

what I could do to relieve her distress. What could I offer that would replace the security of her dear mother's back? I thought about it for a minute, then I popped her on my head. She immediately grabbed hold of my hair with her miniature clenched fists and quieted right down. There she stayed for most of the next month. I named her Blossom.

When friends saw me walking around with a 'possum on my head, it never took long for them to broach the question, "What happens when she has to…um, er….Do you have to wash your hair often?" In my new role as a surrogate mother, I had quickly learned that a baby 'possum does not soil its mother's fur. Whenever she had to answer "nature's call" she insisted on coming down. She would relieve herself and when finished, she would immediately climb back up onto my head. Once I learned this, you can be sure I

a quiet witness to my every move. I could hike in the woods, work on my car, and cook meals. I was teaching school part-time and continued to do so with Blossom on my head. (The kids loved her.) I need not go into all the details, but there is no limit to what you can do with a 'possum on your head.

As she got larger, she usurped an overalls pocket for her daytime sleeping quarters. Then she moved into a shoulder bag and eventually adopted a padded corner in the house or car. She used a cat litter box better than many cats I know. She was very docile and undemanding. She would sleep all day and for a good portion of the night if all her food needs were met. She was unemotional, and never engaged in any playfulness. There was a beautiful existential purity to her being; an acceptance and lack of attachment in her primitive simplicity. She was truly living in the moment. 'Possums are the quintessential Zen animal: No joy, no sorrow, just pure being.

Blossom and I stayed together for more than a year, but I awoke one morning to find her gone. To my dismay, she had wandered off in the night (without even a note on my pillow), and she never returned. So much for these existential, noncommittal relationships.

"The possum is to be met with no where but in America...and is the wonder of all Land Animals," wrote John Brickell, in 1737. Dr. Brickell was a physician who lived in what is now Edenton, North Carolina, in the early 1730s, before the state was even a colony. In his book *The Natural History of North Carolina*, he described the opossum and offered a number of eighteenth-century interpretations of opossum behavior and lore. In that opening sentence to

always allowed her to come down whenever she wanted to. It is amazing how quickly a primitive 'possum can toilet train a human.

During those first few weeks, Blossom always seemed contented and secure when she was riding on my head and I carried on with my daily activities with her clinging there, his section on opossums he could not have written truer words.

In this modern age of specialization and environmental consciousness, it might behoove us to take a closer look at the humble opossum. Opossums are considered to be the oldest living mammals on the continent. Paleontologists tell us that towards the end of the reign of the dinosaurs, some hundred million years ago, the first mammals that appeared were little opossumlike marsupials. (Marsupials are pouched animals and they are considered as more primitive than the somewhat later-appearing eutherian, or placental, mammals.) This was way back during the Cretaceous period, when North America was still connected to the huge land mass known as Gondwanaland. Sometime after the marsupials appeared, Gondwanaland separated from North America and began to break apart. One section of it, the continent we now know as Australia, drifted with its population of marsupials "down under" to its current position. Another section, Antarctica, whose only known mammalian fossil is a marsupial, moved even farther "under" to the South Pole and became covered with ice.

The oldest known, clearly recognizable, marsupial fossils are from Canada. These and other fossils indicate that North America's marsupials evolved into many forms (at least three families, five genera, and thirteen species); however, all these early marsupials became extinct by fifteen million years ago, possibly because "more advanced" placental mammals came on the scene and the competition got too stiff.

In the meantime, the section we know as South America ended up isolated for millions of years in its present location and its population of marsupials evolved and diversi-

fied into a rich variety of species, including huge catlike and hyenalike carnivores, small insect-eaters, and a whole range of medium-sized omnivores.

Then, from two to five million years ago during the Pliocene, North America and South America were reconnected. This suddenly created a land bridge and opened the door to a massive invasion of bears, cats, wolves, and other placental mammals from north to south. Faced with these superior competitors, all of South America's marsupial carnivores were wiped out. However, many of the smaller marsupial insectivores and omnivores managed to hold on, and today, Central and South America are home to almost eighty species of marsupials—almost a third of the world's total. About seventy of these species are part of Didelphidae, the opossum family. (American opossums are not closely related to any of the Australian families of 'possums.)

As South America was being "invaded" by animals from the north, only one marsupial managed to go northward against the flow, and that was the common opossum (*Didelphis marsupialis*). It spread north and colonized Mexico. Then, between one million and seventy-five thousand years ago, during the climatic fluctuations brought on by the North American ice ages, a new species that we know today as the Virginia opossum (*Didelphis virginiana*) diverged from the common opossum and spread north into what is today the southeastern United States.

The opossum still seems to be going against the flow. In the last century, while human population growth, habitat destruction, and industrialization have endangered and extirpated countless species, the opossum has expanded its range to the Pacific states and northward into British Columbia and Ontario, Canada. Opossums can survive in an amazing variety of habitats, from sea level to nine thousand feet above and from vast wilderness areas to downtown business districts. While in other parts of the world the more highly evolved marsupials are rapidly succumbing to pressures from human populations, here in America, Brer 'Possum seems to be rubbing elbows with humanity and actually thriving.

Even though the opossum has now moved north, it is still a southerner at heart (or bodily at least), and it has not quite adapted to its new territory. Most northern opossums, and even some that live in the higher altitudes in the southern Appalachians, lose the tips of their naked tails and ears to frostbite.

In spite of the millions of years that have elapsed since the opossum first made its appearance in the world, the "modern" opossum has retained essentially the same generalized form, habits, and intelligence as its first Cretaceous ancestor that appeared during the end of the Age of Reptiles. In North America, its very generality seems to have been the opossum's key to success. Had the opossum become specialized for a particular type of habitat, food, or behavior, it probably would have had to compete with other, more intelligent, placental mammals and would have lost out.

When Dr. Brickell called the opossum "a very stupid Creature," he was probably not the first, and certainly not the last, person to refer to opossums as slow-witted. Scientists do not like to use the word "stupid," but they will all agree that the opossum has a very low "EQ" (encephalization quotient), that is, very few brains for its size. This EQ was clearly illustrated in the classic "'possum-coon, bean-brain experiment" that is often cited in early opossum literature to indicate its intelligence in comparison to that of a raccoon. The investigators obtained a similar-sized

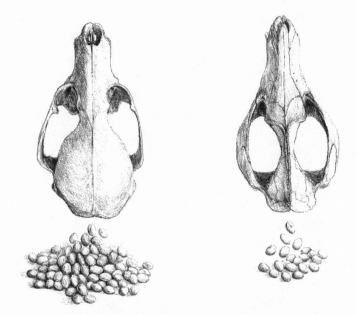

"The Great 'Possum and 'Coon Bean Brain Experiment."

skull of each animal. They filled each skull with beans, and then counted the beans that each skull held. The raccoon's skull held 150 beans and the opossum's skull held 21.

Very little of the opossum's head is occupied with brains. Where the raccoon has brains, the opossum has muscle. The 'possum is the original "meat-head" and good meat it is.

Beulah Perry, an eighty-year-old black woman who was interviewed in the Foxfire books, talked about growing up in the piedmont of South Carolina in the early 1900s. "When I was a kid," she said, "the 'possum head was my favorite. Mother would pay me to do things [by saying], 'Now Beulah, if you do so and so, I'll leave the 'possum head on.' When it got done, she'd cut that head off and give it to me."[2]

Scientists say that opossums have a "limited behavioral repertoire" in that they "do not display complex avoidance responses" in the face of danger. Dr. Brickell explains it more simply, saying that opossums are "altogether negligent of their own Safety, and never strive to flee from their Enemies as it is natural for all other wild Beasts to do."

Opossums have no specialized escape mechanisms. They can climb trees, but they can often be shaken out. They are not fast runners. I have caught many of them after only a short chase.

The most famous defensive behavior of the opossum is, of course, "playing 'possum." (A predator may do less physical harm to a prey animal that seems dead—or it may put it down with the intention of eating it later, only to come back to find its "dead" prey gone.) Dr. Brickell noted the phenomenon and described it this way: "They are hard to kill, for I have known their skulls smashed and broken in pieces, so that they seemed to be quite dead, yet in a few hours they will recover and creep about again."

Among southerners, this behavior is referred to as "sulling up." (As far as I can tell this is a rare verb form of the adjective sullen.) In scientific circles this deathlike condition is known as the "opossum state." Its exact nature has stimulated a great deal of speculation and some scientific investigation, often with contradictory conclusions.

One investigation actually seems to shed more light on the mind of the scientist than it does on the mind of the opossum. Noting that opossums are most commonly induced to play 'possum when grabbed and shaken by a dog, these innovative scientists constructed an artificial dog jaw—a large plierlike apparatus with two jaws that clamped down on the unfortunate opossum. The jaws were then vigorously vibrated, while at the same time recordings of dog barks played over a loudspeaker. Electrodes were implanted on the opossums' skulls so that they could be monitored with an electroencephalograph. (Truly an Orwellian nightmare for any opossum.) When first attacked, the opossum would hiss and growl and try to fight back at the unstoppable mechanical jaw, but then, suddenly, its activity would cease, and the animal would keel over and seem to be dead for as long as two or three minutes. Electroencephalograph records taken before, during, and after this artificially induced opossum state showed no change, except perhaps a heightened arousal level. It was even tried with real dogs and still found no difference in their brain waves during this state and after recovery. These researchers concluded that possums really are just "playing 'possum."[3]

Most other scientific studies, however, conclude the opposite—that the opossum state is not really a "feint" but a true "faint."

I think the opossum state might have two phases. Those scientists with the mechanical dog jaw might have been monitoring only the first phase, which is a sort of deep cringe where the animal remains semiconscious. In the second phase, the opossum conks out into the true oblivion of a genuine catatonic state. In this phase, the body is limp, its heartbeat and breathing are barely perceptible, its salivation increases to a steady drool, it loses bowel control, and it does not respond to rough handling or painful stimulii (even when its eyeballs are touched). It may remain in this state for as long as a few hours or as little as a few minutes. Dr. Brickell reported, "...it is a common saying in Carolina, that if a Cat has nine Lives, a Possum has nineteen."

While in this state, it can withstand a great deal of abuse

and injury. Cahalane reports that of ninety-five opossum skeletons examined in one study, thirty-nine had broken bones that had completely healed. One had survived two broken shoulders, eleven broken ribs (some of the ribs were broken in two or three places) and a badly damaged spinal column.[4]

Another factor in the opossum's success as a species is its high reproductive rate. A female usually raises two litters a year. The sex life and reproduction of the opossum is the source of some of the most bizarre facts, fictions, and folklore in the animal kingdom.

Take, for example, the gestation period of an opossum. For comparison, an elephant's is twenty-three months, a human's is nine months, and a cat's is two months: an opossum's is an incredible thirteen days! This means that when a baby opossum is born, it wasn't even a "gleam in its daddy's eye" two weeks before! ('Possums have notoriously short courtships.)

Though the male opossum lacks a pouch, he is also uniquely endowed when it comes to reproduction. His penis is a forked, or bifurcated, double ender. The two ends are known as *hemi-penes* (half-penises) to wry wildlife biologists. The color is a bluish purple! ("Purple as a 'possum's cod" is a favorite Appalachian folk expression.)

There is one outstanding story about the opossum's sex life that has been told as true many times. It is a unique example of deductive folk reasoning. Folks have noticed the two-ended penis of the male opossum, but have found no corresponding, appropriately located double opening in the female. So the story is that, during the sex act, the male copulates with the female in her nose and she impregnates herself with a sneeze!

The truth is that opossums mate like most other ani-mals. But unlike other animals, the female has a double uterus with two cervices (the generic name, *Didelphis* means double-womb) and the male's bifurcated penis is to better service her. (Now you know what 'possums are always grinning about.)

The male opossum not only has a double copulatory organ but his sperm travel in pairs as well. While still in the testes, two sperm conjugate and swim together through the female reproductive tract and then separate in the oviduct. This is believed to allow exceptionally good sperm efficiency, transport, and survival. The male inseminates the female with only about 3 million sperm, some 5 percent of which reach the site of fertilization; in comparison, a male rabbit inseminates the female with about 150 million, of which .01 percent reach the site of fertilization. As solitary as opossums may be, when they do pair off they get the job done efficiently.

Thirteen days (plus or minus six hours) after conception, anywhere from two to a few dozen baby opossums are born. They look like tiny, translucent preemies, which is actually what they are: quite literally, they are embryos. Each is about half an inch long and weighs less than .2 grams (about the same as a paper match). This is about one ten-thousandth of the body weight of the mother. (A human baby born in the same proportion to the size of its mother would be about the size of a nickel.) They are blind and deaf and have skeletons of cartilage, an incomplete central nervous system, as well as undeveloped, and barely functional, circulatory, respiratory, and digestive systems.

However, these infants are endowed with precociously developed muscular mouth parts and strong front limbs, complete with tiny deciduous claws (which drop off once they are in the safety of the pouch). These are put to use as soon as the infant is born, when it makes its way across the two inches of wet belly fur between the birth canal and the mother's pouch. Using a peculiar swimming motion (sometimes referred to as the Australian crawl), the newborn opossum must travel this distance into the pouch without any maternal help. If the infant falls off or misses the pouch, it is lost. There is no provision in the mother's primeval brain for the rescue of fallen babes. Observers of opossum births report that as many as 40 percent of the young may never reach the pouch.

Once in the pouch, the ordeal is not yet complete. The tiny opossum must locate one of the thirteen pinhead-sized nipples. These are arranged in a horseshoe shape, with six on each side and one in the middle. If all the active nipples are already occupied, it will perish. If the infant does find a nipple, its problems are over until it is about two months old, ready to leave the pouch and ride along with its siblings on the mother's back. (They do not hang with their tails wrapped around hers.) "The young ones...remain sporting in and out of this false Belly till they are able to fend for themselves," Dr. Brickell reported. They are completely weaned and on their own shortly after their third month.

By carrying her young with her, the female opossum has advantages over other mammals in that she can cover a larger foraging territory than she would if she had to return to her den to feed her young every day.

Recently, scientists have learned that opossums control the sex ratios of their offspring in a way that will ensure optimal reproductive success. Though nobody understands how this works, it has been proven that well-fed female opossums in good physical condition will produce more males than their hungrier, weaker sisters. Females that are

'Possum Mother and Infants.

not in good condition will give birth to more female young. This makes sense biologically because male opossums, like many mammals, generally have more than one mate and contribute little parental care. Females, no matter how small, usually do not lack mates and all the females are likely to reproduce, but none will produce as many offspring as the most successful males (who can mate with several females). Weak males, however, may end up with no mates or offspring. So it is advantageous for the strong and healthy mother (capable of high reproductive investment) if she is going to produce stronger and larger young anyway, to produce litters primarily of males. It's also advantageous for less well nourished, or older mothers capable of little reproductive investment, to produce more females. Both these reproductive strategies maximize the spread of their own genes in future generations.

When it comes to reproduction, these so-called primitive beasts are quite sophisticated—and they have to be. It was recently learned that most opossums do not live through more than one breeding season. For their size, opossums are one of the shortest-lived animals in the world. In the past, scientists trying to study opossums were perpetually frustrated because most of the animals they tagged seemed to disappear. Now they know they just died. The few opossums that do live into their second year show many of the classic signs of advanced aging, such as cataracts, weight loss, and lessened motor coordination.

In spite of their apparent primitiveness, it seems that opossums are not exactly living fossils. They do manifest some recently evolved traits and special skills. In spite of their small brain, they have a remarkable talent for finding food and remembering where they found it. When tested for the ability to remember which of four runways was connected to a food box, opossums scored better than cats, dogs, goats, pigs, rabbits, rats, and turtles, though not as well as humans. They can remember the taste of a toxic mushroom a year after a single encounter.

Opossums are immune to the venom of pit vipers (Crotalidae). When an opossum is bitten by a rattlesnake, copperhead, water moccasin, or various other species of tropical pit vipers, it reacts with only a small local swelling, like we might receive from a bee sting. In some parts of the country, in fact, poisonous snakes are an important part of the opossum's diet. Scientists believe that this is a relatively recent adaptive trait, as this immunity does not extend to the venom of Old World snakes like cobras and puff adders.

When I first learned of this immunity I told an old mountain man about it. He thought about it for a minute and said, "You know, that'd be quite the thing if they could take a little 'possum blood and mix it with human blood and make it so people would be immune to snake bites, too." Then he added reflectively, "Yeah, buddy, that'd be somethin' if they could do that. The only thing is that after they got a shot of that stuff, folks'd be drooling all the time at the corner of the mouth!"

Opossum legends and myths are common among many native American groups from the eastern woodlands to the South American jungles. Some tribes view the opossum with little esteem. According to one Cherokee friend of mine, before the white man introduced his complex obscenities, the worst thing one Cherokee could call another was "'possum manure." The Catawbas referred to the opossum with a word that translates as "He who slobbers much fluid."

The following story, from the Tacana Indians of Bolivia, demonstrates the ultimate in the disdain and repugnance with which an opossum can be viewed. They say the opossum was created by a vengeful vulture who flew over an old woman and covered her so thickly with its droppings that she was bent double and could waddle only with great difficulty. The vulture then threw her to the ground, tore out her hair, and used his feces to stick her hair all over her body. Again using his excrement as glue, he affixed a young snake's tail to the unfortunate woman's buttocks. The woman shrank to the size of an opossum. (Wouldn't you, too?!) The vulture then picked up a root, chewed it, and spat it onto the opossum's fur to dye it yellow. (Bolivian opossums are yellowish.) He made her face into an opossum's snout by sticking on a palm bud.

As a contrast, however, the opossum plays an important role in the creation mythology of the Apapocuvas of the Amazon basin. It is viewed with considerably more warmth

Dr. Brickell's 1737 illustration of the 'possum.

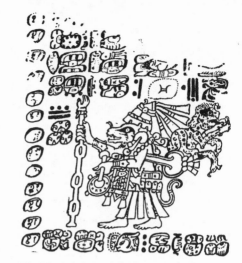

The Mayans depicted the 'possum as a bearer deity in the Dresden Codex.

The 'possum as depicted in the Florentine Codex (circa 1580).

and respect by the people of this tribe, as the following myth illustrates:

> In the beginning, it is told, the first two Apapocuva were born as twins, but their mother died shortly thereafter. The "elder" of the twins was at a loss to feed his little brother, who was still at the breast. So he begged the opossum to help him and the latter, before taking on the task of wet nurse, was careful to lick her chest clean of offensive secretions. As a reward for its service, the opossum was given the marsupial pouch and promised that henceforth she would give birth painlessly.

According to the hieroglyphic codices left by the Aztec and Mayan civilizations, the opossum played an important role. In the Dresden Codex, the Mayans depict opossums as bearer deities called *mams*. (No doubt this was derived from the opossum's habit of carrying its young on its back.) These mams appeared during the last five days of each year and they carried on their backs the prognostications for the new year.

According to the Florentine Codex, the Aztecs not only considered the opossum to be good eating, but the tail was used as a remedy. Made into a tea or salve, it was used as "medicine which expels" to treat everything from splinters to constipation! For difficulty in childbirth, "a little chia seed [and water] is mixed with opossum tail, just a little, perhaps one-half the length of the little finger." The infusion is drunk and "the little child is born quickly."

If you are inclined to judge the Aztecs harshly for prescribing 'possum-tail tea as a remedy, let us realize that the use of animal parts as medicines has a place in our own medical heritage. In fact the good Doc Brickell himself prescribed certain 'possum parts. He says, "the Testicles given with Honey stir up Lust and cause Conception."

Of course, from ancient times to the present, the opossum has been utilized much more as a source of food than of medicine. Dr. Brickell tells us that "their Flesh is generally fat, white and well tasted, several Persons eat of them (and) prefer them before Pork, but their ugly tails are enough to put one out of Conceit with them."

Since no article on opossums would be complete without at least one 'possum song and recipe, I'll include a ditty that includes both.

Dat 'possum meat is good and sweet
I always finds it good to eat
My dog tree, I went to see—
A great big 'possum in that tree.
I reached up and pulled him in.
And dat ol' 'possum begin to grin.
I took him home and dressed him off.
That night I laid him in the frost.
The way I cooked that 'possum sound
Was first parboiled then baked him brown.
With sweet potatoes in the pan,
T'was the finest eating in all the land.

Should you find yourself in the fortunate position of preparing a 'possum for the table, the above stanzas cover the basic procedure. However, a few of the steps could use some elaboration.

Traditionally, 'possums are caught alive either in a box trap or they are simply shaken or pulled out of a tree after being treed by a dog. Then the 'possum is kept in a cage for several weeks and fed cornbread, buttermilk, sweet potatoes, and apples to fatten it and sweeten the meat.

When it is time to eat the 'possum, it is killed by pinning its neck to the ground with a broom handle, the broom handle is stood upon, and the tail is pulled up strongly until the neck snaps. This is somewhat graphic and difficult to read about for those of us with "Bambi complexes," but I include it here because it is considered the most humane method. A 'possum usually cannot be killed with a swift blow to the head because of the thick layer of muscle that protects its brain. Even a bullet to the head might miss the tiny brain and, of course, would spoil the delicious head meat.

Although the opossum can be skinned and prepared like most other game, many traditional people butcher the opossum like a hog. The animal is dipped in boiling water until the hair loosens and can be scraped off. The skin is scrubbed clean and any remaining hairs are singed over a fire. Then the animal is cleaned. The liver is saved. It is tender and delicious with the gall bladder removed. Two kernel-shaped glands located in the "armpits" of the front legs are removed to help alleviate any gamey flavor. The meat is sometimes soaked in a marinade of salt water, vinegar, spices, and herbs. Some people flavor the meat with fresh spicewood (*Lindera benzoin*) twigs. The twigs are sharpened and inserted in the meat "till it looks like a porcupine." After soaking it, as the poem hints, freezing can actually improve the taste. The meat is then parboiled for fifteen to thirty minutes till tender, and then it can be baked, broiled, stewed, barbecued, or fried (any way you would cook chicken). One of my favorite 'possum dishes on those rare occasions when there are leftovers is a 'possum salad sandwich. To make 'possum salad, simply cut up cold cooked 'possum meat and mix it with mayonnaise, chopped celery, pickles, sprouts, tofu, or any other ingredients you would use to make chicken or tuna salad. Because it can be greasy, many people say 'possum reminds them of pork, but I think it tastes more like lamb.

For a number of years in the 1970s, "Eat More 'Possum" bumper stickers were common on many southern automobiles. However, few know that the origin of this catchy slogan is directly traceable to the 'Possum Growers and Breeders Association of America, Inc. The Association, which boasts a membership of over forty thousand, has its headquarters in Clanton, Alabama, where Frank Basil Clark presides as its international president. Clark says he was born and raised in Hanging Dog, a small community out in the far western tip of North Carolina, but he has lived in Alabama since well before the

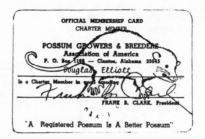

inception of the 'Possum Association. In 1978, I arranged to meet him in Clanton's city hall, where I learned that, along with his duties as president of the 'Possum Growers and proprietor of the town's only drive-in theater, he was also mayor of this bustling central Alabama town of six thousand.

"Yes, it seems my work is never done," he confided. "I'm mayor from nine to five, I run the theater from five to midnight and slop my 'possums from midnight till dawn." Mayor Clark sports a sleek handlebar mustache and snakeskin cowboy boots. He is a blend of southern "good ol' boy," deadpan comedian, and shrewd politician.

"When you join our organization, your whole life is gonna change," he told me emphatically. "You'll be able to do twice as much in half the amount of time and you'll find that you can do things that you never thought possible before you became a member. Now, here's how it works. You know our motto, don't you?"

"'A registered 'possum is a better possum!'" I answered proudly. (I had been a member for a few months.)

"That's right. Well, once you can accept that, you can accept anything, and once you can accept anything, there's no limit to what you can do. Yessir buddy, it stirs your brain up like plowing new ground, like stirring it with a stick. You can think different!"

He pointed out that membership is not open to just anyone, that indeed there are strict criteria that one must meet in order to join. The most noteworthy of these is that members must "prove that they can raise a 'possum to maturity without eating said 'possum." "And not everyone can do that," the Mayor added.

Some rather prestigious people are members, among them Jimmy Carter (who was president at the time) and former president Richard Nixon. He said that Carter became a member before he ever ran for the presidency. But once he became a member, Clark recalls, he said, "I'll just have to go up there and get them Republicans out of Washington!"

"That's all right, Jimmy," Clark had said. "You got the power to do so now." And the rest is history.

"Now, as for ol' Richard—well, being a member of the 'Possum Breeders saved his life! When that Watergate thing started, what did he do? Why he just sulled up! Yep, he played 'possum! And they'd a hung him sho' nuff if he hadn't." I guess the rest of that is history as well.

I spent most of the afternoon with the gracious mayor while he regaled me with the most detailed and voluminous account of 'possum esoterica that I have ever run across. This intensive course in "'possumology," as the mayor calls it, covered everything from the most intimate details of 'possum courtship (like how you can tell if a sow 'possum is in heat—"'Possums are always grinning," he said, "so when that grin breaks into a smile, she's in heat and that's when you put her in with the boar"), to some early American history detailing how the 'possum got its name—"It was Cap'n John Smith that named 'em o-possum 'cause he heard the

Indians point at 'em and say, 'uhh...'possum, uhh... 'possum." Them Indians grunted a lot y'see and ol' Cap'n Smith thought they was from Ireland. So he called 'em o'possum. The real name is just 'possum."

Well, after all this, I finally had to say it: "Mayor Clark, are you really serious about this? I mean is there really such a thing as a 'possum ranch?"

"Yessir, we're dead serious," he said solemnly. "We think we might have the answer to the world's food problems."

Mayor Clark and Jimmy Carter at a meeting of the Possum Growers and Breeders Association.

He made a phone call and arranged for a tour of his buddy Curtis Smith's 'possum ranch that evening.

As we drove over, he told me that Curtis had just sold off most of his possums and he had only a dozen or so left. (These were his breeding stock.) But at least I would get an idea of the layout of the place.

Curtis greeted us as we pulled into the driveway of his modern brick ranch house and escorted us to a wooded grove where the 'possum cages were arranged around and in a barn. While he went from cage to cage, feeding and watering the animals, he explained that he was now getting fifty dollars apiece (the highest prices ever) for his "registered" possums.

"That's about eight dollars a pound for the meat," I calculated. "Who can 'eat more 'possum' at those prices?"

"We can't even afford to eat them anymore," Clark lamented. "Medical research labs are buying them up as fast as we can produce 'em."

Apparently, because of its unusual life cycle, its embryonic young, and its easily induced catatonia, the opossum has become an important experimental animal for medical and psychiatric researchers who are studying ways to combat birth defects, psychological disorders, and other diseases in humans. Registered 'possums, since they are raised in captivity, are healthy, easy to handle, and have pleasant dispositions.

"There's nothing sweeter than a peach-fed 'possum," said Clark.

Curtis Smith had also been successful in the political arena. He was a newly elected Alabama state representative. He, of course, attributed his political success to his involvement with the 'Possum Growers and Breeders Association. Both he and Clark summed it up this way: "If you put your 'possum first, everything else will fall right into place."

What Frank Clark and Curtis Smith are to 'possums as livestock, Craig and Fanny Phillips are to 'possums as household pets. When I was in the Washington, D.C., area I gave the Phillipses a call on the phone.

"Yes, indeed, we are 'possum people," Fanny assured me cheerily. "We only have four 'possums now, but we have had as many as nine. How we love the little creatures! How nice it is that you called at this time because Craig and I were just planning on having all of our 'possum friends over this Sunday afternoon for a Didelphorama, that is, a

Successful politicians Frank Clark(left) and Curtis Smith proudly display Beauregard and Stonewall Jackson, two handsome, world champion, registered stud 'possums.

'possum-party-on-the-lawn. We'd love to meet your little Blossom. She sounds terribly sweet. Could you both come?"

"We wouldn't miss it for the world," I assured her. When the big day arrived, I brushed Blossom's hair, scrubbed her tail, and put on her best neckerchief. We piled into the ol' V-Dub and followed the directions into the shady, tree-lined streets of a swanky suburban Silver Spring (Maryland) neighborhood. The house was unmis-

takable because in front it had a 'possum coat-of-arms. "*Ergo possum*" read the inscription.

I braced myself and knocked. The door flew open and a voice said, "Oh, Blossom's here!" We were graciously ushered into a casual gathering of people sipping beer and iced tea and munching snacks. I was handed a small dish of grapes. I took a few and tossed them into my mouth simultaneously realizing that I had just committed my first faux pas. The grapes were for the 'possums!

And 'possums there were! Sniffing, slobbering, and shuffling about, courting and quarreling, climbing over the furniture, peeing in the corner, gobbling grapes with bulging cheeks, great smacking lips, and vacant gazes. There were roly-poly, indulgent, suburban opossums, some so fat that their eyes bulged. There were wiry wild opossums, light-furred opossums, and dark-furred opossums. One was named Whitesocks because he had white "leggings" and another was named Butterfly because of her large floppy ears. Chasmo was the largest, weighing some thirty pounds. He lay in his owner's arms panting and snoring with his head on her shoulder and his two long snaggly canine teeth protruding down on either side of his hoary snout.

Blossom was the smallest. Just coming into the bloom of adolescence at about four pounds, all agreed that she was indeed the fairest of them all (and the best

Fanny Phillips holds Chasmo.

dressed until she wriggled out of her ker-chief).

The 'possum people were as diverse as their pets: doctors, lawyers, scientists, office workers, musicians, homemakers, and hippies. Snatches of their conversations drifted in and out of my consciousness as I tried to grasp the scene.

"And how did you get your 'possum?"

"You mean our first 'possum?"

"Oh…yes, of course."

"Well, our first 'possum came walking up out of the basement with a rat trap on its head. We knew there was something down there! My husband took the trap off its little head and put it in a box with a dish of milk thinking that we'd have to bury it in the morning. Well, the next morning it had drunk all the milk and was in the corner of the box grinning at us…."

"Yes, our 'possums come when we call, 'Kitty-kitty.'"

"Oh, isn't that nice. Mine never answers to anything…."

"You know, our poor Wiley died two weeks ago. He was suffering from severe arthritis in his hindquarters. He couldn't even move his back legs, poor dear. He just lay in his box all day. I used to take him out on the lawn in the evenings and hold his hindquarters up by the tail. Like a little furry wheelbarrow he was. Even in his last days, he would have a marvelous time sniffing around and drooling over everything…"

"I've read that 'possums eat frogs and insects in the wild

"Of course when you walk a 'possum, you mostly stand around…"

but I don't think mine could hardly catch a slug!"

"One veterinarian, when I told him I had a sick 'possum in my bag, refused to even look at it! I guess the Hippocratic oath doesn't apply to opossums…."

"When my 'possum was little, he would sleep in my trouser pocket and whenever I entered the room, no matter how many people were there, this old girlfriend of mine would always say in her most sultry, Mae West voice, 'Hey, big boy is that a 'possum in your pocket or are you glad to see me?!'"

"Yes, we found these small dog harnesses work quite well for walking opossums. Of course, when you walk a 'possum, you mostly stand around…."

On and on it went into the afternoon. A few of us posed for a group portrait on the lawn. Toward evening, things started to wind down. I prepared to leave and thanked the Phillipses for a delightfully different afternoon. They each gave Blossom a farewell buss on the ear and we departed. Yes, we wouldn't have missed it for the world!

1 John Brickell, *The Natural History of North Carolina* (Murfreesboro, N.C.: Johnson Publishing 1968), p. 125-126.

2 Eliot Wigginton, ed., *Foxfire 3* (Anchor Press/Doubleday, Garden City, N.Y.: 1975), p. 404.

3 Science and the Citizen, *Scientific American* (December, 1964), p. 64.

4 Victor Cahalane, *Mammals of North America* (New York: Macmillan Co., 1947), p. 107-108.

19

Matching the Hatch

A Twentieth-Century Fish Story

The hatchery truck just delivered a batch of five hundred fingerling rainbow trout for our pond. This is the second year that my wife, Yanna, and I have raised trout. Even though our pond is spring fed, it is still somewhat marginal as a habitat for trout. Trout need cool, highly oxygenated water—the kind of water found in rushing mountain streams and cold northern lakes. Our pond water gets warm in summer—great for swimming but too warm for a large population of trout. So we stock the pond with young four-inch fish in October. We feed them commercial feed all during the cooler months and harvest them in May and June as handsome thick-bodied creatures with a rosy blush down their twelve- to fifteen-inch glistening silver flanks. They weigh a pound or more each and make absolutely

Rainbow Trout

delicious eating however they are cooked. Sometimes we bake or broil them. Occasionally, we poach them with ginger, garlic, and soy sauce, and other times we grill them over hickory charcoal with a dash of barbecue sauce.

Last spring, when the water was still cool, the trout were growing fast and they were ravenous. It seemed like you could stand there all day throwing feed at them and they would never stop their frenzied churning of the water as they greedily devoured those pellets.

They sure loved their Purina Trout Chow. We bought it in fifty-pound bags from the local feed store. By reading the ingredient list on the bags, we learned that these feed pellets contain fish meal, soybeans, corn, brewer's yeast, a dozen or two vitamin and mineral supplements with, of course, the ever-present preservative or two added to protect freshness.

Preservatives! Isn't that ironic? Here we were trying to clean up our diet and raise our own food, so we could avoid all the preservatives in grocery-store foods, and it turned out that we were feeding those same preservatives to the fish that were going to feed us.

So we thought that we might try to get our trout on a natural foods diet. We figured that a fish that had been eating worms, bugs, and other natural fare would be a healthier fish than one raised on an exclusive diet of manufactured pellets. This fish might be heathier for us to eat and perhaps even taste better.

Rather than spend our days running through the fields flailing insect nets or furiously digging for grubs and earthworms under the compost piles, we decided we would cultivate fish worms. We ordered some Georgia Wriggler red worms from none other than the Carter Worm Farm in Plains, Georgia. It seemed like a poetic and wholistic idea to feed our household garbage to the worms and then feed the worms to the trout, and thereby turn our household garbage into healthy, high-protein, gourmet dinners.

A thousand one-inch worms arrived one day in a container half the size of a shoe box. We released them into a bin full of leaves, vegetable parings, and other organic garbage, which was situated right next to the trout pond. Every day, we would add more garbage and the worms began to grow. When some of the worms attained "eating"

size, we selected a few fat, lively ones, carried them to the edge of the pond, and prepared to watch the action.

We tossed the first one into the expectant school of trout. And then another. And another. We noticed something strange happening. As soon as a worm hit the water, fish came streaking towards it from all directions. But when they realized that it was not a pellet of trout chow but something as weird and unfamiliar as a worm, they would just glide right on by. The worm would slowly sink down, inch by inch, right in the midst of this school of hungry trout. Wild trout love worms, but these fish were so accustomed to pellets that they didn't even recognize a worm as food!

However, before the worm hit bottom, an ancient, atavistic memory would usually awaken in one of the fish. In a streak of quivering silver, a trout would erupt from the edge of this unthinking mass of totally conditioned, worm-naive, fish flesh and that slowly sinking worm would become fish food. We waited to see if the hundredth monkey phenomenon* would occur: When enough of them learned to recognize a worm, would this knowledge automatically be transferred to the whole population and would they all suddenly recognize a worm as food? But this never seemed to happen before the water warmed up and the fish stopped eating.

As soon as word filtered out that our trout were getting large, friends offered to bring their fishing rods and help us harvest. One day, a fellow came with his fly rod and a tackle box full of flies. He tried dry flies and wet flies of various

*The hundredth monkey concept is derived from the observations of biologists who were working with populations of monkeys on small islands in the Pacific. They supposedly observed that once a critical number of individuals ("the hundredth monkey") had learned a set of behaviors, this new knowledge would automatically be conveyed through the entire species—even to monkeys living on remote islands separated from the others. This concept has been popularly embraced as a metaphor for world peace.

shapes and colors, but nothing seemed to work. It is amazing how narrow and finely honed a trout's perception of appropriate food can be. This is, of course, the challenge of trout fishing. We eventually tied a small #10 treble hook on to his line and wedged one of the pellets into the tines of the hook. We managed to catch a few that way—but it was still quite difficult. The weight of the hook caused the pellet to sink unnaturally and the trout were reluctant to bite this suspicious morsel. In fact, the only way it worked with any consistency was to toss in a handful of feed first. If the pellet with the hook was dropped into the midst of the ensuing frenzy, a trout would often take it. As the water warmed, fishing for these trout became more and more difficult, so when it came time for a serious harvest, we resorted to a seine net. After each harvest, we clean and freeze several months supply and divide them among friends. Sometimes we smoke a few dozen. These smoked trout keep well and we use them as travel or camping food.

After our fish were harvested that summer, I thought little about trout until I went on a camping trip along the Beaverkill River in the Catskill Mountains of upstate New York. The Catskills are where fly-fishing in America was born, and there is still a strong fly-fishing tradition in the area. Anglers know the Beaverkill as one of the best trout rivers in the East. Many times during the warmer months, hatches of mayflies, stoneflies, and other aquatic insects rise from its clear rushing waters to mate, lay eggs, and fall back into the water to become food for hungry wild trout.

Fly-fishing enthusiasts stalk the waters with extensive collections of carefully tied flies, trying to "match the hatch"—to select just the right-sized hook, adorned with just the proper combination of feathers, thread, and hair to duplicate the shape and color of the insects that are hatch-

Black Gnat

Black Gnat Fly

Epeorus Mayfly

Quill Gordon Fly

Grasshopper

Grasshopper Fly

Sculpin

Muddler Minnow Fly

ing during that particular hour of the day. These could be dry flies as tiny as the Black Gnat, as distinctive as the Quill Gordon, which is tied to resemble a particular species of tawny mayfly *(Epeorus pleuralis)*, or as large and obvious as the Grasshopper, with its yellow cotton body and its straight turkey-quill wings. Wet flies are also used. Unlike dry flies, these flies are allowed to sink. They are made to resemble various underwater nymphal insects and other creatures. A favorite Catskill wet fly, the Muddler Minnow, has a trimmed wad of tan deer hair at the front, with mottled feathers and squirrel-tail hair trailing behind. It is made to imitate a sculpin, a small bottom-dwelling fish.

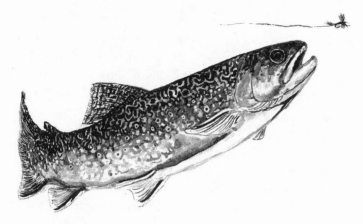

Brook Trout

A trout fly must be "presented" in such a way that it lands naturally in the pool. If it is a dry fly, it must be cast so that it will float naturally on the surface and not be dragged in any unnatural way by the current. A wet fly must be fished with just the right twitching action at the rod's tip in order to imitate the movements of an underwater creature. Foiling the finely tuned instincts of a wily and cautious wild trout is no simple matter. A trout fisherman must not only be tuned in to the fish he is trying to catch, but also to the nuances of the environment in which the fish lives.

Should you ever manage to catch a wild trout, I know of no better way to prepare it than to skewer it on a green sapling of sweet-flavored wood (such as maple or spicebush) and cook it over the coals of a small hardwood fire right next to the stream.

Most of the Beaverkill River where I was camping is owned and posted by long-established trout-fishing clubs. Their primarily male members seek relaxation and renewal by wading the clear bubbling waters with finely crafted split-bamboo fly rods in pursuit of nature's most elegant fish. They find a pulse-quickening euphoria in the feel of a dancing arc of bamboo enlivened by the desperate life and death struggles of a trout on the other end of a thin strand of synthetic line.

Even the line on the fly-fishing reel is the product of decades of tradition, experimentation, craftsmanship, and industrial technology. Most of the reel is filled with a braided nylon fly-casting line. It is the weight of this line that carries the fly in its intended direction. The last six feet or so of line, made of a synthetic polymer, is a nearly invisible monofilament leader tied directly to the fly. This leader is as thin as possible so as not to interfere with the natural appearance of the fly. Because it is so delicate this threadlike line also serves to prolong the fisherman's moment of ecstasy after the trout engulfs the fly, by making it impossible to quickly "horse" the fish in. The fisherman must carefully "play" the fish until it is exhausted and can be landed. In this way the landing of even a small trout can be drawn out into an epic encounter of mythic proportions—complete with a startling strike, spectacular leaps, long runs, and dogged struggles before the exhausted, quivering being, bearing all the colors of the rainbow and the subtle pearlescent glow of a winter sunset, is gently slid into the landing net.

For many fishermen, the power and intensity of this moment holds a greater allure than the sumptuous flesh of the trout. It is this experience they are fishing for; the trout is often released unharmed to its pool to continue its life. The fisherman, also, will soon return home with a deepened awareness, and the hope that perhaps he might be able to tap into that wildness and meet that same trout again one day. Both the fish and the fisherman go back to

"The landing of even a small trout can be an epic encounter of mythic proportions…"

their lives, but both are changed in a subtle but profound way. The fish will be more wary than ever. For the fisherman, however, this experience is religious in nature. The quest for trout is a quest for God in the sense that a trout provides the fisherman with a link to a wild and pristine place in himself, as well as a connection to nature as the source. Catching a trout puts him in direct contact with the cycle of life and death of which we are all a part.

These club members guard their exclusive fishing rights with the fervor of a religious crusade and their trout with the vigilance of secret-service agents. They manage their section of the stream to create as much prime trout habitat as possible. This can mean bringing in heavy equipment to move boulders and logs in order to dam the stream and create the "natural" pools trout so like to inhabit. The several miles of stream they own is virtually lined with No Trespassing signs, and the land is patrolled by a full-time resident caretaker who has the power to arrest trespassers.

The stream is regularly stocked with full-grown trout. In the last few years, in order to maintain this abnormally large trout population, the club has taken to feeding the trout. Mechanized feeders, hung on cables at several locations over the stream, at certain times release a load of floating trout pellets. Like drowned insects, these pellets drift down the stream, sliding over rocks, bouncing in the eddy currents, and floating on pools, where they are snatched up along the way by hungry, ever-watchful trout. The feeders have timers, so that the trout can be fed on a regular schedule during the week, but they are not fed on weekends to ensure that they will be good and hungry for the club's weekend fishermen.

I asked the club's caretaker if the trout become reluctant to bite an artificial fly after a steady diet of trout pellets.

"No problem," he told me, "We use a pellet fly."

"A pellet fly?"

"Sure, it's made with trimmed deer hair on a number ten hook, like the head on a Muddler Minnow. It works like a charm," he said with a wink.

What an irony that the industrial-age fly-fisherman, who goes to great lengths stocking and feeding the fish as

Trout Chow Pellet

Pellet Fly

well as posting, patrolling, and manipulating the environment, all in a desperate attempt to control and make this wildness accessible, finds that to the extent he controls it, he can no longer attain it. The wildness recedes, and rather than tuning into the nuances of the natural world, he finds himself reduced to matching a mechanized hatch of his own creation.

Another example of the extent to which our culture reveres the trout as a symbol of this precious wildness is illustrated by the struggles of a citizens' environmental group in a Maryland suburb of Washington, D.C. They have been working to protect the pristine watershed of a meandering piedmont stream from development. The wooded floodplain along this stream provides habitat for dozens of species of birds and other animals. The stream itself has been found to have populations of some twenty-five different species of fish, including bass, sunfish, catfish, darters, sculpins, suckers, chubs, shiners, and dace. Some of these fish are good eating sport fish, some are quite beautiful, some are unusual, and a couple species are somewhat rare. But as far as the state wildlife commission was concerned, none of them counted for much. It was only when one of the neighborhood youngsters caught a rainbow trout in the stream that the wildlife commission took notice. Nobody is sure how that trout came to be in the stream. Rainbow trout are not even native east of the Rockies. But the environmentalists quickly learned that if their little stream could support a few trout then it could be classed as a "Use 3" trout water and it would thereby be eligible for the most stringent environmental protections that the state offers. Only a stream that has trout is considered worth protecting. So the environmental group stocked the stream with brown trout. The brown trout is a European fish that

The Brown Trout is a European Fish.

was long ago introduced to this continent. Biologists determined that this was the species most likely to adapt to the conditions of the stream. As of this writing, they are all spending the summer waiting to see if the trout survive.

While we await the outcome of this experiment, I cannot help but marvel at the role the trout plays in our lives. For some of us, the trout is darn good eating. For others, it's great sport. For still others, the trout becomes, like the Holy Grail, a symbolic object of a spiritual quest. And in that peaceful suburban community being engulfed by urban sprawl, the quality of human life for generations to come (not to mention the property values), as well as the health, integrity, and well-being of an entire watershed hinges entirely upon the survival of this highly symbolic non-native fish.

For millennia, the trout has lived its life bathed in clear waters. No matter how we see it, the trout remains...a trout.

20

Mud Turkle Medicine

"My country uncle sure did like turtle meat," our friend was saying. She told us that when she was a young teenager, she and her family would occasionally go out to the farm to visit her slightly eccentric uncle. One weekend when they were visiting, he caught a large snapping turtle and they decided to have it for Sunday dinner. She watched her uncle kill and clean the turtle. When he came to the heart, he carefully lifted it out of the turtle and placed it in the palm of her hand. It looked like a small piece of liver. Then, to her astonishment, it began to move—a slow, unmistakable undulation. And then another. And another. There in the palm of her hand, the heart was still beating. She watched it in awe while her uncle finished cutting up

Snapping Turtle

the meat. Then he put the still-beating heart on a scrap of board in his smokehouse. They carried the panful of turtle meat into the kitchen, where the rest of the folks were chopping vegetables for the soup, washing greens, and mixing up cornbread. Soon the soup and the greens were simmering away on the stove; the cornbread was in the oven, and the table was set.

During the lull while it all was cooking, her uncle took her back out to the smokehouse to look at the heart. It was still beating.

They went back to the house and, before long, the meal was on the table. The turtle soup was delicious. Chunks of meat floated in a rich broth with tomatoes, carrots, and potatoes. She had two helpings. After the dinner dishes

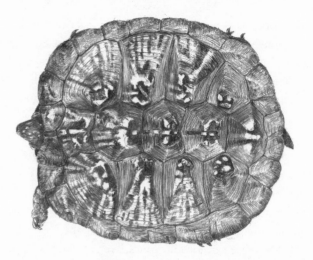

Dancing lady turtle is the Cherokee name for the box turtle because woman dancers tie turtle shell rattles to their ankles. It is said that if you look closely at the patterns on a box turtle's shell, you can see the dancing ladies and many other things as well.

were all cleaned up, she and her uncle returned once more to look at the heart.

As they peered in at the heart, her uncle said, "Look Honey, that turtle's heart is still beating." Then he looked her right in the eye and said, "Now I want to ask you something. Is that turtle you ate for dinner still alive?"

This question was a puzzler for her. She felt the satisfying fullness of Sunday dinner settling in her stomach, and at the same time, she watched the heart of the creature she had eaten continue to beat. It was an important lesson about the interconnectedness of life and death.

There is an old saying among country folks that if you can swallow that snapping turtle's heart while it is still beating, you'll never feel fear again. I can believe that. In fable and in fact, turtles have long been a symbol of steadfastness and longevity. Even the common box turtle has

been known to live more than one hundred years. Just as Aesop's tortoise finishes ahead of the hare through its humility and persistence, the turtle's heart persists in beating long after being removed from its body.

Snapping turtles are great swamp monsters that have always held a special fascination and allure for me. For a number of years in my youth, I knew of no greater sport than turtle hunting. My friends and I would wade the swamps with a gunny sack and a long-handled net or "turtling pole." The best turtle swamps in our area were shallow bodies of water rimmed with cattails and other marsh grasses. The water was usually less than a foot deep over another foot or so of oozy silt, which belched sulfurous bubbles as we slogged through it. This soft bottom was the perfect medium for registering the tracks of submerged turtles. Since snapping turtles are usually active at night, we would start in the morning before the daytime breezes disturbed the waters. We would scan the bottoms of the pools for fresh tracks. When we found a turtle trail, we'd figure out its direction and estimate the turtle's size. We were glad for any turtles we found, whether they were the small ornery mud turtles, ornate painted turtles, or delicate spotted turtles. But the big game—the high adventure—was the snapping turtle. When we found a set of tracks where the left and the right prints were more than a foot apart, we knew we were on the trail of a big one: a true swamp monster. We would follow along as the trail wound its way over the silty bottom, between tussocks of marsh grass and under logs. We probed the mud continuously with our turtle poles, listening for the telltale, hollow-sounding "thunk" of a snapper's shell, and feeling for a slight movement of the beast as it cringed in response to our rude invasion.

Painted Turtle

When we finally located our sequestered quarry, our next task was to determine which way the head was pointing (an essential step) before anyone would dare to reach blindly into the mud to actually grab the turtle. We developed a form of "turtle-pole braille," using the pole to feel around the edge of the turtle's shell for the teeth on the back of the shell. Then, before the beast could turn around, we'd reach down into the mire, feel under the shell for the thick, fleshy, scale-studded tail and pull the furious beast, with its flailing limbs, lunging head, and snapping jaws, out of the mud. Sometimes, a turtle would lose patience with the indignities of our clumsy "braille" process and attempt an escape. It would erupt out of the depths, paddling madly, streaming clouds of silt, heading for the next county, with me and my buddies slogging madly behind in riotous hot pursuit.

I caught quite a few snappers in my youth; some of them were quite large. Sometimes I would keep one in a barrel for a while. I marked and released a number of them and occasionally, I caught hatchlings that I kept as pets. In those days, I never actually had the heart to kill one to eat. It wasn't that I was averse to the idea of eating turtle meat—on a number of occasions I did eat snappers that others had killed. But the turtles I handled just seemed too special to me. They were so large, so powerful, so nonrational, and so tenacious. They were ancient and primordial and untameable. Very little in my life was like that. The idea of this giant beast lurking in the primal ooze, dwelling in the depths of my neighborhood marsh, touched something deep within me. It was like a call from my own depths, reaching me in a way that little else in my life of school, TV, and homework could. I felt like snappers were something precious and that we needed to take care of them.

"[T]here are sermons in stones, aye and mud [snapping] turtles at the bottoms of pools…," Thoreau observed.[1]

Perhaps it is this same mythic turtle that emerges from the depths to form Turtle Island, which is the name by which many Indians refer to the North American continent. Their legends tell of how, a long time ago, the land was formed on the back of a giant turtle.

There was a classic exchange on this subject that has been attributed to the philosopher William James when he interviewed an elderly Indian woman about her spiritual beliefs in the early twentieth century. She told him of how the land rested on the back of a giant turtle.

He asked her what that turtle stood upon.

"Another turtle," she replied.

"And that turtle," he asked, "what is it standing on?"

"Why another turtle, of course," she informed him.

"And that turtle, is it on yet another turtle?" he asked.

"Yes sir," she replied, pleased that he finally seemed to be getting it. "There's turtles all the way down…"

"I wonder if you'd let me put a hook in your pond. I'm wanting to catch me a mud turkle (this is the Appalachian name for the common snapping turtle)," Roy was saying as he looked at the mashed-down grass and mud that marked the trail made by a large snapping turtle when it crossed the narrow spit of land between our two ponds.

Roy was our country neighbor. He came from a long line of "turkle hunters." He said he was "'bout raised on turkle soup." He and his wife, Edith, had been very friendly and welcoming to us when we moved into the neighborhood a few years previously.

Roy had a heart condition. He had undergone heart surgery and had spent several months in the hospital in the last few years. Now he was having serious back trouble and was facing another hospitalization and more surgery. As weak as he was feeling, he dreaded the thought of another major surgical ordeal. He had been taking a dozen different kinds of expensive prescription pills but they only made him feel weaker. He needed something to give him strength. He needed turkle meat. He was going into the hospital the next week, so he needed it soon.

He twisted large hooks onto wire leaders, baited them with fresh chicken liver, and staked them to the bank of the pond. Every day he came and checked the hooks, but the hooks never produced. He often found fresh tracks

There's an old country saying: "If you see a turtle on a fence post, you know it didn't get there by itself."

between the ponds. Roy knew there was a large turtle in there. He was frustrated, disheartened, and disappointed at his failure to catch it. The day he was due at the hospital came too soon and Roy had not gotten his turtle. He and Edith had to drive five hours to the large hospital in Durham and stay overnight in a motel, so they would be there for his appointment the next morning.

When the head surgeon saw Roy's weakened condition and examined his medical records, he realized the risks involved. He told them flatly that surgery would kill Roy. Although they were both somewhat relieved that he didn't have to undergo more surgery, they were profoundly depressed about his poor health. As soon as they got home Roy went straight to bed. When Yanna called that afternoon to check on him, Edith said Roy was feeling pretty low. He was in the bed. He didn't feel like talking to anybody.

Later that afternoon, Yanna heard our dog barking frantically out by the pond. She ran out to see what the dog had found. She was astounded to see a huge snapping turtle. As she approached, the turtle raised up on its thick scaly front legs and faced her. Its powerful jaws gaped. Its sharp, menacing eaglelike beak framed a soft pink gullet.

The dog leapt and danced in front of the turtle, making false attacks and barking frantically while the turtle lunged savagely at the dog. This was Roy's turtle! She wanted desperately to catch it for him, but she had never seen such a large turtle before. She had seen me capture snapping turtles by grabbing the tail, but I was away that week. She didn't know if she could handle this monster by herself. While the dog held the turtle at bay, she found a fifty-five gallon barrel and managed to invert it over the turtle. She then piled heavy rocks on top to hold it down and drove iron stakes into the ground to keep it in place.

Then she ran to the phone and called. Edith answered and as soon as she heard how out of breath Yanna was, Edith interrupted, "What's the matter honey? Are you snake bit?"

"No, I got Roy's turtle! What do I do now?"

"Oh, I don't know. He's still in the bed. I'll go tell him."

In a few minutes Edith came back to the phone. "He says he's a comin' right over. He's a puttin' on his shoes right now," she said in astonishment. A few minutes later Roy arrived.

He had a pair of channel-lock pliers in his back pocket, a cigarette dangling out of the corner of his mouth, and he was carrying a small butcher knife in his hand.

They went over to the turtle and Roy lifted off the barrel and said, "That's that turkle I was tellin' you about. I knew he was a big 'un." He casually reached down, picked it up by the tail, and carried it out into an open area in the yard. "I reckon he'll run eighteen or twenty pounds."

He set it down in the yard and came around to face the turtle's gaping jaws. He adjusted the pliers and expertly clamped them onto the lower jaw and instructed Yanna, "Now, you hold onto them pliers tight and pull hard. If you let go it'll hurt

him worse."

As she grabbed hold of the pliers and looked into the wide-open expressionless eyes of this massive, silent reptile, Yanna held her breath.

Roy unsheathed his butcher knife, grabbed the turtle by the tail and started to pull. Yanna knew she would have to muster a great deal of both psychic and physical strength to be able to hold on to the turtle's jaw with those pliers and literally pull that great beast's head out of its shell.

"Roy, can you stop just a minute? I think I want to say a prayer." She was slightly embarrassed that Roy might think her somewhat strange, but he bowed his head respectfully. She looked into that turtle's eyes through her own watery eyes and said, "Bless you little one. May your flesh, your life, and your spirit give strength, life, and healing to Roy.

"Okay, Roy, I guess I'm ready," she said and held onto those pliers with all her might and they both pulled until the neck was extended. Roy reached around with his sharp knife and expertly severed the neck right behind the head.

Roy flipped the turtle onto its back.

The turtle's jaws were still clamped onto the pliers Yanna held in her hand. Roy removed the disembodied head from the pliers. The jaws still gaped. He placed a stick in the mouth and the jaws snapped onto the stick and held tightly. He handed Yanna the stick with the head attached and told her to go bury it somewhere where the dog couldn't dig it up. The head was too dangerous to leave lying around because it could still bite. She buried it with a large rock on top.

When she got back, Roy was trying to skin the turtle. The headless beast was still kicking and thrashing about, responding to every prick of Roy's knife.

They worked on that turtle, cutting around the upper shell, separating it from the bottom. They used pliers and a great deal of tugging to remove the skin. As they struggled, Yanna was astounded at how much strength and stamina it took to prepare this meat. She was concerned about Roy. She felt like she had pulled him out of his sickbed, and here he was wrestling with a huge, incredibly tough reptile. She brought him over to the shade and set up a table and a chair. Roy appreciated these comforts, but he did not seem to be suffering.

It seemed that the more he worked on this turtle, the better he felt. This experience was strengthening him in some very deep way. As he worked, he talked and talked. He told Yanna about how they used to catch turtles when he was a boy. He told her about the seven kinds of meat in the turtle. He showed her the beef in the back of the shell, the fatty pork around the hind legs, the squirrel and the rabbit meat in the front legs, as well as the chicken, duck, and groundhog meat. There are four kinds of meat in the neck, he explained. He removed the heart and placed it in her hand, and they watched it continue to beat and marveled at the strength of such an animal. He removed the lungs and the liver and carefully set them aside. Yanna scurried about, as busy and attentive as a surgical nurse, sharpening his knife, fetching dishpans and pots, as well as pulling and cutting as he liberated one chunk of flesh after another. She carefully listened to all of Roy's instructions on how to deal with the various internal organs. (She even went so far as to clean out all the intestines—turtle chit'lins. She also saved his "goober." That was Roy's daddy's favorite part.) If this turtle was to be Roy's medicine, she wanted to prepare all the usable parts and make sure it was treated with respect. She froze the liver and those other organs, and later we ran them through a meat grinder and cooked it all up with cornmeal, sage, pepper, and other spices to make "turkle-liver mush" as is the tradition with home-butchered hogs. This liver mush is then pan-fried, like sausage patties.

It took them at least two hours of solid work to get that turtle dressed out. Roy stuck with it the whole time. Yanna parboiled some of the turtle meat and sent him home with it so Edith could make it into soup. He ate some every day for more than a week.

Roy insisted that Yanna keep some of it. So she saved it for me when I came home. Roy and Edith came over and joined us one evening for turtle soup. Roy took me aside and said, "One thing I never will forget is that little Yanna prayin' over that mud turkle 'fore we kilt it. It reminded me of my momma."

Roy never did go back into the hospital after that. For the rest of his days he was usually seen cruising the neighborhood, visiting neighbors, lending a hand where he could. On one occasion he helped pull a car out of a ditch. On another occasion he spotted a neighbor's house on fire. After calling the fire department, he then crawled into the burning building alone to be sure that there was no one in the beds. I am still amazed when I think of how he lived his last days—they were filled with deeds of helpfulness, neighborliness, and even quiet heroism. The shell of that turtle still sits on our bookshelf and I marvel at how the strength and spirit of its original owner was shared. For us, it is a memorial to a special man and a special beast as well as a symbol of the interconnectedness of all life.

[1] Henry David Thoreau. *Journals*, Vol. II., 1850, 14–15.

21

The Serpent and the Egg

"A little piece of paradise"—that's what my wife, Yanna, and I call our little homestead on the southeastern edge of the Blue Ridge Mountains. Along with our ponds, we have a small orchard and a large organic garden. Of course, it wouldn't be paradise without a serpent or two. And do we have serpents! This place is downright snaky! "Some of 'em are big enough to put sidesaddles on!" one of the local old-timers told us. Our area is home to at least twenty kinds of nonpoisonous snakes—not to mention the occasional copperhead or rattlesnake.

One of our neighbors recommended that we put out "snake boards" to monitor the population. Snake boards are pieces of board, plywood, paneling, or sheet metal, scattered around the edge of our garden and in the orchard. Each piece is raised a few inches, propped up on a few rocks or a piece of two-by-four. This creates an ideal habitat for snakes. It is warm, dry, dark, and protected—and it attracts rodents, which snakes like to eat.

Every now and then, we check the boards. If there are copperheads around, I want to know about it, and we dispose of them in various ways. The nonpoisonous snakes we enjoy and want to encourage. Not only are they beautiful but they help control the many mice, voles, and other hungry rodents that reside in our house, garden, and chicken coop. Over the last few years we have found king snakes, mole snakes, racers, garter snakes, water snakes, and corn snakes under our boards.

When I lifted one of the boards early this summer, I was amazed and pleased to find not one, but two, large black rat snakes. These are one of the largest and most handsome of our nonpoisonous snakes. Seeing these glistening, heavy-bodied reptiles coiled under this board was like the answer to a snake boy's dream. Each of these individuals was at least six feet in length. I very gently lowered the board back down. I felt honored to have them in the area and wanted to disturb them as little as possible. One of them had recently eaten a meal. We could tell by the bulge in its body. Could it have been one of those pesky voles that had been ravaging the potatoes? This was a big lump...maybe it had eaten the rat that had been hanging around the chicken coop. There was no way of telling for sure. We were glad they were there and we were thrilled that they were eating our rodents.

I knew from observing captive snakes that a large meal such as the one this snake had swallowed can take as long as a week to digest. During this process the snake retreats to a secluded place, where it can rest and not have to move its distended body. That's just what this snake was doing.

Every day we would go out and gently lift the board, just enough to check on them. Whenever friends visited, we took them over to see "our" snakes. They were an awesome sight indeed, as they raised their heads and calmly peered out at us. Their tongues flickered curiously above the sprawl of glistening black coils. We always noted the bulge in the one snake's body. It seemed that even after a week the lump was still the same size.

One morning, our friend T. J. was visiting. T. J. is an older woman, a city apartment dweller who visits us regularly. She wanted to see the snakes, so right after breakfast we went out to the board. On the way, as we passed the chicken coop, we were telling her that when we had gotten the chickens the month before, we had placed a fake plastic egg in the nesting box as a "nest egg," to encourage the hens to lay eggs there. It was strange, we told her, how the egg had simply disappeared. We couldn't find it anywhere, even when we cleaned out the coop.

"The snake ate it," she said with conviction.

"No!" I protested, not even wanting to consider such weirdness in my own backyard. "A snake wouldn't be stupid enough to swallow a plastic egg...would it?"

"A chicken's stupid enough to sit on a plastic egg," she retorted. "Why wouldn't a snake swallow one?"

When we lifted the board, that was all the proof T. J. needed. "There's your egg in that snake," she concluded.

I gently lowered the board, still not wanting to accept what was becoming increasingly obvious. It had been weeks since the plastic egg had disappeared. I hated to consider the distress of this unfortunate instinct-bound creature suffering from this Grade A hunk of plastic lodged in its gut. Nor did I want to consider the additional suffering I would cause if I made some clumsy attempt at surgery.

"We've got to catch that snake and do something!" both she and Yanna insisted.

Procrastination was doing no good. I knew I had to act. I went back and captured the snake. Often a wild snake, when first caught, will struggle or strike defensively but this snake was as gentle as could be. I felt the lump in the snake's body. This was no half-digested rodent—it was exactly the size and shape of our missing plastic hen's egg. We measured the snake. It was six feet long. The egg was lodged thirty-two inches from the head—almost halfway down the snake.

What to do? Surgery? How would I cut it open? If I did cut it open, how would I sew it back up? My mind raced ahead, trying to think of a solution.

"I have an idea," I said and started gently squeezing behind the egg. The snake writhed about in my hands (but never attempted to bite). Could it be? The egg was responding to the pressure. It was moving! Soon Yanna was in there with me. We just kept cradling the snake in our arms and gently squeezing its body behind the egg, forcing it slowly forward inside the snake. Inch by inch, the egg

wrapping its unhinged jaws around the egg and reversing the process we had witnessed the day before. It swallowed the egg whole. We watched the egg distend the neck as it moved down the snake. After the egg had traveled about six inches, it stopped. The snake flexed its body to make a right angle bend at the egg. Then we heard the muffled yet unmistakable sound of an egg cracking, and soon there was no longer any visible evidence of the meal the snake had just eaten.

It's hard to read a snake's expression but something about its demeanor after this meal seemed to say, "Ahh, now, that's the way things are supposed to be."

We kept the snake for a few more days, fed it a few more eggs, and then we released it.

A year later, while taking a break from the final preparations for this book, I was walking by the garden. What should I see but a large black rat snake. I followed from a distance as it meandered across the garden with flickering tongue and graceful undulations. Just before it crawled off into a thicket I picked it up. It was so gentle, I felt sure it

was moving forward. As the egg approached the last foot or so, the snake's own peristalsis took over and it continued the process on its own. We held the snake and watched in awe as the lump continued toward the neck. The snake's head hung limply forward. Its mouth was open, and it drooled viscous saliva while making a soft-toned gagging noise. In a few minutes the egg appeared in the snake's greatly distended mouth. The snake gave one final flick of its head and the egg dropped to the ground. The snake appeared weak and exhausted. We felt that way too. The plastic egg was completely unchanged after more than two weeks in the belly of the snake.

We put the snake in a cage to rest and recover. It avidly drank water from a dish. The snake had gone for weeks without food and we knew that it was hungry. The next day we placed a fresh warm egg in with the snake, wondering how it would respond. Would it ever trust an egg again? Soon its tongue started flickering and, before long, it was

was the one I had helped the summer before. I brought it to the house and presented it with a fresh egg. To my astonishment, it took the egg right from my hand. We kept the snake for a few days more and fed it several more eggs. It would coil up on my lap and take eggs from my fingers. We released the snake, and we look forward to our next meeting. That plastic egg has become one of our treasured possessions. Sometimes it sits on our bookshelf, where it serves as a reminder that as much as we try to live in a harmonious way with the natural world, we've still got a lot to learn. Sometimes it travels with me in my storytelling bag as a reminder that, with nature as the source, the stories will never end.

A Few Last Words

Of More Snakes, More Eggs, and a Cast-off Skin

As we come to the end of this book, I hope I've conveyed to you some of the joy and truth I've found in the natural world. I also hope I have demonstrated that you don't have to trek for weeks into the back country to experience nature and seek these mythic truths (though it's great when you can). Like Theron said during the ginseng hunt, "The still hog gets the slop." Wherever we are, whether it be on the street in a city, in a suburban backyard, or a wilderness camp, we just need to look around. Whether we encounter a boreal spruce grouse or an urban pigeon, a soaring eagle or a dead skunk in the road, a ginseng plant hidden in a dark "holler" or a wood sorrel poking up through a crack in the sidewalk, we just need to open ourselves and remember, "It's all there."

In the last chapter, I left you with a snake, an egg, and a comment about how the natural world provides a never-ending source of stories. And sure enough while trying to write this conclusion, I find myself launching into another story, a true tale, about more snakes and more eggs.

Well, you see, it happened like this: When I came home this summer from an extensive traveling stint, leading wilderness adventures and back-country camping trips, my sweet wife, Yanna, who had chosen to stay home and immerse herself in the vast, untamed wilderness of her half-acre garden, presented me with an aquarium tank full of leaves and compost.

Yanna, you see, is a bit of an alchemist; she is constantly mixing and layering various herbs, grass clippings, garden debris, household garbage, and various manures into simmering, sacred heaps. She later spreads this compost in her garden and turns it into some of the best food I have ever eaten.

In the leafy depths of one of these piles, she uncovered a clutch of seven eggs. Each egg was about two inches long and an inch in diameter. The shells were leathery and dull white in color. She gathered them up and reburied them in the tank. In late September, they hatched into slender, delicately marked, foot-long black rat snakes.

These young snakes were not black, like their parents, but were elegantly patterned with dark blotches on a gray background. This pattern serves as excellent camouflage; the irregular blotches break up the outlines of the snakes, allowing them to blend in with a tangle of vegetation or the dappled pattern of sunlight on the forest floor. As the snakes get older and larger, however, they become almost solid black. (Only the belly and some of the interstitial skin between the scales retain vestiges of the pattern.)

It is intriguing to think of black as a protective coloration. It imitates darkness or shadow—nothingness. If you have ever watched a black snake disappear into a thicket, you know this is true. A black snake is an embodiment of negative space. As you try to keep your eye on the snake crawling through the tangle, you find that what one minute is a black snake, the next minute becomes a black hole of negative space. The snake is so difficult to discern in this setting because we are not accustomed to seeing negative space—the space around and between things.

My art teacher, many years ago, emphasized that the negative space is as important as the objects that occupy the space; in fact, it is the negative space that defines the objects we see. But when I studied the scales of the black snake I realized that there is more to it than that. The black scales of the black rat snake represent the darkness. Yet when the snake's body is stretched or distended, like after a meal, the interstitial spaces between the scales reveal the light, the colors, and the pattern.

I realized that what I could see so clearly on the body of this snake is also true of the world. Sometimes we need to look between the cracks to see the colors and the pattern. The matrix that holds this world together and gives it

form, substance, and texture is often revealed in the interstices. A single scale is insignificant unto itself, but combined with others and held together in the form of a serpent, it becomes something to be reckoned with.

After the little snakes in our leaf-filled tank had all hatched, we thought they would be hungry so we presented them with an assortment of worms and insects. But they had no interest in food. They had emerged from the egg well nourished by the yolk. We learned that one of the first things newborn snakes do after coming into the world is shed their skin. They usually do this before they eat.

As a snake grows, it will shed its skin at regular intervals, perhaps as often as a few times a year. As the new skin forms under the old, the snake's entire body loses its luster and seems dull and clouded over. The eyes turn bluish and cloudy, and the snake becomes almost blind for a few days. As shedding time approaches, the snake retires to a moist place, sometimes it will even soak in water for hours on end. This softens the outer skin. Then it rubs its lips on something rough, like a stone or a stick. The skin separates around the mouth, and the snake literally crawls out of its skin, peeling it off, inside out, in a slow, sensual way, like a striptease artist might peel off a silk stocking. Inch by inch and scale by scale, the skin peels back over each and every curve of its sinuous body. Even the transparent "spectacle," the scale that once covered the eye, is shed with the skin. At the last moment, before the snake has parted with its old skin, the two tail tips are together, pointing at each other, until one last tug separates them. The old skin remains, inside out, facing back the way it came, clinging to twigs, rocks, and other rough spots in the terrain, like an intricate, textured shadow of the being it once enveloped. The shed

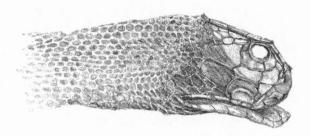

skin is rich in proteins and will soon be broken down and absorbed by organisms in the soil.

The snake slithers off to meet its destiny, with a bright, newborn, and resplendent quality. This is only one of the many kinds of sensual unveilings—celebrations of newness, growth, and maturation—that the natural world provides for us on a regular basis if we tune ourselves in to its wonder.

Previously I recounted the various times snakes have crawled in and out of my life, providing me with regular metaphors for my own growth. As I work here on these last few paragraphs, I feel like a snake shedding its skin. Like the shedding snake, I, too, started at the mouth, because most of what I have written comes from the spoken word— my own anecdotes, as well as stories from the oral tradi-

tion. Little by little, I have peeled off these stories, experiences, legends, and lore and laid them before you—intricate, textured, and full of detail. A part of me has occupied every part of them. I hope that as I've peeled back at least one cloudy layer I've also revealed some newness, growth, and richness. I hope you have been able to peek at the world through my "spectacles" and through the eyes of the characters I've introduced.

Now, I'm right at the end of the process, where the two tail tips are together, pointing at each other. I'm pointing back at it and it is pointing at me. One more tug and we are on our way. Perhaps, like the microorganisms in the earth that absorb the snake's skin, you, too, will be nourished by what I have left here.

Index